THE INQUISITION OF FRANCISCA

THE OTHER VOICE IN EARLY MODERN EUROPE

A Series Edited by Margaret L. King and Albert Rabil Jr.

RECENT BOOKS IN THE SERIES

GIULIA BIGOLINA
Urania: A Romance
Edited and Translated by Valeria Finucci

MADDALENA CAMPIGLIA
Flori, a Pastoral Drama: A Bilingual Edition
Edited with an Introduction and Notes by Virginia Cox and Lisa Sampson
Translated by Virginia Cox

GABRIELLE DE COIGNARD
Spiritual Sonnets: A Bilingual Edition
Edited and Translated by Melanie E. Gregg

MARIE DENTIÈRE
Epistle to Marguerite de Navarre and Preface to a Sermon by John Calvin
Edited and Translated by Mary B. McKinley

MADAME DE MAINTENON
Dialogues and Addresses
Edited and Translated by John J. Conley, S.J.

OLYMPIA MORATA
The Complete Writings of an Italian Heretic
Edited and Translated by Holt N. Parker

ISOTTA NOGAROLA
Complete Writings: Letterbook, Dialogue on Adam and Eve, Orations
Edited and Translated by Margaret L. King and Diana Robin

MADELEINE DE SCUDÉRY
Selected Letters, Orations, and Rhetorical Dialogues
Edited and Translated by Jane Donawerth and Julie Strongson

MADELEINE DE SCUDÉRY
The Story of Sapho
Translated and with an Introduction by Karen Newman

ARCANGELA TARABOTTI
Paternal Tyranny
Edited and Translated by Letizia Panizza

ELISABETTA CAMINER TURRA
Selected Writings of an Eighteenth-Century Venetian Woman of Letters
Edited and Translated by Catherine M. Sama

MADAME DE VILLEDIEU
(Marie-Catherine Desjardins)
Memoirs of the Life of Henriette-Sylvie de Molière: A Novel
Edited and Translated by Donna Kuizenga

Francisca de los Apóstoles

THE INQUISITION
OF FRANCISCA

*A Sixteenth-Century
Visionary on Trial*

و

*Edited and Translated by
Gillian T. W. Ahlgren*

THE UNIVERSITY OF CHICAGO PRESS
Chicago & London

Francisca de los Apóstoles, 1539–after 1578

Gillian T. W. Ahlgren is professor of theology at Xavier University. She is the author of three books, most recently *Entering Teresa of Avila's "Interior Castle."*

The University of Chicago Press, Chicago 60637
The University of Chicago Press, Ltd., London
© 2005 by The University of Chicago
All rights reserved. Published 2005
Printed in the United States of America

14 13 12 11 10 09 08 07 06 05   1 2 3 4 5

ISBN: 0-226-14222-1 (cloth)
ISBN: 0-226-14224-8 (paper)

The University of Chicago Press gratefully acknowledges the generous support of the Program for Cultural Cooperation between Spain's Ministry of Culture and United States Universities toward the publication of this book.

Library of Congress Cataloging-in-Publication Data

The inquisition of Francisca : a sixteenth-century visionary on trial / edited and translated by Gillian T.W. Ahlgren.—1st ed.
p. cm. — (The other voice in early modern Europe)
Includes bibliographical references and index.
ISBN 0-226-14222-1 (hardcover : alk. paper) — ISBN 0-226-14224-8 (pbk. : alk. paper)
1. Francisca, de los Apóstoles, b. 1539?—Trials, litigation, etc.   2. Trials (Heresy)—Spain—Toledo.   3. Inquisition—Spain—History—Sources.
I. Ahlgren, Gillian T. W., 1964–   II. Series.
KBR128.5.F73   2005
272'.2'094643—dc22
2004022020

♾ The paper used in this publication meets the minimum requirements of the American National Standard for Information Sciences—Permanence of Paper for Printed Library Materials, ANSI Z39.48-1992.

CONTENTS

ACKNOWLEDGMENTS

This project has a long gestational history. I first discovered Francisca de los Apóstoles's story in 1991 while working at the Archivo Histórico Nacional in Madrid. At that time, I was examining inquisitional trials of *alumbradas* in order to locate Teresa of Avila's inquisitional encounters in a broader context of female religious experience and inquisitorial prosecution. The story was compelling. It seemed important to recover Francisca's voice for history and to learn from her trial. I returned to Madrid in 1995 on a Xavier University Faculty Research Sabbatical, which allowed me to transcribe the trial and begin to analyze its contents. At that time, I also received grant support from the American Academy of Religion and the Program for Cultural Cooperation between Spain's Ministry of Culture and U.S. Universities. A second faculty research sabbatical in the fall of 1999 enabled me to prepare the manuscript for publication.

Conversations with many colleagues over these years have made this publication possible. I am particularly indebted to Marcia Colish, Mary E. Giles, Kathleen Granrose, Elizabeth Rhodes, Ricardo Saez, Alain Saint-Saens, and Alison Weber. I would also like to express my appreciation to María Dolores Alonso Roldán, who is in charge of the Inquisitional Section of the Archivo Histórico Nacional, for her professionalism, expertise, and kindness. Xavier University has provided me with a number of excellent undergraduate research assistants. My thanks to Karin Rademaker, Nancy McDonald, and Lea Minniti for their careful and painstaking work.

Equally important in the genesis of this particular book was the solidarity, prayer, and good wishes of friends and colleagues. My thanks go to all who have fielded telephone inquiries, have seen me squinting at the microfilm reader and suggested I go home and rest, or have listened and made suggestions as I hammered out interpretive theories. During the final pushing stages, your prayers were profoundly important to me, turning the whole project into a labor of love.

This study is hardly the definitive work on Francisca. Further study of her trial will surely elicit more conversations and a deeper understanding of the complex web of social, political, and religious movements in sixteenth-century Spain. It is certainly my hope that Francisca's voice, lost to us for over four centuries, will continue to speak to us for some time in the future.

Gillian T. W. Ahlgren

THE OTHER VOICE IN
EARLY MODERN EUROPE:
INTRODUCTION TO THE SERIES

Margaret L. King and Albert Rabil Jr.

THE OLD VOICE AND THE OTHER VOICE

In western Europe and the United States, women are nearing equality in the professions, in business, and in politics. Most enjoy access to education, reproductive rights, and autonomy in financial affairs. Issues vital to women are on the public agenda: equal pay, child care, domestic abuse, breast cancer research, and curricular revision with an eye to the inclusion of women.

These recent achievements have their origins in things women (and some male supporters) said for the first time about six hundred years ago. Theirs is the "other voice," in contradistinction to the "first voice," the voice of the educated men who created Western culture. Coincident with a general reshaping of European culture in the period 1300–1700 (called the Renaissance or early modern period), questions of female equality and opportunity were raised that still resound and are still unresolved.

The other voice emerged against the backdrop of a three-thousand-year history of the derogation of women rooted in the civilizations related to Western culture: Hebrew, Greek, Roman, and Christian. Negative attitudes toward women inherited from these traditions pervaded the intellectual, medical, legal, religious, and social systems that developed during the European Middle Ages.

The following pages describe the traditional, overwhelmingly male views of women's nature inherited by early modern Europeans and the new tradition that the "other voice" called into being to begin to challenge reigning assumptions. This review should serve as a framework for understanding the texts published in the series the Other Voice in Early Modern Europe. Introductions specific to each text and author follow this essay in all the volumes of the series.

TRADITIONAL VIEWS OF WOMEN, 500 B.C.E.—1500 C.E.

Embedded in the philosophical and medical theories of the ancient Greeks were perceptions of the female as inferior to the male in both mind and body. Similarly, *ix* the structure of civil legislation inherited from the ancient Romans was biased against women, and the views on women developed by Christian thinkers out of the Hebrew Bible and the Christian New Testament were negative and disabling. Literary works composed in the vernacular of ordinary people, and widely recited or read, conveyed these negative assumptions. The social networks within which most women lived—those of the family and the institutions of the Roman Catholic Church—were shaped by this negative tradition and sharply limited the areas in which women might act in and upon the world.

GREEK PHILOSOPHY AND FEMALE NATURE. Greek biology assumed that women were inferior to men and defined them as merely childbearers and housekeepers. This view was authoritatively expressed in the works of the philosopher Aristotle.

Aristotle thought in dualities. He considered action superior to inaction, form (the inner design or structure of any object) superior to matter, completion to incompletion, possession to deprivation. In each of these dualities, he associated the male principle with the superior quality and the female with the inferior. "The male principle in nature," he argued, "is associated with active, formative and perfected characteristics, while the female is passive, material and deprived, desiring the male in order to become complete."[1]

Men are always identified with virile qualities, such as judgment, courage, and stamina, and women with their opposites—irrationality, cowardice, and weakness.

The masculine principle was considered superior even in the womb. The man's semen, Aristotle believed, created the form of a new human creature, while the female body contributed only matter. (The existence of the ovum, and with it the other facts of human embryology, was not established until the seventeenth century.) Although the later Greek physician Galen believed there was a female component in generation, contributed by "female semen," the followers of both Aristotle and Galen saw the male role in human generation as more active and more important.

In the Aristotelian view, the male principle sought always to reproduce itself. The creation of a female was always a mistake, therefore, resulting from an imperfect act of generation. Every female born was considered a "defective" or "mutilated" male (as Aristotle's terminology has variously been translated), a "monstrosity" of nature.[2]

---

1. Aristotle, *Physics* 1.9.192a20–24, in *The Complete Works of Aristotle*, ed. Jonathan Barnes, rev. Oxford trans., 2 vols. (Princeton, 1984), 1:328.

2. Aristotle, *Generation of Animals* 2.3.737a27–28, in *The Complete Works*, 1:1144.

For Greek theorists, the biology of males and females was the key to their psychology. The female was softer and more docile, more apt to be despondent, querulous, and deceitful. Being incomplete, moreover, she craved sexual fulfillment in intercourse with a male. The male was intellectual, active, and in control of his passions.

These psychological polarities derived from the theory that the universe consisted of four elements (earth, fire, air, and water), expressed in human bodies as four "humors" (black bile, yellow bile, blood, and phlegm) considered, respectively, dry, hot, damp, and cold and corresponding to mental states ("melancholic," "choleric," "sanguine," "phlegmatic"). In this scheme the male, sharing the principles of earth and fire, was dry and hot; the female, sharing the principles of air and water, was cold and damp.

Female psychology was further affected by her dominant organ, the uterus (womb), *hystera* in Greek. The passions generated by the womb made women lustful, deceitful, talkative, irrational, indeed—when these affects were in excess—"hysterical."

Aristotle's biology also had social and political consequences. If the male principle was superior and the female inferior, then in the household, as in the state, men should rule and women must be subordinate. That hierarchy did not rule out the companionship of husband and wife, whose cooperation was necessary for the welfare of children and the preservation of property. Such mutuality supported male preeminence.

Aristotle's teacher Plato suggested a different possibility: that men and women might possess the same virtues. The setting for this proposal is the imaginary and ideal Republic that Plato sketches in a dialogue of that name. Here, for a privileged elite capable of leading wisely, all distinctions of class and wealth dissolve, as, consequently, do those of gender. Without households or property, as Plato constructs his ideal society, there is no need for the subordination of women. Women may therefore be educated to the same level as men to assume leadership. Plato's Republic remained imaginary, however. In real societies, the subordination of women remained the norm and the prescription.

The views of women inherited from the Greek philosophical tradition became the basis for medieval thought. In the thirteenth century, the supreme Scholastic philosopher Thomas Aquinas, among others, still echoed Aristotle's views of human reproduction, of male and female personalities, and of the preeminent male role in the social hierarchy.

ROMAN LAW AND THE FEMALE CONDITION. Roman law, like Greek philosophy, underlay medieval thought and shaped medieval society. The ancient belief that adult property-owning men should administer households and make decisions affecting the community at large is the very fulcrum of Roman law.

About 450 B.C.E., during Rome's republican era, the community's customary law was recorded (legendarily) on twelve tablets erected in the city's central forum. It was later elaborated by professional jurists whose activity increased in the imperial era, when much new legislation was passed, especially on issues affecting family and inheritance. This growing, changing body of laws was eventually codified in the *Corpus of Civil Law* under the direction of the emperor Justinian, generations after the empire ceased to be ruled from Rome. That *Corpus*, read and commented on by medieval scholars from the eleventh century on, inspired the legal systems of most of the cities and kingdoms of Europe.

Laws regarding dowries, divorce, and inheritance pertain primarily to women. Since those laws aimed to maintain and preserve property, the women concerned were those from the property-owning minority. Their subordination to male family members points to the even greater subordination of lower-class and slave women, about whom the laws speak little.

In the early republic, the *paterfamilias*, or "father of the family," possessed *patria potestas*, "paternal power." The term *pater*, "father," in both these cases does not necessarily mean biological father but denotes the head of a household. The father was the person who owned the household's property and, indeed, its human members. The *paterfamilias* had absolute power—including the power, rarely exercised, of life or death—over his wife, his children, and his slaves, as much as his cattle.

Male children could be "emancipated," an act that granted legal autonomy and the right to own property. Those over fourteen could be emancipated by a special grant from the father or automatically by their father's death. But females could never be emancipated; instead, they passed from the authority of their father to that of a husband or, if widowed or orphaned while still unmarried, to a guardian or tutor.

Marriage in its traditional form placed the woman under her husband's authority, or *manus*. He could divorce her on grounds of adultery, drinking wine, or stealing from the household, but she could not divorce him. She could neither possess property in her own right nor bequeath any to her children upon her death. When her husband died, the household property passed not to her but to his male heirs. And when her father died, she had no claim to any family inheritance, which was directed to her brothers or more remote male relatives. The effect of these laws was to exclude women from civil society, itself based on property ownership.

In the later republican and imperial periods, these rules were significantly modified. Women rarely married according to the traditional form. The practice of "free" marriage allowed a woman to remain under her father's authority, to possess property given her by her father (most frequently the "dowry," recoverable from the husband's household on his death), and to inherit from her father. She could also bequeath property to her own children and divorce her husband, just as he could divorce her.

Despite this greater freedom, women still suffered enormous disability under Roman law. Heirs could belong only to the father's side, never the mother's. Moreover, although she could bequeath her property to her children, she could not establish a line of succession in doing so. A woman was "the beginning and end of her own family," said the jurist Ulpian. Moreover, women could play no public role. They could not hold public office, represent anyone in a legal case, or even witness a will. Women had only a private existence and no public personality.

The dowry system, the guardian, women's limited ability to transmit wealth, and total political disability are all features of Roman law adopted by the medieval communities of western Europe, although modified according to local customary laws..

CHRISTIAN DOCTRINE AND WOMEN'S PLACE. The Hebrew Bible and the Christian New Testament authorized later writers to limit women to the realm of the family and to burden them with the guilt of original sin. The passages most fruitful for this purpose were the creation narratives in Genesis and sentences from the Epistles defining women's role within the Christian family and community.

Each of the first two chapters of Genesis contains a creation narrative. In the first "God created man in his own image, in the image of God he created him; male and female he created them" (Gn 1:27). In the second, God created Eve from Adam's rib (2:21–23). Christian theologians relied principally on Genesis 2 for their understanding of the relation between man and woman, interpreting the creation of Eve from Adam as proof of her subordination to him.

The creation story in Genesis 2 leads to that of the temptations in Genesis 3: of Eve by the wily serpent and of Adam by Eve. As read by Christian theologians from Tertullian to Thomas Aquinas, the narrative made Eve responsible for the Fall and its consequences. She instigated the act; she deceived her husband; she suffered the greater punishment. Her disobedience made it necessary for Jesus to be incarnated and to die on the cross. From the pulpit, moralists and preachers for centuries conveyed to women the guilt that they bore for original sin.

The Epistles offered advice to early Christians on building communities of the faithful. Among the matters to be regulated was the place of women.

Paul offered views favorable to women in Galatians 3:28: "There is neither Jew nor Greek, there is neither slave nor free, there is neither male nor female; for you are all one in Christ Jesus." Paul also referred to women as his coworkers and placed them on a par with himself and his male coworkers (Phlm 4:2–3; Rom 16:1–3; 1 Cor 16:19). Elsewhere, Paul limited women's possibilities: "But I want you to understand that the head of every man is Christ, the head of a woman is her husband, and the head of Christ is God" (1 Cor 11:3).

Biblical passages by later writers (although attributed to Paul) enjoined women to forgo jewels, expensive clothes, and elaborate coiffures; and they forbade women to "teach or have authority over men," telling them to "learn in silence with all submissiveness" as is proper for one responsible for sin, consoling them, however, with the thought that they will be saved through childbearing (1 Tm 2:9–15). Other texts among the later Epistles defined women as the weaker sex and emphasized their subordination to their husbands (1 Pt 3:7; Col 3:18; Eph 5:22–23).

These passages from the New Testament became the arsenal employed by theologians of the early church to transmit negative attitudes toward women to medieval Christian culture—above all, Tertullian (*On the Apparel of Women*), Jerome (*Against Jovinian*), and Augustine (*The Literal Meaning of Genesis*).

THE IMAGE OF WOMEN IN MEDIEVAL LITERATURE. The philosophical, legal, and religious traditions born in antiquity formed the basis of the medieval intellectual synthesis wrought by trained thinkers, mostly clerics, writing in Latin and based largely in universities. The vernacular literary tradition that developed alongside the learned tradition also spoke about female nature and women's roles. Medieval stories, poems, and epics also portrayed women negatively—as lustful and deceitful—while praising good housekeepers and loyal wives as replicas of the Virgin Mary or the female saints and martyrs.

There is an exception in the movement of "courtly love" that evolved in southern France from the twelfth century. Courtly love was the erotic love between a nobleman and noblewoman, the latter usually superior in social rank. It was always adulterous. From the conventions of courtly love derive modern Western notions of romantic love. The tradition has had an impact disproportionate to its size, for it affected only a tiny elite, and very few women. The exaltation of the female lover probably does not reflect a higher evaluation of women or a step toward their sexual liberation. More likely it gives expression to the social and sexual tensions besetting the knightly class at a specific historical juncture.

The literary fashion of courtly love was on the wane by the thirteenth century, when the widely read *Romance of the Rose* was composed in French by two authors of significantly different dispositions. Guillaume de Lorris composed the initial four thousand verses about 1235, and Jean de Meun added about seventeen thousand verses—more than four times the original—about 1265.

The fragment composed by Guillaume de Lorris stands squarely in the tradition of courtly love. Here the poet, in a dream, is admitted into a walled garden where he finds a magic fountain in which a rosebush is reflected. He longs to pick one rose, but the thorns prevent his doing so, even as he is wounded by arrows from the god of love, whose commands he agrees to obey. The rest of this part of the poem recounts the poet's unsuccessful efforts to pluck the rose.

The longer part of the *Romance* by Jean de Meun also describes a dream. But here allegorical characters give long didactic speeches, providing a social satire on a variety of themes, some pertaining to women. Love is an anxious and tormented state, the poem explains: women are greedy and manipulative, marriage is miserable, beautiful women are lustful, ugly ones cease to please, and a chaste woman is as rare as a black swan.

Shortly after Jean de Meun completed *The Romance of the Rose*, Mathéolus penned his *Lamentations*, a long Latin diatribe against marriage translated into French about a century later. The *Lamentations* sum up medieval attitudes toward women and provoked the important response by Christine de Pizan in her *Book of the City of Ladies*.

In 1355, Giovanni Boccaccio wrote *Il Corbaccio*, another antifeminist manifesto, although ironically by an author whose other works pioneered new directions in Renaissance thought. The former husband of his lover appears to Boccaccio, condemning his unmoderated lust and detailing the defects of women. Boccaccio concedes at the end "how much men naturally surpass women in nobility" and is cured of his desires.[3]

WOMEN'S ROLES: THE FAMILY. The negative perceptions of women expressed in the intellectual tradition are also implicit in the actual roles that women played in European society. Assigned to subordinate positions in the household and the church, they were barred from significant participation in public life.

Medieval European households, like those in antiquity and in non-Western civilizations, were headed by males. It was the male serf (or peasant), feudal lord, town merchant, or citizen who was polled or taxed or succeeded to an inheritance or had any acknowledged public role, although his wife or widow could stand as a temporary surrogate. From about 1100, the position of property-

---

3. Giovanni Boccaccio, *The Corbaccio, or The Labyrinth of Love*, trans. and ed. Anthony K. Cassell, rev. ed. (Binghamton, NY, 1993), 71.

holding males was further enhanced: inheritance was confined to the male, or agnate, line—with depressing consequences for women.

A wife never fully belonged to her husband's family, nor was she a daughter to her father's family. She left her father's house young to marry whomever her parents chose. Her dowry was managed by her husband, and at her death it normally passed to her children by him.

A married woman's life was occupied nearly constantly with cycles of pregnancy, childbearing, and lactation. Women bore children through all the years of their fertility, and many died in childbirth. They were also responsible for raising young children up to six or seven. In the propertied classes that responsibility was shared, since it was common for a wet nurse to take over breast-feeding and for servants to perform other chores.

Women trained their daughters in the household duties appropriate to their status, nearly always tasks associated with textiles: spinning, weaving, sewing, embroidering. Their sons were sent out of the house as apprentices or students, or their training was assumed by fathers in later childhood and adolescence. On the death of her husband, a woman's children became the responsibility of his family. She generally did not take "his" children with her to a new marriage or back to her father's house, except sometimes in the artisan classes.

Women also worked. Rural peasants performed farm chores, merchant wives often practiced their husbands' trades, the unmarried daughters of the urban poor worked as servants or prostitutes. All wives produced or embellished textiles and did the housekeeping, while wealthy ones managed servants. These labors were unpaid or poorly paid but often contributed substantially to family wealth.

WOMEN'S ROLES: THE CHURCH. Membership in a household, whether a father's or a husband's, meant for women a lifelong subordination to others. In western Europe, the Roman Catholic Church offered an alternative to the career of wife and mother. A woman could enter a convent, parallel in function to the monasteries for men that evolved in the early Christian centuries.

In the convent, a woman pledged herself to a celibate life, lived according to strict community rules, and worshiped daily. Often the convent offered training in Latin, allowing some women to become considerable scholars and authors as well as scribes, artists, and musicians. For women who chose the conventual life, the benefits could be enormous, but for numerous others placed in convents by paternal choice, the life could be restrictive and burdensome.

The conventual life declined as an alternative for women as the modern age approached. Reformed monastic institutions resisted responsibility for related female orders. The church increasingly restricted female institutional life by insisting on closer male supervision.

Women often sought other options. Some joined the communities of laywomen that sprang up spontaneously in the thirteenth century in the urban zones of western Europe, especially in Flanders and Italy. Some joined the heretical movements that flourished in late medieval Christendom, whose anticlerical and often antifamily positions particularly appealed to women. In these communities, some women were acclaimed as "holy women" or "saints," whereas others often were condemned as frauds or heretics.

In all, although the options offered to women by the church were sometimes less than satisfactory, they were sometimes richly rewarding. After 1520, the convent remained an option only in Roman Catholic territories. Protestantism engendered an ideal of marriage as a heroic endeavor and appeared to place husband and wife on a more equal footing. Sermons and treatises, however, still called for female subordination and obedience.

THE OTHER VOICE, 1300–1700

When the modern era opened, European culture was so firmly structured by a framework of negative attitudes toward women that to dismantle it was a monumental labor. The process began as part of a larger cultural movement that entailed the critical reexamination of ideas inherited from the ancient and medieval past. The humanists launched that critical reexamination.

THE HUMANIST FOUNDATION. Originating in Italy in the fourteenth century, humanism quickly became the dominant intellectual movement in Europe. Spreading in the sixteenth century from Italy to the rest of Europe, it fueled the literary, scientific, and philosophical movements of the era and laid the basis for the eighteenth-century Enlightenment.

Humanists regarded the Scholastic philosophy of medieval universities as out of touch with the realities of urban life. They found in the rhetorical discourse of classical Rome a language adapted to civic life and public speech. They learned to read, speak, and write classical Latin and, eventually, classical Greek. They founded schools to teach others to do so, establishing the pattern for elementary and secondary education for the next three hundred years.

In the service of complex government bureaucracies, humanists employed their skills to write eloquent letters, deliver public orations, and formulate public policy. They developed new scripts for copying manuscripts and used the new printing press to disseminate texts, for which they created methods of critical editing.

Humanism was a movement led by males who accepted the evaluation of women in ancient texts and generally shared the misogynist perceptions of their culture. (Female humanists, as we will see, did not.) Yet humanism also opened the door to a reevaluation of the nature and capacity of women. By calling authors, texts, and ideas into question, it made possible the fundamental rereading of the whole intellectual tradition that was required in order to free women from cultural prejudice and social subordination.

A DIFFERENT CITY. The other voice first appeared when, after so many centuries, the accumulation of misogynist concepts evoked a response from a capable female defender: Christine de Pizan (1365–1431). Introducing her *Book of the City of Ladies* (1405), she described how she was affected by reading Mathéolus's *Lamentations:* "Just the sight of this book . . . made me wonder how it happened that so many different men . . . are so inclined to express both in speaking and in their treatises and writings so many wicked insults about women and their behavior."[4]

These statements impelled her to detest herself "and the entire feminine sex, as though we were monstrosities in nature."[5]

The rest of *The Book of the City of Ladies* presents a justification of the female sex and a vision of an ideal community of women. A pioneer, she has received the message of female inferiority and rejected it. From the fourteenth to the seventeenth century, a huge body of literature accumulated that responded to the dominant tradition.

The result was a literary explosion consisting of works by both men and women, in Latin and in the vernaculars: works enumerating the achievements of notable women; works rebutting the main accusations made against women; works arguing for the equal education of men and women; works defining and redefining women's proper role in the family, at court, in public; works describing women's lives and experiences. Recent monographs and articles have begun to hint at the great range of this movement, involving probably several thousand titles. The protofeminism of these "other voices" constitutes a significant fraction of the literary product of the early modern era.

THE CATALOGS. About 1365, the same Boccaccio whose *Corbaccio* rehearses the usual charges against female nature wrote another work, *Concerning Famous Women*. A humanist treatise drawing on classical texts, it

---

4. Christine de Pizan, *The Book of the City of Ladies*, trans. Earl Jeffrey Richards, foreword by Marina Warner (New York, 1982), 1.1.1, pp. 3–4.

5. Ibid., 1.1.1–2, p. 5.

praised 106 notable women: ninety-eight of them from pagan Greek and Roman antiquity, one (Eve) from the Bible, and seven from the medieval religious and cultural tradition; his book helped make all readers aware of a sex normally condemned or forgotten. Boccaccio's outlook nevertheless was unfriendly to women, for it singled out for praise those women who possessed the traditional virtues of chastity, silence, and obedience. Women who were active in the public realm—for example, rulers and warriors— were depicted as usually being lascivious and as suffering terrible punishments for entering the masculine sphere. Women were his subject, but Boccaccio's standard remained male.

Christine de Pizan's *Book of the City of Ladies* contains a second catalog, one responding specifically to Boccaccio's. Whereas Boccaccio portrays female virtue as exceptional, she depicts it as universal. Many women in history were leaders, or remained chaste despite the lascivious approaches of men, or were visionaries and brave martyrs.

The work of Boccaccio inspired a series of catalogs of illustrious women of the biblical, classical, Christian, and local pasts, among them Filippo da Bergamo's *Of Illustrious Women*, Pierre de Brantôme's *Lives of Illustrious Women*, Pierre Le Moyne's *Gallerie of Heroic Women*, and Pietro Paolo de Ribera's *Immortal Triumphs and Heroic Enterprises of 845 Women*. Whatever their embedded prejudices, these works drove home to the public the possibility of female excellence.

THE DEBATE. At the same time, many questions remained: Could a woman be virtuous? Could she perform noteworthy deeds? Was she even, strictly speaking, of the same human species as men? These questions were debated over four centuries, in French, German, Italian, Spanish, and English, by authors male and female, among Catholics, Protestants, and Jews, in ponderous volumes and breezy pamphlets. The whole literary genre has been called the *querelle des femmes*, the "woman question."

The opening volley of this battle occurred in the first years of the fifteenth century, in a literary debate sparked by Christine de Pizan. She exchanged letters critical of Jean de Meun's contribution to *The Romance of the Rose* with two French royal secretaries, Jean de Montreuil and Gontier Col. When the matter became public, Jean Gerson, one of Europe's leading theologians, supported de Pizan's arguments against de Meun, for the moment silencing the opposition.

The debate resurfaced repeatedly over the next two hundred years. *The Triumph of Women* (1438) by Juan Rodríguez de la Camara (or Juan Rodríguez del Padron) struck a new note by presenting arguments for the superiority of women to men. *The Champion of Women* (1440–42) by Martin Le Franc addresses once again the negative views of women presented in *The Romance of the Rose* and offers counterevidence of female virtue and achievement.

A cameo of the debate on women is included in *The Courtier,* one of the most widely read books of the era, published by the Italian Baldassare Castiglione in 1528 and immediately translated into other European vernaculars. *The Courtier* depicts a series of evenings at the court of the duke of Urbino in which many men and some women of the highest social stratum amuse themselves by discussing a range of literary and social issues. The "woman question" is a pervasive theme throughout, and the third of its four books is devoted entirely to that issue.

In a verbal duel, Gasparo Pallavicino and Giuliano de' Medici present the main claims of the two traditions. Gasparo argues the innate inferiority of women and their inclination to vice. Only in bearing children do they profit the world. Giuliano counters that women share the same spiritual and mental capacities as men and may excel in wisdom and action. Men and women are of the same essence: just as no stone can be more perfectly a stone than another, so no human being can be more perfectly human than others, whether male or female. It was an astonishing assertion, boldly made to an audience as large as all Europe.

THE TREATISES. Humanism provided the materials for a positive counterconcept to the misogyny embedded in Scholastic philosophy and law and inherited from the Greek, Roman, and Christian pasts. A series of humanist treatises on marriage and family, on education and deportment, and on the nature of women helped construct these new perspectives.

The works by Francesco Barbaro and Leon Battista Alberti—*On Marriage* (1415) and *On the Family* (1434–37)—far from defending female equality, reasserted women's responsibility for rearing children and managing the housekeeping while being obedient, chaste, and silent. Nevertheless, they served the cause of reexamining the issue of women's nature by placing domestic issues at the center of scholarly concern and reopening the pertinent classical texts. In addition, Barbaro emphasized the companionate nature of marriage and the importance of a wife's spiritual and mental qualities for the well-being of the family.

These themes reappear in later humanist works on marriage and the education of women by Juan Luis Vives and Erasmus. Both were moderately sympathetic to the condition of women without reaching beyond the usual masculine prescriptions for female behavior.

An outlook more favorable to women characterizes the nearly unknown work *In Praise of Women* (ca. 1487) by the Italian humanist Bartolommeo

Goggio. In addition to providing a catalog of illustrious women, Goggio argued that male and female are the same in essence, but that women (reworking the Adam and Eve narrative from quite a new angle) are actually superior. In the same vein, the Italian humanist Mario Equicola asserted the spiritual equality of men and women in *On Women* (1501). In 1525, Galeazzo Flavio Capra (or Capella) published his work *On the Excellence and Dignity of Women*. This humanist tradition of treatises defending the worthiness of women culminates in the work of Henricus Cornelius Agrippa *On the Nobility and Preeminence of the Female Sex*. No work by a male humanist more succinctly or explicitly presents the case for female dignity.

THE WITCH BOOKS. While humanists grappled with the issues pertaining to women and family, other learned men turned their attention to what they perceived as a very great problem: witches. Witch-hunting manuals, explorations of the witch phenomenon, and even defenses of witches are not at first glance pertinent to the tradition of the other voice. But they do relate in this way: most accused witches were women. The hostility aroused by supposed witch activity is comparable to the hostility aroused by women. The evil deeds the victims of the hunt were charged with were exaggerations of the vices to which, many believed, all women were prone.

The connection between the witch accusation and the hatred of women is explicit in the notorious witch-hunting manual *The Hammer of Witches* (1486) by two Dominican inquisitors, Heinrich Krämer and Jacob Sprenger. Here the inconstancy, deceitfulness, and lustfulness traditionally associated with women are depicted in exaggerated form as the core features of witch behavior. These traits inclined women to make a bargain with the devil—sealed by sexual intercourse—by which they acquired unholy powers. Such bizarre claims, far from being rejected by rational men, were broadcast by intellectuals. The German Ulrich Molitur, the Frenchman Nicolas Rémy, and the Italian Stefano Guazzo all coolly informed the public of sinister orgies and midnight pacts with the devil. The celebrated French jurist, historian, and political philosopher Jean Bodin argued that because women were especially prone to diabolism, regular legal procedures could properly be suspended in order to try those accused of this "exceptional crime."

A few experts such as the physician Johann Weyer, a student of Agrippa's, raised their voices in protest. In 1563, he explained the witch phenomenon thus, without discarding belief in diabolism: the devil deluded foolish old women afflicted by melancholia, causing them to believe they had magical powers. Weyer's rational skepticism, which had good credibility in the community of the learned, worked to revise the conventional views of women and witchcraft.

WOMEN'S WORKS. To the many categories of works produced on the question of women's worth must be added nearly all works written by women. A woman writing was in herself a statement of women's claim to dignity.

Only a few women wrote anything before the dawn of the modern era, for three reasons. First, they rarely received the education that would enable them to write. Second, they were not admitted to the public roles—as administrator, bureaucrat, lawyer or notary, or university professor—in which they might gain knowledge of the kinds of things the literate public thought worth writing about. Third, the culture imposed silence on women, considering speaking out a form of unchastity. Given these conditions, it is remarkable that any women wrote. Those who did before the fourteenth century were almost always nuns or religious women whose isolation made their pronouncements more acceptable.

From the fourteenth century on, the volume of women's writings rose. Women continued to write devotional literature, although not always as cloistered nuns. They also wrote diaries, often intended as keepsakes for their children; books of advice to their sons and daughters; letters to family members and friends; and family memoirs, in a few cases elaborate enough to be considered histories.

A few women wrote works directly concerning the "woman question," and some of these, such as the humanists Isotta Nogarola, Cassandra Fedele, Laura Cereta, and Olympia Morata, were highly trained. A few were professional writers, living by the income of their pens; the very first among them was Christine de Pizan, noteworthy in this context as in so many others. In addition to *The Book of the City of Ladies* and her critiques of *The Romance of the Rose*, she wrote *The Treasure of the City of Ladies* (a guide to social decorum for women), an advice book for her son, much courtly verse, and a full-scale history of the reign of King Charles V of France.

WOMEN PATRONS. Women who did not themselves write but encouraged others to do so boosted the development of an alternative tradition. Highly placed women patrons supported authors, artists, musicians, poets, and learned men. Such patrons, drawn mostly from the Italian elites and the courts of northern Europe, figure disproportionately as the dedicatees of the important works of early feminism.

For a start, it might be noted that the catalogs of Boccaccio and Alvaro de Luna were dedicated to the Florentine noblewoman Andrea Acciaiuoli and to Doña María, first wife of King Juan II of Castile, while the French translation of Boccaccio's work was commissioned by Anne of Brittany, wife of King Charles VIII of France. The humanist treatises of Goggio, Equicola, Vives, and Agrippa were dedicated, respectively, to Eleanora of Aragon, wife of Ercole I d'Este, Duke of Ferrara; to Margherita Cantelma of Mantua; to Catherine of Aragon, wife of King Henry VIII of England; and to Margaret, Duchess of Austria and regent of the Netherlands. As late as 1696, Mary Astell's *Serious Proposal to the Ladies, for the Advancement of Their True and Greatest Interest* was dedicated to Princess Anne of Denmark.

These authors presumed that their efforts would be welcome to female patrons, or they may have written at the bidding of those patrons. Silent themselves, perhaps even unresponsive, these loftily placed women helped shape the tradition of the other voice.

THE ISSUES. The literary forms and patterns in which the tradition of the other voice presented itself have now been sketched. It remains to highlight the major issues around which this tradition crystallizes. In brief, there are four problems to which our authors return again and again, in plays and catalogs, in verse and letters, in treatises and dialogues, in every language: the problem of chastity, the problem of power, the problem of speech, and the problem of knowledge. Of these the greatest, preconditioning the others, is the problem of chastity.

THE PROBLEM OF CHASTITY. In traditional European culture, as in those of antiquity and others around the globe, chastity was perceived as woman's quintessential virtue—in contrast to courage, or generosity, or leadership, or rationality, seen as virtues characteristic of men. Opponents of women charged them with insatiable lust. Women themselves and their defenders—without disputing the validity of the standard—responded that women were capable of chastity.

The requirement of chastity kept women at home, silenced them, isolated them, left them in ignorance. It was the source of all other impediments. Why was it so important to the society of men, of whom chastity was not required, and who more often than not considered it their right to violate the chastity of any woman they encountered?

Female chastity ensured the continuity of the male-headed household. If a man's wife was not chaste, he could not be sure of the legitimacy of his offspring. If they were not his and they acquired his property, it was not his household, but some other man's, that had endured. If his daughter was not chaste, she could not be transferred to another man's household as his wife, and he was dishonored.

The whole system of the integrity of the household and the transmission of property was bound up in female chastity. Such a requirement pertained only to property-owning classes, of course. Poor women could not expect to maintain their chastity, least of all if they were in contact with high-status men to whom all women but those of their own household were prey.

In Catholic Europe, the requirement of chastity was further buttressed by moral and religious imperatives. Original sin was inextricably linked with the sexual act. Virginity was seen as heroic virtue, far more impressive than, say, the avoidance of idleness or greed. Monasticism, the cultural institution that dominated medieval Europe for centuries, was grounded in the renunciation of the flesh. The Catholic reform of the eleventh century imposed a similar standard on all the clergy and a heightened awareness of sexual requirements on all the laity. Although men were asked to be chaste, female unchastity was much worse: it led to the devil, as Eve had led mankind to sin.

To such requirements, women and their defenders protested their innocence. Furthermore, following the example of holy women who had escaped the requirements of family and sought the religious life, some women began to conceive of female communities as alternatives both to family and to the cloister. Christine de Pizan's city of ladies was such a community. Moderata Fonte and Mary Astell envisioned others. The luxurious salons of the French *précieuses* of the seventeenth century, or the comfortable English drawing rooms of the next, may have been born of the same impulse. Here women not only might escape, if briefly, the subordinate position that life in the family entailed but might also make claims to power, exercise their capacity for speech, and display their knowledge.

THE PROBLEM OF POWER. Women were excluded from power: the whole cultural tradition insisted on it. Only men were citizens, only men bore arms, only men could be chiefs or lords or kings. There were exceptions that did not disprove the rule, when wives or widows or mothers took the place of men, awaiting their return or the maturation of a male heir. A woman who attempted to rule in her own right was perceived as an anomaly, a monster, at once a deformed woman and an insufficient male, sexually confused and consequently unsafe.

The association of such images with women who held or sought power explains some otherwise odd features of early modern culture. Queen Elizabeth I of England, one of the few women to hold full regal authority in European history, played with such male/female images—positive ones, of course—in representing herself to her subjects. She was a prince, and manly, even though she was female. She was also (she claimed) virginal, a condition absolutely essential if she was to avoid the attacks of her opponents. Catherine de' Medici, who ruled France as widow and regent for her sons, also adopted such imagery in defining her position. She chose as one symbol the figure of

Artemisia, an androgynous ancient warrior-heroine who combined a female persona with masculine powers.

Power in a woman, without such sexual imagery, seems to have been indigestible by the culture. A rare note was struck by the Englishman Sir Thomas Elyot in his *Defence of Good Women* (1540), justifying both women's participation in civic life and their prowess in arms. The old tune was sung by the Scots reformer John Knox in his *First Blast of the Trumpet against the Monstrous Regiment of Women* (1558); for him rule by women, defects in nature, was a hideous contradiction in terms.

The confused sexuality of the imagery of female potency was not reserved for rulers. Any woman who excelled was likely to be called an Amazon, recalling the self-mutilated warrior women of antiquity who repudiated all men, gave up their sons, and raised only their daughters. She was often said to have "exceeded her sex" or to have possessed "masculine virtue"—as the very fact of conspicuous excellence conferred masculinity even on the female subject. The catalogs of notable women often showed those female heroes dressed in armor, armed to the teeth, like men. Amazonian heroines romp through the epics of the age—Ariosto's *Orlando Furioso* (1532) and Spenser's *Faerie Queene* (1590–1609). Excellence in a woman was perceived as a claim for power, and power was reserved for the masculine realm. A woman who possessed either one was masculinized and lost title to her own female identity.

THE PROBLEM OF SPEECH. Just as power had a sexual dimension when it was claimed by women, so did speech. A good woman spoke little. Excessive speech was an indication of unchastity. By speech, women seduced men. Eve had lured Adam into sin by her speech. Accused witches were commonly accused of having spoken abusively, or irrationally, or simply too much. As enlightened a figure as Francesco Barbaro insisted on silence in a woman, which he linked to her perfect unanimity with her husband's will and her unblemished virtue (her chastity). Another Italian humanist, Leonardo Bruni, in advising a noblewoman on her studies, barred her not from speech but from public speaking. That was reserved for men.

Related to the problem of speech was that of costume—another, if silent, form of self-expression. Assigned the task of pleasing men as their primary occupation, elite women often tended toward elaborate costume, hairdressing, and the use of cosmetics. Clergy and secular moralists alike condemned these practices. The appropriate function of costume and adornment was to announce the status of a woman's husband or father. Any further indulgence in adornment was akin to unchastity.

THE PROBLEM OF KNOWLEDGE. When the Italian noblewoman Isotta Nogarola had begun to attain a reputation as a humanist, she was accused of incest—a telling instance of the association of learning in women with unchastity. That chilling association inclined any woman who was educated to deny that she was or to make exaggerated claims of heroic chastity.

If educated women were pursued with suspicions of sexual misconduct, women seeking an education faced an even more daunting obstacle: the assumption that women were by nature incapable of learning, that reasoning was a particularly masculine ability. Just as they proclaimed their chastity, women and their defenders insisted on their capacity for learning. The major work by a male writer on female education—that by Juan Luis Vives, *On the Education of a Christian Woman* (1523)—granted female capacity for intellection but still argued that a woman's whole education was to be shaped around the requirement of chastity and a future within the household. Female writers of the following generations—Marie de Gournay in France, Anna Maria van Schurman in Holland, and Mary Astell in England—began to envision other possibilities.

The pioneers of female education were the Italian women humanists who managed to attain a literacy in Latin and a knowledge of classical and Christian literature equivalent to that of prominent men. Their works implicitly and explicitly raise questions about women's social roles, defining problems that beset women attempting to break out of the cultural limits that had bound them. Like Christine de Pizan, who achieved an advanced education through her father's tutoring and her own devices, their bold questioning makes clear the importance of training. Only when women were educated to the same standard as male leaders would they be able to raise that other voice and insist on their dignity as human beings morally, intellectually, and legally equal to men.

THE OTHER VOICE. The other voice, a voice of protest, was mostly female, but it was also male. It spoke in the vernaculars and in Latin, in treatises and dialogues, in plays and poetry, in letters and diaries, and in pamphlets. It battered at the wall of prejudice that encircled women and raised a banner announcing its claims. The female was equal (or even superior) to the male in essential nature—moral, spiritual, and intellectual. Women were capable of higher education, of holding positions of power and influence in the public realm, and of speaking and writing persuasively. The last bastion of masculine supremacy, centered on the notions of a woman's primary domestic responsibility and the requirement of female chastity, was not as yet assaulted—although visions of productive female communities as alternatives to the family indicated an awareness of the problem.

During the period 1300–1700, the other voice remained only a voice, and one only dimly heard. It did not result—yet—in an alteration of social patterns. Indeed, to this day they have not entirely been altered. Yet the call for justice issued as long as six centuries ago by those writing in the tradition of the other voice must be recognized as the source and origin of the mature feminist tradition and of the realignment of social institutions accomplished in the modern age.

We thank the volume editors in this series, who responded with many suggestions to an earlier draft of this introduction, making it a collaborative enterprise. Many of their suggestions and criticisms have resulted in revisions of this introduction, although we remain responsible for the final product.

PROJECTED TITLES IN THE SERIES

Isabella Andreini, *Mirtilla*, edited and translated by Laura Stortoni

Tullia d'Aragona, *Complete Poems and Letters*, edited and translated by Julia Hairston

Tullia d'Aragona, *The Wretch, Otherwise Known as Guerrino*, edited and translated by Julia Hairston and John McLucas

Francesco Barbaro et al., *On Marriage and the Family*, edited and translated by Margaret L. King

Laura Battiferra, *Selected Poetry, Prose, and Letters*, edited and translated by Victoria Kirkham

Francesco Buoninsegni and Arcangela Tarabotti, *Menippean Satire: "Against Feminine Extravagance" and "Antisatire,"* edited and translated by Elissa Weaver

Rosalba Carriera, *Letters, Diaries, and Art*, edited and translated by Catherine M. Sama

Madame du Chatelet, *Selected Works*, edited by Judith Zinsser

Vittoria Colonna, Chiara Matraini, and Lucrezia Marinella, *Marian Writings*, edited and translated by Susan Haskins

Princess Elizabeth of Bohemia, *Correspondence with Descartes*, edited and translated by Lisa Shapiro

Isabella d'Este, *Selected Letters*, edited and translated by Deanna Shemek

Fairy Tales by Seventeenth-Century French Women Writers, edited and translated by Lewis Seifert and Domna C. Stanton

Moderata Fonte, *Floridoro*, edited and translated by Valeria Finucci

Moderata Fonte and Lucrezia Marinella, *Religious Narratives*, edited and translated by Virginia Cox

Catharina Regina von Greiffenberg, *Meditations on the Life of Christ*, edited and translated by Lynne Tatlock

In Praise of Women: Italian Fifteenth-Century Defenses of Women, edited and translated by Daniel Bornstein

Louise Labé, *Complete Works*, edited and translated by Annie Finch and Deborah Baker

Lucrezia Marinella, *L'Enrico, or Byzantium Conquered*, edited and translated by Virginia Cox

Lucrezia Marinella, *Happy Arcadia*, edited and translated by Susan Haskins and Letizia Panizza

Chiara Matraini, *Selected Poetry and Prose*, edited and translated by Elaine MacLachlan

Alessandro Piccolomini, *Rethinking Marriage in Sixteenth-Century Italy*, edited and translated by Letizia Panizza

Christine de Pizan, *Debate over the "Romance of the Rose,"* edited and translated by Tom Conley and Virginie Greene

Christine de Pizan, *Life of Charles V*, edited and translated by Nadia Margolis

Christine de Pizan, *The Long Road of Learning*, edited and translated by Andrea Tarnowski

Madeleine and Catherine des Roches, *Selected Letters, Dialogues, and Poems*, edited and translated by Anne Larsen

Oliva Sabuco, *The New Philosophy: True Medicine*, edited and translated by Gianna Pomata

Margherita Sarrocchi, *La Scanderbeide*, edited and translated by Rinaldina Russell

Justine Siegemund, *The Court Midwife*, edited and translated by Lynne Tatlock

Gabrielle Suchon, *"On Philosophy" and "On Morality,"* edited and translated by Domna Stanton with Rebecca Wilkin

Sara Copio Sullam, *Sara Copio Sullam: Jewish Poet and Intellectual in Early Seventeenth-Century Venice*, edited and translated by Don Harrán

Arcangela Tarabotti, *Convent Life as Inferno: A Report*, introduction and notes by Francesca Medioli, translated by Letizia Panizza

Laura Terracina, *Works*, edited and translated by Michael Sherberg

Katharina Schütz Zell, *Selected Writings*, edited and translated by Elsie McKee

VOLUME EDITOR'S
INTRODUCTION

THE OTHER VOICE

On October 5, 1575, Francisca de los Apóstoles, a thirty-six-year-old *beata*,[1] was summoned from her prison cell to appear before the Toledan Inquisitor Juan de Llano de Valdés. She was about to defend herself against charges of *alumbradismo*, or claims to direct, illuminative experiences of God, in a trial that would last over two years.[2] Perhaps this encounter had become unavoidable. For nearly two years Francisca and her sister, Isabel Bautista, had been attracting public attention in their attempts to found a new religious

---

1. The word *beata* refers to religious women of Spain who fell into several categories. Some were independent laywomen who aspired to live pious lives of prayer and service. Others were lay associates of formal religious orders. Still others formed small communities similar to convents but without taking formal religious vows. For a discussion of this phenomenon, see Mary Elizabeth Perry, *Gender and Disorder in Early Modern Seville* (Princeton: Princeton University Press, 1990), 97–117.

2. Perhaps no single term is as confusing as the term *alumbrado*, which clearly meant very different things to different people. The term was a technical category for prosecution by the Spanish Inquisition, and there were formal edicts against *alumbrados* as early as 1525. Broadly speaking, it referred to those who had religious experiences that led them to speak about what God had revealed to them in prayer. They were tried by the Inquisition because they were accused of having been "falsely illumined" in prayer and at times because they were accused of attempting to deceive others through their recourse to prayer. For a discussion of the definition of *alumbradismo*, especially as it pertained to Inquisitional cases against women, see Gillian T. W. Ahlgren, "Negotiating Sanctity: Holy Women in Sixteenth-Century Spain," *Church History* 64 (1995): 373–88; see also Ahlgren, *Teresa of Avila and the Politics of Sanctity* (Ithaca, NY: Cornell University Press, 1996), 9–15; Mary Giles, ed., *Women in the Inquisition: Spain and the New World* (Baltimore: Johns Hopkins University Press, 1998); Alistair Hamilton, *Heresy and Mysticism in Sixteenth-Century Spain* (Toronto: University of Toronto Press, 1992); Alvaro Huerga, *Historia de los alumbrados, 1570–1620*, 5 vols. (Madrid: Fundación Universitaria Española, 1972–94); and Alison Weber, "Demonizing Ecstasy: Alonso de la Fuente and the *Alumbrados* of Extremadura," in *The Mystical Gesture: Essays on Medieval and Early Modern Spiritual Culture in Honor of Mary E. Giles*, ed. Robert Boenig (Burlington, VT: Ashgate, 2000), 141–58.

community for women without dowries and another for the priests who would minister to them. Their reform efforts contained some pointed criticisms of the contemporary state of the Toledan church, which at that point had been managed by a governor and his council for sixteen years during the absence of its archbishop, Bartolomé de Carranza. Francisca's apocalyptic visions foretelling the return of Carranza from his imprisonment in Rome and her poignantly articulated concern for the state of the disadvantaged in light of the suspension of many of Carranza's initiatives toward poor relief in the archdiocese alternately struck chords of sympathy in some and fear or defensiveness in others. After a grueling trial lasting over three years, Francisca was condemned for false mysticism, forced to appear in a public auto de fe, given one hundred lashes, and exiled from the city of Toledo for three years; as a result she disappeared from recorded history.

Inquisitorial interrogation would silence Francisca's voice for both her contemporaries and for historians, but we have much to learn by recovering and listening carefully to this "other voice" as we attempt to reconstruct that ever-shifting landscape of early modern Europe. As tempting as it might be to interpret the verdict against this bold and determined visionary as inevitable, the dynamics of Francisca's Inquisitional trial are as illuminating as the testimony she offers about the nature of her religious experiences.

Although Francisca is a woman unknown to us, she apparently exerted considerable public influence in her day until her demise after inquisitorial prosecution.[3] This circumstance is not entirely unusual, as recent studies of women and their influence in the intertwined spheres of social, political, and religious life in sixteenth-century Spain have begun to reveal. Women religious, whether avowed nuns or other kinds of holy women, played many important roles among their contemporaries. The *beata* María de Santo Domingo (d. 1524), a charismatic woman whose raptures, stigmata, and spiritual power were controversial in her day, dictated a book of prayer and was frequently consulted by her contemporaries.[4] The Franciscan nun Juana de

---

3. A preliminary study of Francisca is available in Giles, *Women in the Inquisition*, 119–33. Alvaro Huerga mentions her case briefly in *Historia de los alumbrados* 1: 232–33, and Juan Blázquez Miguel considers her briefly in *Sueños y procesos de Lucrecia de León* (Madrid: Tecnos, 1987), 65–66, and *La Inquisición en Castilla-La Mancha* (Madrid: Universidad de Córdoba, 1986), 114–15. From their comments it appears that neither scholar has actually read the transcript or even the summary of her case, which is contained in the Archivo Histórico Nacional (AHN), Madrid, Inquisición, leg. 113, no. 5.

4. María was investigated for heterodoxy in 1509–10 and defended by her confessors Diego de Vitoria and Antonio de la Peña; she was exonerated by Inquisitor General Franciscao Ximénez de Cisneros and the Consejo of the Inquisition in March of 1510. For a study of her life and works, see Mary E. Giles, ed., *The Book of Prayer of Sor María of Santo Domingo: A Study and Translation*

la Cruz (d. 1534) was known for her sermons, apparently revealed to her directly by God while she was in ecstatic prayer.[5] The *beata* Mari Diaz (d. 1572) was an important influence on the Jesuit Baltasar Alvarez and many young priests in her day.[6] And at the early stages of her career, before her commitment to full claustration as part of the reform of the Carmelite order, Teresa of Avila (d. 1582) had occasion to spend time with influential women in Toledo, including Doña Luisa de la Cerda, who served as an important patron and enabled Teresa's consultation with Juan de Avila.[7] As an administrator of the reform movement, Teresa grew to exert considerable influence through her correspondence and writings.

Other women, while effective and influential for some time, found their prophetic reforming careers cut short by Inquisitional condemnation. The *beata* Francisca Hernández, associated with members of the Franciscan order and professors at the University of Alcalá, was consulted for her interpretation of scripture and her prophetic utterances until she was arrested by the Toledan tribunal of the Inquisition in 1529.[8] The stigmatic nun María de la Visitación was asked to bless the Spanish Armada before its fateful departure from Lisbon in 1588. Shortly afterward, she was investigated by the Inquisitional tribunal in Lisbon and condemned to reclusion as a false mystic.[9] The laywoman Lucrecia de León's influence as a political prophet was similarly cut short by inquisitorial investigation.[10]

(Albany: State University of New York Press, 1990). Jodi Bilinkoff, after studying María's case, suggests that María de Santo Domingo and her supporters represented a "Catherinist" movement, i.e., a Spanish movement with a charismatic orientation to prayer and penance, in imitation of the recently canonized Catherine of Siena, which challenged contemporary Thomistic revival in the universities; see Jodi Bilinkoff, "Charisma and Controversy: The Case of María de Santo Domingo," in *Spanish Women in the Golden Age: Images and Realities*, ed. Magdalena S. Sánchez and Alain Saint-Saens (Westport, CT: Greenwood Press, 1996), 23–35 at 30–31.

5. For a study of Juana de la Cruz, see Ronald E. Surtz, *The Guitar of God: Gender, Power, and Authority in the Visionary World of Mother Juana de la Cruz (1481–1534)* (Philadelphia: University of Pennsylvania Press, 1990).

6. For a discussion of Mari Diaz's career, see Jodi Bilinkoff, *Avila of Saint Teresa: Religious Reform in a Sixteenth-Century City* (Ithaca, NY: Cornell University Press, 1989), and Baldomero Jiménez Duque, *Maridiaz: La "santa de Avila" en el siglo XVI* (Avila: Tau, 1989).

7. For a discussion of Teresa's associations with Luisa de la Cerda and other notable women, see Alison Weber, "Saint Teresa's Problematic Patrons," *Journal of Medieval and Early Modern Studies* 29 (1999): 357–78.

8. For a discussion of Francisca's case, see Mary E. Giles, "Francisca Hernández and the Sexuality of Religious Dissent," in Giles, *Women in the Inquisition*, 75–97.

9. See Luis de Granada, *Historia de Sor María de la Visitación y Sermón de las caídas públicas*, ed. Alvaro Huerga (Barcelona: Juan Flors, 1962).

10. See Richard Kagan's study, *Lucrecia's Dreams: Politics and Prophecy in Sixteenth-Century Spain* (Berkeley: University of California Press, 1990).

What these examples suggest is that women like Francisca, whose religious experiences inspired a lifetime of activities dedicated to religious reform, had few platforms that allowed them to sustain a public role. The religious status of these women, while by no means a guarantor of their orthodoxy (and resultant exoneration after Inquisitional investigation), is not insignificant. Increasingly, religious vows and claustration were seen to be critical in establishing the institutional allegiance that lent credibility to a woman's message of reform. But this way of life was not open to all. Many women lacked a dowry and were therefore precluded from marriage or the convent. Some of these became *beatas*, women who sought to lead holy lives in the world. At times they attached themselves to already formed religious communities as third-order participants, and at other times they formed small congregations that maintained themselves financially through some sort of trade and then formed an association with a parish priest or a cleric from some religious institution.[11]

Because they often taught catechism to young women, the *beatas* could be incorporated into the larger program of Tridentine reform, and many were provided with financial support by bishops and other religious officials. Although many of them used their charismatic power in creative ways, in general the more public religious space they appropriated, the more institutional challenges they encountered. The charismatic influence of *beatas* was increasingly viewed as problematic, particularly because there were few mechanisms to guarantee the stability of the community or the women's obedience to ecclesiastical figures. After the Council of Trent (1545–63), which declared in its decree on religious orders that all women religious should be cloistered, there was increasing pressure on *beatas* to associate themselves with recognized religious orders and to take formal vows.

THE SPANISH INQUISITION

In Spain more specifically, investigation of the orthodoxy and desirability of the activities and message of religious women was made possible by the various tribunals of the Spanish Inquisition. This institution, while comparable to other Inquisitional offices, had several characteristics unique to Spain and its religious culture. Throughout the medieval period, three religious traditions flourished in Spain—Christianity, Judaism, and Islam—a situation that

---

11. For more discussion of the religious roles of *beatas* and the challenges they faced, see Mary Elizabeth Perry, "Beatas and the Inquisition in Early Modern Seville," in *Inquisition and Society in Early Modern Europe*, ed. Stephen Haliczer (London: 1986), 147–68, and Perry, *Gender and Disorder*.

had allowed for a great deal of intellectual and cultural interaction. With the exception of the kingdom of Granada, the gradual *reconquista*, or reconquering, of the Iberian Peninsula by Christian forces had been essentially accomplished by the time Ferdinand and Isabella united the kingdoms of Castile and Aragon with their marital union. It was believed that a common religion held the key to the elusive political unity of these two regions that had significant linguistic and cultural barriers. A concerted effort at proselytizing in the fifteenth century had led to an increase in the number of Jewish converts to Christianity. But by the 1470s, many disputed the authentic conversion of the *cristianos nuevos*, or new Christians, also called *conversos*. In 1478, Pope Sixtus IV granted the request of Catholic monarchs Ferdinand and Isabella to appoint officials who could investigate and proceed against those suspected of corrupting the purity of the Catholic faith, laying the foundations for the gradual institutional structure known as the Spanish Inquisition. The monarchs retained the right to appoint the Inquisitor General, who set policy and headed the *Suprema*, or main tribunal, but the operation and management of the institution was in the hands of ecclesiastical officials (religious hierarchs, priests, cathedral canons, and avowed religious), who served a multitude of functions as the Inquisition grew in scope and influence. Throughout the 1480s, regional tribunals were established in twenty-three cities including Seville, Córdoba, Zaragoza, Valencia, Jaén, Ciudad Real, Avila, Segovia, and Toledo.

    Established initially to monitor the activity of *conversos*, the Spanish Inquisition found its activities magnified by the same religious and political movements that shaped other European nations early in the sixteenth century, most particularly the Protestant Reformation. When the early works of Luther began to filter into the Peninsula, raising concerns about the social and political unrest that might follow, the Spanish Inquisition provided an effective network for censorial control—a result that was likely unintended by its founders, but one that led to increased inquisitorial influence over religious culture and Christian theological writing. In the 1520s, concern over the emergence of individualistic prayer techniques that were perhaps contributing to a rejection of the authority of the papacy and the disparagement of the sacraments—clear signals to inquisitors of Lutheranism—led to the prosecution of a group of *alumbrados* in Toledo and an Inquisitional edict against them in 1525.[12] The variety of *alumbrado* practices contained in the

---

12. The 1525 edict against the *alumbrados* is found in Antonio Márquez, *Los alumbrados: Orígines y filosofía, 1525–1559* (Madrid: Taurus, 1980), 229–38. The characteristics of *alumbradismo* contained in the edict—from "Lutheran" tendencies to disparage the sacraments, veneration of the saints, and respect for the papacy to prayer techniques encouraging radical abandonment to

edict, many of which may be distorted representations of the intentions of the group, reflect the complexity of the phenomenon of *alumbradismo*. For example, the attempt to practice self-abandonment in prayer (called *dejamiento*) may not be in such acute tension with the practice of recollective meditation and the turning over of the self to the insights that may come out of such reflection. Certainly, the focus on prayer led to the development of a rich interior life, and the spiritual growth that attended it might lead to serious questions about the more ordinary practice of the Christian faith. Indeed, such a program of reflective reform was precisely what the Franciscan revival of the 1510s hoped to accomplish. After the promulgation of the Edict of 1525 and the prosecution of several *alumbrados* throughout the 1520s and 1530s, *alumbradismo* became a punishable offense in and of itself and, perhaps more importantly, there was an increased suspicion of mental prayer and greater scrutiny of religious figures whose authority was rooted in revelation or claims to access to the knowledge of God.

A relative lack of Inquisitional activity during the 1530s and 1540s was followed by an explosion of activity under Inquisitor General Fernando de Valdés, who took office in 1547. Informed by the appearance of other indices, Valdés formulated a general Index of Prohibited Books considered injurious to the Catholic faith.[13] The Valdés Index of Prohibited Books, published in 1559, affected Spanish Catholicism by effectively limiting access to spiritual classics that would allow lay Catholics to learn techniques of mental prayer. After expressing a reserved indignation over the Valdés Index of Prohibited Books in *The Book of Her Life*, Teresa of Avila devoted a writing career to filling the void caused by the Valdés Index,[14] but her works were not published until after her death and the extent of their influence on contemporary women outside her religious order (i.e., on women like Francisca) is unclear.

During the 1570s, another wave of Inquisitional activity against *alumbradismo* erupted, engaging primarily the tribunals of Toledo, Llerena, and Seville. This wave of investigations for false mysticism included Teresa of Avila and Francisca. At the same time, institutional concern over the auton-

---

God—reveal the many ambiguities in defining, recognizing, and prosecuting illuminism. For a discussion of some of the figures in this early group of illuminists prosecuted by the Inquisition, see Márquez, *Los alumbrados*, 58–94; and Milagros Ortega Costa, *Proceso de la Inquisición contra María de Cazalla* (Madrid: Fundación Universitaria Española, 1978).

13. For a summary of the evolution of the Valdés Index and a review of its sources, see Virgilio Pinto Crespo, *Inquisición y control ideológico en la España del siglo XVI* (Madrid: Taurus, 1983), 149–72.

14. See discussion in Ahlgren, *Teresa of Avila and the Politics of Sanctity*, 39–42.

omy and charismatic authority of *beatas* was expressed clearly by the Supreme Council of the Inquisition, which sought to assess the influence of *beatas* throughout Spain and to achieve consensus about limiting their freedom of movement. In a letter of October 25, 1575, the Council solicited the advice of other tribunals on the problem of uncloistered religious women to see if this practice ought to be prohibited.[15]

The response of the tribunal of Toledo is interesting. Although this correspondence arrived in the middle of the inquisitorial investigation of Francisca, Isabel, and their confessor Miguel Ruíz, officials there still appeared unconcerned about *beatas* and their potentially destabilizing effects on the institutional church.[16] "With regard to the *beatas*," they wrote on November 10, 1575, "we do not have news of there being so many of them in this district, nor are they so disorderly as to make it necessary to force them to live in community." The tribunal promised to notify the *Suprema* of any difficulties associated with the *beatas* as they arose.[17] The Inquisitional tribunal of Seville, however, responded quite differently. In a letter dated December 17, 1575, officials there advocated the suppression of all *beatas* who were not members of third orders (i.e., lay associates of recognized religious orders). Although the evidence reflects quite a range of perspectives on the acceptance of *beatas* within church structures, it seems clear that, as a religious status or way of being, *beatas* were considered less "normative" during the 1570s; as Mary Elizabeth Perry argues, their status would continue to decline into the next century.[18]

<hr />

15. AHN, lib. 578, fol. 341v: "Muy reverendos señores: Aqui se a tenido relacion que en algunos lugares dese distrito ay muchas mugeres que handan en avito de veatas y viven como tal sin estar en comunidad y clausura y que algunas dellas dan obediencia a algunas personas y porque se entiende que de permitirse lo susodicho se an seguido y siguen algunos ynconbinientes y adelante podrian rresultar otros mayores si no se remediase con tiempo. Consultado el reverendisimo señor inquisidor general a parecido que vosotros señores nos aviseis que ynconbenientes resultan de permitir que las d[ic]has mugeres anden en el d[ic]ho abito de veatas sin estar encerradas y de que bivan en casa de por sy y apartadas de la comunidad y dar la d[ic]ha obediencia como lo azen y si sera bien prohibir esta manera de bivir y que orden os parece se podra tener para ello para que visto v[uest]ro parecer se provea del remedio que mas convenga."

16. See AHN, Inquisicion, leg. 3072, no. 35: Carta al Consejo de 1 septiembre 1575.

17. AHN, Inquisicion, leg. 3072, no. 44: Carta de 10 noviembre 1575: "Resçebimos las de V. s. de 25 del pasado y de 2, 3, y 8 del p[rese]nte y qua[n]to a las beatas, no hemos tenido Rel[aci]on que aya tanto numero dellas en lugar alg[un]o deste districto, sin tanto deshorden en esto q sea necessario reduzir las a que bivan en comunidad. Estaremos advertidos delo de aqui adelante y entendiendo algun inconveniente daremos delo aviso a V. s."

18. See Perry, *Gender and Disorder*, 97–117.

THE SOCIAL AND ECONOMIC SITUATION
OF WOMEN IN TOLEDO

If becoming a *beata* was one of the few socioreligious options Francisca and her sister Isabel had, they were hardly alone in their predicament. Indeed, Francisca's public role as a visionary reformer and the inquisitorial proceedings against her cannot be understood outside the context of Toledo with its specific social, economic, and religious problems. Geographically, politically, and economically, Toledo was the heart of Castile, and, like Castile, over the course of the sixteenth century it experienced significant change. Under Charles V, the city was the location for the meetings of the Cortes. But in 1561, his son Philip II left Toledo definitively to establish his court in Madrid, with serious political and economic consequences for Toledo. In her detailed study *Poverty and Welfare in Habsburg Spain: The Example of Toledo*, Linda Martz describes how, during the 1570s, "the city experienced a long depression caused by the crown's suspension of payments, an enormous increase in taxation that struck particularly hard at the cloth industries, and an outbreak of sickness that was one of the worst of the sixteenth century."[19] Indeed, by 1575 the city council had become "more and more concerned about the number of poor persons in the city, especially 'the Galicians and the people from the mountains.' In June *corregidor* Juan Gutierrez Tello mentioned that there were more than 300 sick people who could not be admitted to the already overcrowded city hospitals and thus they were left 'to die on the streets.'"[20]

These problems of poverty were most often addressed through various forms of relief for the poor administered by the church. Toledo was by far the wealthiest archdiocese in Spain; its income in 1577 totaled 200,000 ducats, two and a half times the income of the archdiocese of Seville and four to five times the size of the other Spanish dioceses.[21] It also had a solid infrastructure of religious communities to assist the poor. A relatively large population of clerics, religious, *beatas*, and lay confraternities served in some thirteen hospitals throughout the city.[22] Relief for the poor was a source of

---

19. Linda Martz, *Poverty and Welfare in Habsburg Spain: The Case of Toledo* (New York: Oxford University Press, 1972), 4.

20. Martz, *Poverty and Welfare*, 139.

21. See V. Vazquez de Prada, *Historia económica y social de España*, vol. 3, *Los siglos XVI y XVII* (Madrid, 1978), 188–89.

22. The Hospital de la Misericordia, where Francisca and the *beatas* went for liturgical acts, was one of the more important in the city, containing approximately sixty beds. The hospital was one of two in the city devoted to treating noncontagious ailments like wounds, broken bones, intestinal problems, fevers, and toothaches. Founded by Lope Gaytán in the mid-fifteenth cen-

concern for Bartolomé Carranza, who was appointed archbishop of Toledo in 1558 while still living in Brussels. Carranza paid his first visit to the archdiocese in October 1558 where, among other duties, he oversaw plans for bread distribution to the poor for 1559. But his administration of the important archdiocese was cut short when, in August 1559, he was arrested by the Inquisitional Tribunal of Toledo. The formal charge was heretical statements in the catechism he had developed after the Council of Trent.[23]

Carranza's trial lasted for nearly twenty years,[24] and his absence proved economically advantageous to Philip II. Throughout the 1570s in particular, archdiocesan revenues appear to have been diverted to the crown in a desperate attempt to address Philip's larger financial crisis. In 1576, the crown suspended all payments to Toledo prior to declaring bankruptcy in 1578. Also in 1576, the crown raised the tax rate to 10 percent (up from 5 percent).[25] By all accounts, therefore, the need for socioreligious reform in Toledo during the 1570s was pressing. Although there appeared to be a substantial religious infrastructure already in place (according to Manuel Fernández Alvarez, in the mid-sixteenth century Toledo's population of 55,000 included 739 clerics and 1,942 members of religious orders[26]) foundations did not address the

tury, the hospital was well organized and housed a confraternity that included some of the better families of Toledo. See Martz, *Poverty and Welfare*, 160–61. See also Francisco de Pisa, *Apuntamientos para la IIa Parte de la "Descripción de la Imperial Ciudad de Toledo,"* ed. José Gómez-Menor Fuentes (Toledo: Insituto Provincial de Investigaciones y Estudios Toledanos, 1976), 58–59.

23. The case is well documented by José Ignacio Tellechea Idígoras, *El arzobispo Carranza y su tiempo*, 2 vols. (Madrid: Guadarrama, 1968), but its effects on church life in Spain still need consideration. For documentation and discussion of the initial accusations against Carranza, see Idigoras, 1: 237–66.

24. Carranza's formal appeal to Rome led to a transfer of jurisdiction to the Roman Inquisition, but the case languished on for nearly two decades and through several popes, complicating the diplomatic and political issues involved in resolving it. Philip II's interventions ranged from the extremes of a formal declaration of support for Carranza, payment of the expenses of Martin de Azpilcueta, who was sent to Rome in 1567 to defend Carranza, and a denunciation of Carranza in 1574. Gregory XIII, the pope who passed sentence on Carranza on April 14, 1576, declared rather enigmatically that he was neither innocent nor a heretic but suspected of heresy. His determination encapsulates the problematic politics of the case. To have declared Carranza a heretic after he had represented the church at the Council of Trent and served the church well as archbishop would have been a travesty of justice; but to have absolved him would have been a condemnation of the Spanish Inquisition and would have cost Gregory the favor of Philip II. See Alvaro Huerga, "La muerte de Carranza: Informes confidenciales del Cardenal de Como, Secretario de Estado de Gregorio XIII," in *Cuadernos de investigación histórica* 7 (1981): 15–27 at 18. For a detailed account of the trial see Idigoras, *El Arzobispo Carranza y su tiempo*.

25. See Martz, *Poverty and Welfare*, 139.

26. See Manuel Fernández Alvarez, "El entorno histórico de Santa Teresa," *Studia Zamorensia* 3 (1982): 357–447, at 379.

socioreligious needs of women adequately. Indeed, in her assessment of Toledan society, Linda Martz notes,

> Toledo appears to have been a man-poor society, or, as Luis Hurtado observed, there was "an excessive number and notable quantity of women" (Memorial, 498). One consequence of this surfeit was the proliferation of female religious orders. In 1576 and 1591 the number of female religious was more than double that of the males, though many women included in these estimates did not take formal religious vows.[27]

The gendered implications of poverty have been amply studied by Perry in her work on sixteenth-century Seville, all of which are applicable to the Toledan situation and also affirmed by what we can understand of Francisca's story. Women's options beyond marriage and the cloister—both of which necessitated a dowry—meant that, as Perry concludes, "social and economic changes combined to disrupt the other traditional roles of women and promote prostitution as a livelihood."[28] When local industry and small-scale agriculture declined, as they did in the 1570s, the economic survival of women was a particular problem: fully 20 percent of parishioners in Toledo were reported to be widows, women who would have been hard hit by consistent shortages in the grain supply of the city throughout the decade.[29] Forms of religious life, particularly that of the *beata*, were often seen to provide another avenue for women.

Hurtado's 1576 inventory of the city of Toledo provides us with an excellent description of the state of religious life in Toledo, and it suggests that Francisca and Isabel's desire to provide religious enclosure for poorer women so that they would not "lose their virtue" was neither original nor superfluous. A similar endeavor had been undertaken in the 1550s in the form of an institution known as *Nuestra Señora de los Remedios*, founded by the then archbishop of Toledo, Cardinal Juan Martínez Siliceo.[30] Later, Gaspar de Quiroga,

27. Martz, *Poverty and Welfare*, 105.

28. For a general introduction to these issues, see Mary Elizabeth Perry, *Crime and Society in Early Modern Seville* (Hanover, NH: University Press of New England, 1980).

29. For a discussion of the situation of widows in Toledo, a summary of parish records listing the numbers of widows, and an attempt to account for these figures, see Martz, *Poverty and Welfare*, 103–5. Martz notes that Toledo does not seem to have a particularly high percentage of widows compared with other cities in Spain at this time.

30. Francisco de Pisa, *Apuntamientos*, 61–62: "En este distrito cae el insigne colegio y iglesia de las Doncellas con título de nuestra Señora de los Remedios, que fundó y dotó magníficamente y espléndidamente el Illmo. Cardenal don Juan Martínez Siliceo, arzobispo de Toledo, donde se crían e instituyen en buenas costumbres las niñas o doncellas pobres, y viven en recogimiento y son ayudadas para su dote y casamiento o para religión, que se comenzó esta obra en el año

cardinal-archbishop of Toledo, founded *Nuestra Señora del Refugio*, a house where twenty-four lay women—widows, young women awaiting marriage, or married women involved in divorces or other legal proceedings with their absent spouses—might live a cloistered life under the supervision of the Augustinian prioress of Santa Monica.[31]

The portrait of religious reform available in the Inquisitional testimony of Francisca de los Apóstoles provides us with a unique insider's perspective on this situation. Francisca's narrative testifies poignantly to the acute problems of poverty the Toledan people faced, the expectation that religious officials would be concerned about remedying such problems, and the intense frustration many religious people felt at the economic administration of the archdiocese, which was, to all appearances, being run contrary to Carranza's initial impulse toward greater infrastructural organization for relief for the poor. The apocalyptic visions Francisca experienced in the chapel of *Nuestra Señora del Sagrario*, a Marian pilgrimage shrine located in the heart of the Toledan cathedral, reflected God's displeasure with the current situation in Toledo. Her visions were then a prophetic denunciation of social and ecclesiastical forms of sin among her own neighbors. Francisca, her sister Isabel, and their supporters appear to be key players in the dramatic struggles to transform or to maintain social and ecclesiastical structures and to monitor their effectiveness. The voice of Francisca, as it emerges from the Inquisitional trial transcript, should provide us with much food for thought about the nexus of relationships that undergird such struggles.

FRANCISCA: THE WOMAN

We know nothing more about Francisca herself than what is contained in the Inquisitional case against her. She was born in the town of Noves, probably in 1539. Her father, Cebrián de Avila, was a painter, and her mother, Juana Diez, died when Francisca was still a child, precipitating her residence with a noblewoman of Noves named Francisca Sarmiento and her father's eventual move to Madrid to pursue work. When Francisca was sixteen, she was sent to Toledo to live at the church of Santa María la Blanca, a former synagogue,

---

de 1551 en las casas [que ahora son] de Arias Pardo, que son a San Román, y después de 1557 se pasaron de asiento en las casas muy principales de D. Diego de Mendoza, conde de Mélito; esta casa y obra tiene por patronos a los Reyes de España y Arzobispo de Toledo que por tiempo fueren. Es la dotación de cien doncellas, aunque no está todo el número cumplido." Palomares, who edited the text, scratched out "cien" and wrote instead "cinquenta y cinco."

31. Martz, *Poverty and Welfare*, 105.

with a community of *beatas*.[32] She remained there for eight years until she left to live with several of her sisters, perhaps serving as a chaperone figure for them. In her genealogical information, Francisca claimed never to have known her paternal grandparents, whom she could not name. She named her maternal grandfather, Alberto Cerezo, but not her maternal grandmother and claimed to know little of their origins. Given both the vague information and her artisan class standing, it is a distinct possibility that Francisca came from a *converso* background.[33]

Francisca appears to have remained faithful to the lifestyle she had learned at Santa María la Blanca. As early as 1565, working out of her home, Francisca began to teach young women to support themselves, since "she understood the way in which many young girls and women lost their virtue, so she occupied herself in gathering together some of them and teaching them needlepoint."[34]

Around 1570, Francisca's sister, Isabel Bautista, fell ill and was bedridden for a full year. After various medical treatments failed to help Isabel, Francisca was referred to Alonso Hernández, a cleric at the church of San Juan de los Reyes who specialized in the cure of *endemoniadas*, or women possessed by the devil. Hernández performed exorcisms on Isabel for a period of five months, at times publicly. The exorcisms were apparently quite grueling, and Francisca describes both her discomfort with Hernández's treatment of her sister[35] and her concern that he had little success in curing her. Isabel was often observed wandering the streets aimlessly and was perhaps considered immoral or mentally unbalanced. Eventually, Francisca was advised to consult with a cleric named Miguel Ruíz, chaplain of the Hospital of the Misericordia, who helped

---

32. The description of Santa María la Blanca in Francisco de Pisa, *Apuntamientos*, 71 reads, "Asimismo hay otra iglesia intitulada de Santa María la Blanca, que es de mugeres recogidas, al presente. Esta iglesia fue antiquísima sinagoga de judíos, por ellos edificada en esta ciudad después de su primera dispersión, antes que Zorobabel reedificase el Templo de Jerusalem. . . Perseveró esta iglesia en forma de ermita o oratorio hasta que el cardenal don Juan Martínez Siliceo, arzobispo de Toledo, en nuestra edad la hizo aderezar y renovar juntando con ella algunas casas cercanas en forma de monasterio, y trajo a esta casa las mugeres recogidas para que se sirviesen de esta iglesia, dándole por título N. Sa de la Piedad."

33. Indeed, it is quite possible that Francisca did not name them because they were known *conversos* or had a common *converso* name. *Conversos*, individuals whose families had converted from Judaism to Christianity, either recently or within several generations, were often suspected of maintaining their former Jewish customs and even beliefs. Inquisitional trials of *conversos* were common throughout the sixteenth century.

34. Fol. 171r: "tenia entendido el camino por donde se perdian muchas donzellas y mugeres que andavan perdidas se empleava en rrecoger algunas y ensenarles labor que savia."

35. See fol. 171r: "sentia grandes fatigas de berlo."

endemoniadas heal from spiritual illness through increased devotional practices like prayer and the sacraments. Miguel Ruíz advised Isabel to change her lifestyle by dressing with modesty, keeping herself enclosed, and devoting herself to prayer and communion. This more pastoral approach appeared to address the problem: within eight days of her association with Miguel Ruíz, Isabel experienced a remarkable improvement, characterized by the return of sound judgment and a more normal domestic life. She conversed with her sister as she had before she was ill, and had enough concentration to do her needlework.[36]

As Isabel increasingly gave herself over to prayer, she encouraged Francisca to become more devoted to spiritual practices including fasting and penance "on behalf of the state of the church and for the growth of the Catholic faith."[37] Throughout 1572 and 1573, Isabel became even more devoted to penance, walking barefoot, fasting, and taking communion frequently. Isabel made plans to found a convent dedicated to these practices. She consulted with a noblewoman from Madrid about endowing the convent, engaged in a seventy-day fast over this intention, and wrote a monastic rule for the community she wanted to establish.

On November 1, 1573, Isabel left Toledo to travel to Rome to secure a patent for the convent, presumably because she did not receive permission to found it from the governor. In her sister's absence, Francisca began to establish a penitential relationship with Miguel Ruíz, taking him as a spiritual director. She began to spend time with several other women who confessed with him, and they began to pray intensely for the foundation of the convent. The women prayed together, fasted, received communion, and said novenas at many of the local churches, praying especially for the reform of the church.

After two months of this greater dedication to religious life, Francisca began to experience deeper, more visionary forms of prayer. At the Chapel of Nuestra Señora del Sagrario, in the main cathedral of Toledo, Francisca had her first experience of rapture during which she saw a vision of Our Lady interceding before Christ on behalf of the church of Toledo and on behalf of Archbishop Carranza, imprisoned in Rome. The following week Francisca experienced another vision, this time of God's wrath at the corrupted church. In this second vision, Christ asked her if she would be willing to allow the

---

36. Fol. 172r: "dentro de ocho dias estubo bueno y en su juyzio y hacia su labor y tratava con ella como de antes."

37. Fol. 172r: " y de aqui se bino a dar a muchos ayunos y penitenzias y a persuadir a esta confesante q[ue] hiciese mas de lo que hazia por el estado eclesiastico por ensalsamiento de la fe catolica."

demons who were tormenting the world to enter into her and give an account through her of all the world had done to offend God. Francisca spent six months in prayer discerning whether or not to accept such torments by devils in the service of God. During this process of discernment, Francisca came across a similar experience recounted of Catherine of Siena in Raymond of Capua's *Life of Catherine of Siena*, in which Catherine was tormented by demons on behalf of the church.[38] This reading gave Francisca the courage she needed to "accept with good will whatever His Majesty wanted, as long as He gave her His grace so that she would never offend Him."[39]

From June through October 1574, Francisca experienced a series of torments in which demons entered her body and spoke to Miguel Ruíz through her mouth, identifying themselves as demons associated with pride or other forms of sin. Thus, in a form of universal confession, Francisca in effect dictated to Ruíz a catalogued account of humanity's offenses against God. After this experience, Francisca was given to understand that she should make a vow to commit herself to uphold the virtue that remedied each of the sins that the demons represented. To counteract the power of the demons who represented examples of humanity's sin of pride, for example, Francisca vowed to commit herself to greater humility.

The vows to which Francisca referred in her narrative, translated in this volume, expressed clearly her reform ideals. They reveal that she understood Christ's life on earth, much like her own, to be one of repeated conflict with demonic forces, to which he responded by continually calling humanity toward greater virtue. Francisca viewed the monastery of Corpus Christi and the convent of the Encarnación, the convents that she and her sister Isabel intended to found, as altars of sacrifice on behalf of human sin. This intercessory vocation was rooted in her strong conviction that humanity remained in bondage to sin and that the redemptive process initiated by Christ was not fully completed. Thus she writes that the women who enter her religious houses "should have the intent to imitate and follow Jesus Christ," their vocation being "to awaken the passion of Christ because it has been frozen by continual sin and our desire to flee from troubles and our love of our bodies."[40]

---

38. See Raimundo de Capua, *Vida de la bienaventurada sancta Catharina de Sena*, trans. Antonio de la Pena (Medina del Campo: Francistco de Canto, 1569), fols. 92r–93v. A similar example, this one rooted in Antony's temptation by demons in the desert, is described in the *Suma de los solicitos enganos de nuestros tiempos*, Biblioteca de la Real Academia de Historia, MS 12–26-7.D 185, fol. 191.

39. Fol. 173v. Francisca's language here recalls that of Teresa of Avila in her description of her conversion before the statue of Christ in *Vida* 9.1–8.

40. Fol. 158v.

Theologically speaking, Francisca's understanding of human existence was that people go through life conflicted by temptation toward vices and attraction to the positive, passionate energy of Christ. While Francisca realistically and pragmatically affirmed that humans could indeed reject or ignore God's constant call to a deeper engagement in prayer and virtue, she also believed that some people would choose to imitate Christ and thus model and embody his redemptive activity in the world. Her model of reform introduced women as intercessors and agents in a redemptive process that continually invites all humanity into a greater imitation of Christ.

For Francisca, the *beatas'* dedication to poverty and humility were key indicators of their commitment to a deeper relationship with God and greater service to humankind. Furthermore, the women could dedicate themselves to cultivating specific virtues in direct exchange for pardon for specific sins. In one of her vows, for example, Francisca offered her own "perpetual rectitude of spirit," or her sincere intention to please God through all of her actions, in exchange for the corruption of ecclesiastical leaders. Francisca's criticism of such corruption was pointed. Although she acknowledged that all humanity was subject to hypocrisy, she particularly called attention to a lack of sincerity and authenticity in the behavior of priests who "serve and love God with hypocrisy, pretending to be holy with half-hearted works." As Francisca saw things, such behavior was in fact a daily, ongoing crucifixion of Christ.[41]

In her testimony, Francisca states that her conflicts with demons ended when she took her vows on November 1, 1574. As she describes it, Francisca understood that she had achieved a victory over the demons, a sign of which she felt in the form of deep interior peace. Her desire to dedicate herself to prayer, fasting, and communion increased, and she sought for herself a greater intercessory role. In prayer, she asked God how she could contribute to the salvation of humanity. A second, more intense experience of visionary prayer would provide her with new directions.

In early December 1574, Francisca fell ill and had an embodied prayer experience witnessed by several family members. As she describes it,[42] she awoke suddenly one night, cried out, and felt "transported out of herself." In this state, she experienced a vision of the final judgment in which Francisca felt the wrath of God, witnessed the suffering of Christ on the cross with Mary at his side, and grew to fear the condemnatory sentence God would impose on the entire world in response. This experience lasted about three hours and left Francisca bedridden for three days afterward. On the following Friday

41. Fol. 160v.
42. What follows is a paraphrase of Francisca's testimony of October 8, 1575, fols. 174v–177v.

evening, Francisca experienced yet another rapture and vision in which she herself played a more integrated role in the intercessory process. She saw scenes from the life of Christ that were emblematic of particular virtues, and she vowed to embody those virtues in order to take on the same redemptive role as Christ. After observing many scenes from Christ's passion, Francisca saw a procession of priests dressed in coarse, woolen cloth and black hoods and a procession of nuns dressed in white with white capes, and Our Lord said to her, "These are the religious who I want to make satisfaction to me in the same way you yourself have vowed [to make it]."[43]

Shortly after this vision of the judgment confirming Francisca's divine mandate to found the monastery and convent, Francisca's sister Isabel returned from Rome with an unnamed Portuguese woman who had promised to finance the religious houses. The sisters enlisted the help of Pedro González de Mendoza, a cathedral canon in Toledo who had spoken with Isabel in Rome, to have him ask the governor of Toledo to grant permission to establish a community of twelve women under the rule of Saint Jerome. In addition, Isabel Bautista visited a noblewoman in Madrid, Doña Isabel Osorio, who had indicated a willingness to endow the convent.[44] However, Isabel Osorio eventually decided not to endow a convent outside of Madrid; instead, she supported the women by presenting their case to the Royal Council, who referred the matter back to the governor of Toledo. Public scandal in the city kept the women from receiving approval from the governor. Although the transcripts do not describe the nature of this scandal, it is clear that the city was divided in its support for Carranza and for the provisional leadership of the church. Francisca's visionary prayers, which were experienced in one of the main chapels of the cathedral and which included bodily manifestations and prophetic utterances, had the potential to galvanize support for Carranza at the expense of the authority of those administering the church in his absence. Whatever doubts her contemporaries had about the authenticity of Francisca's religious experiences, concerns about her charismatic appeal clearly hindered the success of her attempts at monastic reform. On November 19, 1574, a year after Isabel had left for Rome to secure ecclesiastical approval for the foundation of the convent, the first formal denunciations against Francisca were lodged at the Inquisitional tribunal.

---

43. Fol. 177r.

44. Isabel Osorio corresponded with Teresa about entering a Carmelite foundation. While there is no evidence that she did, her sister, Inés de la Encarnación, did. See E. Allison Peers, *Handbook to the Life and Times of Teresa of Avila and John of the Cross* (London: Burns Oates, 1954), 208.

By this time the sisters had consulted with a discalced Franciscan friar named Juan Bautista who supported their desire to establish the convent. Juan Bautista apparently thought that approval for the convent would be forthcoming once the scandal passed and church officials recognized the pious devotion of the women. He suggested that they enclose themselves and give themselves over to prayer and contemplation according to the rule of Saint Jerome. He offered himself as an advocate in their case, saying that he would go to Rome on their behalf. He also asked the sisters to take in a woman he knew who wanted to pursue religious life. Others joined the community throughout the spring, and various religious attempted to move the sisters' reform plans through the administrative system of the Toledan archdiocese. However, an investigation by the governor, combined with previous Inquisitional denunciations of the women, led to the initiation of a formal hearing against Francisca, Isabel, and Miguel Ruíz, beginning on October 1, 1575.

By then, eleven months had passed since the initial complaint against the sisters. Such a delay was not unusual. Inquisitional tribunals were often remarkably thorough and followed established prosecutorial procedures.[45] After receiving complaints from two *beatas* who had been associated with Francisca's religious community, Catalina de Jesús and Luisa de Aguilera, in November 1574, the tribunal chose not to proceed until after they had received testimony from another, more authoritative witness, the Jesuit Sebastián Hernández, who testified on February 11, 1575. Hernández was the confessor of Luisa de Aguilera, and his testimony describes the dire concerns about Francisca that lay on Luisa's conscience that she confided to him in her deathbed confession. In spite of these several complaints against the sisters, it appears that at first the Inquisitional tribunal took little notice of Francisca and Isabel, considering their religious aspirations a disciplinary matter pertaining to the archdiocese and the vicar of religious orders.

However, by September 1, 1575, Toledan Inquisitor Juan de Llano de Valdés was in the awkward position of having to account to the Supreme Council of the Inquisition for his apparent negligence in prosecuting them. His correspondence reveals that the tribunal had had its hands full with other matters and was short on theologians who served as consulters. As he explained in a letter to the Supreme Council of the Inquisition, since originally he had been "of the opinion that they might be under the influence of [evil] spirits and because of the weakness of the testimony against them, we

---

45. For a review and discussion of these procedures, see Henry Kamen, *Inquisition and Society in Spain in the Sixteenth and Seventeenth Centuries* (Bloomington: Indiana University Press, 1985).

did not pursue the matter."[46] As more witnesses testified, however, the tribunal turned the testimony over to theologians for an assessment. Independent of the Inquisitional investigation, Valdés knew that the vicar of religious orders in the archdiocese was investigating the women for having founded a religious community without permission and he was awaiting the results of that investigation. The vicar's concern over the public scandal of the matter moved Valdés to faster action. In his letter to the Council, Valdés explained, "And the vicar urged us to act with haste to determine what we ought to do, saying that there was great scandal seeing that those women had joined together in the form of a convent without permission from the ordinary [i.e., the archbishop's representative]." Valdés felt that the danger of public scandal was much greater if there were questions of heterodoxy involved, so he asked the vicar to suspend his investigation until he received the theologians' report. Now, pending review of the evidence and approval from the Supreme Council, he intended to prosecute them rapidly.[47]

The Supreme Council responded on September 27, 1575. They considered the matter to be a priority and urged Valdés to proceed individually with the prosecutions of Francisca, Isabel, and Miguel Ruíz. To help him in the determination, the Council sent him a copy of the proceedings and propositions of *alumbrados* currently being prosecuted in Llerena.[48] On September

46. AHN, Inq., leg. 3072, no. 35, Carta al Consejo 1 septiembre 1575 de Joan de Llano de Valdés: "por estar en oppinion q aun no estava fuera de tener [e]sp[irit]us y por la infor[maci]on flaca no hezimos dilig[enci]a en ello."

47. AHN, Inq., leg. 3072, no. 35: "Y el vicar[i]o nos ha dado mucha priessa y muchas vezes para q[ue] determinassemos lo que [h]aviamos de hazer, diziendo q[ue] hera grande escandalo q[ue] viessen que aquellas mugeres estuviessen en forma de monaster[i]o sin lic[enci]a del ordin[ari]o, hasele respondido q[ue] no es de mucho inconveniente que esten quinze o veinte dias mas de lo que han estado: pues q[ue] el daño so viene a parar en q[ue] estan juntas sin licençia del ordinario. Y serialo muy grande si fuesse neg[oci]o que importasse al sancto offi[ci]o entenderlo y castigarlo y por hazerse tan açeleradamente se perdiesse quanto mas que se [h]avia de ver en consulta, y despues consultarlo a v. s. porque paresçia que por ser neg[oci]o desta qualidad: no se podia entender en el sin [h]averlo primero v. s. en este estado estava el neg[oci]o quando ayer llego la de v. s."

48. AHN, Inq., Lib. 578, fol. 334r: "Muy R[everen]dos señores Aqui se [h]a visto el proçeso criminal contra françisca de los Apóstoles e ysavel baptista su hermana veatas y miguel Ruíz clerigo y se os tornan a embiar para que en sus causas [h]agais señores justiçia [h]aziendo a cada uno su proçesso aparte yendo en los neg[oci]os con el ciudado que la calidad dellos requiere y para que con mas claridad se pueda proçeder en las causas se os embian las proposiçiones que han resultado de las testificaçiones que se [h]an Reçivido en la ynquisiçion de llerena tocantes al esta doctrina de los alumbrados y las qualificaçiones que sovre ellas se han echo converna que luego [h]agais señores sacar copias de todo para quedaros con ellas y las originales nos remitireys y siempre yreis avisando al consejo de lo que en estos neg[oci]os se fuere [h]aziendo guarde n[uest]ro s[eño]r en madrid a xxvii de septiembre 1575. Los d[ic]hos señores." Nota marginal:

28, 1575, Valdés reported back to the Council that he was arresting Ruíz and the two sisters and opening formal proceedings against them.[49]

THE TRIAL

The Inquisitional trial against Francisca consisted of three major stages. First there was the initial examination, known as the *moniciones*, in which defendants were given three opportunities to confess their offenses before they knew the charges against them. In Francisca's case this took the form of an extensive two-month interview between the inquisitor and the accused in which Francisca primarily narrated her religious life and experiences. In the next stage, the *publicación*, the inquisitorial prosecutor presented formal accusations against the defendant. In Francisca's case, the prosecutor assembled an overwhelming 144 accusations, taken from the testimony of witnesses gathered in 1575 and from Francisca's own testimony during her interrogation sessions. Before beginning her point-by-point defense to each accusation, Francisca repeatedly requested a defense attorney. However, in inquisitorial proceedings the accused had recourse to consultation with an Inquisitional official known as the *abogado de los presos* only after making an initial response to the formal accusations. As Henry Kamen notes, while many of these lawyers probably fulfilled their duties conscientiously, "they were hindered by the restrictions of the tribunal and by the subtle and dangerous task of defending the prisoner while condemning his heresy."[50] Despite such strict procedural parameters, Francisca initially mounted a spirited defense, which she maintained over the course of several months until she was eventually beaten down in arguments with the inquisitor.

The crux of the Inquisitional case against Francisca hinged upon a decision regarding the orthodoxy of her visions. Initially allowed to narrate her life experience in her own way, Francisca experienced greater scrutiny and challenge from the inquisitor as she detailed her visionary experiences. On December 1, 1575, in response to Francisca's description of the judgment and

---

"Estas proposiçiones son diez pieças y tienen çinquenta y çinco ojas escriptas en todo o en parte." Most likely these attachments included the propositions in AHN, Inquisición, leg. 4443, no. 24: Proposiciones de los alumbrados de Extremadura.

49. AHN, Inq., leg. 3072, no. 41, Carta al Consejo, 28 septiembre 1575: "Resçevimos las de V. S. de 20 y beinte y siete deste y en lo que toca a fran[cis]ca de los Apóstoles y su hermana y miguel Ruíz se hara como V. s. manda y las proposiçiones y califiçaçiones que [h]an Resultado de las testificaçiones contra los alumbrados se trasladaran con mucha brevedad y se rremitiran a v. s. y se hara la puerta y çerraduras para el secreto."

50. Kamen, *Inquisition and Society*, 179.

execution visions outlined above, Inquisitor Valdés began an inquiry regarding the authenticity of her visions, asking her to explain why she trusted them and thought them divinely inspired. This conversation addressed two key issues in the prosecution of *alumbrados* in this decade: the discernment of true visions and the delicate balance between humility and prophetic authority.[51]

In providing Valdés with more details regarding her subjective experience of the visionary phenomenon, Francisca identified several criteria for recognizing authentic religious visions. First, she was careful to identify her visions as internal and therefore distinct from anything she might see with her eyes.[52] In this way, Francisca also attempted to separate the visions from any relationship with her body, except for the suspension of her faculties in rapture. She also differentiated her visionary experiences from that of a dream and, by way of defending their veracity, explained that they often occurred directly following the moment she received communion at mass.[53] Finally, she explained that in her visions, the significance or meaning of what was seen was communicated to her soul at the same time that she saw it. Thus she claimed that "[w]hen she is enraptured, the meaning of each thing is also impressed in the soul, so much so that it is as if they were to see a known person and they were to say, 'That is that person.'"[54]

51. For a review of Teresa of Avila's strategies regarding this balance, see Ahlgren, *Teresa of Avila and the Politics of Sanctity*, 68–84.

52. The distinction between corporeal and imaginary (i.e., image-based) visions is rooted in the threefold visionary typology developed by Augustine in *De Genesi ad litteram*, book 12, chap. 14, sec. 29, where corporeal visions are judged less reliable than spiritual visions, seen within the depths of the soul or *intellectus*. Augustine's teachings on visions were relatively accessible in sixteenth-century Spain through various manuals on visions, revelations, and the discernment of spirits. Jean Gerson's *De probatione spirituum* (1415) was considered the Latin authority for theologians and was often cited in theological assessments of visionary experiences commissioned by the Spanish Inquisition.

53. Fol. 186r: "Dixo que por verdadero tiene que vio aquello y que no fue sueño porque fue en el momento que acabo de comulgar . . ." Francisca's point of departure—that visions are located in a particular devotional and liturgical context—is important because it demonstrates her consistency with a long tradition of female visionary experience, in which rapture, visions, and other experiences of embodied prayer followed the reception of the Eucharist. For an analysis of this phenomenon and its meaning, see Caroline Walker Bynum, *Holy Feast and Holy Fast: The Religious Significance of Food to Medieval Women* (Berkeley: University of California Press, 1987). See also the introductory material in Elizabeth Alvilda Petroff, ed., *Medieval Women's Visionary Literature* (New York: Oxford University Press, 1986), 3–48. Teresa's visions and raptures were also often triggered by reception of the Eucharist. See, e.g., *Vida* 28.1.

54. Fol. 186v: "Dixo que quando esta arrebatada se asienta en el alma la significacion de cada cosa ques [sic] tan de asiento como si viesen una persona conozida diexesen aq[ue]llo es aquella persona." Cf. fol. 187v: "ansi se dan a entender al alma q[ue] son aquellas cosas y la significacion dellas en un muy poco tiempo." Teresa of Avila, when describing signs of an authentic locution in the *Interior Castle*, VI.3.15–16, writes, "Fourth, the words [of a locution] are very dif-

After several other introductory questions about the nature of her visions, the inquisitor began to express doubts about the veracity of Francisca's visionary experiences and to discredit the signs she had described to associate them with the supernatural. Valdés challenged Francisca to give more reasons to demonstrate that her visions were from God rather than a dream or product of her own imagination. He also suggested that tying them to an experience of communion was not sufficient proof of their being a gift from God, for "in that time and before it and even during that same communion and in all times, the devil is always seeking an opportunity to deceive people."[55] At this point, because she was moving into a more defensive mode, Francisca's testimony became a clearer statement of her visionary theology and the criteria she used for the discernment of spirits, a statement that can be summarized and compared with the teachings of Francisca's noteworthy contemporary Teresa of Avila.[56]

As we analyze Francisca's initial testimony, we can see five major principles for the verification of authentic visionary experience. First, the experience of the vision is an internal one that suspends the person's normal faculties and suggests a noncorporeal experience of visions. Second, the vision's supernatural source is apparent to the soul because the visions are marked by a feeling of tenderness, even joy, at the time of the rapture.[57] Third, visions trigger a recognition of the soul's baseness and reinforce the soul's humility after their reception. Fourth, they invigorate the soul in the pursuit of virtue. Finally, the visions increase the soul's love for God and neighbor and enable it to take on suffering or hardship out of love.[58]

---

ferent, and with one of them much is comprehended. Our intellect could not compose them so quickly. Fifth, together with the words, in a way I wouldn't know how to explain, there is often given much more to understand than is ever dreamed of without words." See also VI.4.5: "When the soul is in this suspension, the Lord likes to show it some secrets, things about heaven, and imaginative visions. It is able to tell of them afterward, for these remain so impressed on the memory that they are never forgotten." And VI.4.6: "But, you will insist, if there is no image and the faculties do not understand, how can the visions be remembered? I don't understand this either, but I do understand that some truths about the grandeur of God remain so fixed in this soul that even if faith were not to tell it who God is and of its obligation to believe that He is God, from that very moment it would adore Him as God, as did Jacob when he saw the ladder."

55. Fol. 188r: "[N]o es bastante seguridad lo que [h]a d[ic]ho y declarado en dezir que porque le [h]a acaecido en acabando de comulgar porque en ese tiempo y antes y en la mesma comunion y en todos tiempos el demonio anda buscando como engañar a las personas."

56. A summary introduction to Teresa's visionary theology is available in Ahlgren, *Teresa of Avila and the Politics of Sanctity*, 97–104.

57. Fol. 188r.

58. See fol. 188r: "She said that one could see that this was a thing from God and not from the devil first because the spirit is enraptured with great sweetness and in that time the senses do not feel any corporeal thing, nor do they disturb the soul."

As Francisca concluded her list of "proofs" that her visions came from God, she described a certain "surety" the soul has about the origin of its visions, stating, "In this security that remained in her soul she could understand if it [i.e., its experience] was good and was from Our Lord."[59] This certitude was to become a problematic issue in Francisca's trial because to the inquisitor it represented all the pitfalls of spiritual pride. However, Francisca asserted that she derived this certainty about the origins of her experiences primarily from the effects they had on her soul, stating, "If this were something from the devil, it would give occasion to be prideful and presumptuous and to detest anything that was wearisome or difficult."[60]

Although she had a clear list of criteria for discerning spirits and affirms that a confidence in their veracity remains in the soul after the visions, Francisca also described the need for a continuing relationship with a spiritual director. This conviction might have allayed the inquisitor's concern that Francisca's description of certainty did not necessarily equal pride or even complete autonomy. In her trial, Francisca explained that she consulted with her confessor about every vision she experienced and that he recognized the authenticity of her religious experiences because he observed her growth in virtue.[61]

To all of these reasons that Francisca gave to defend the authenticity of her visions, the inquisitor replied that Francisca had erred in balancing humility and prophetic authority by attracting public attention. He argued that the authenticity of such experiences was often doubted even in known saints, who responded to such experiences with increased penance and humility, knowing that they could in no way merit the extraordinary spiritual experiences they had received. Valdés contrasted Francisca's case with theirs, saying that Francisca had not been a humble recipient of the visions but that she and her sister had used their religious experiences to become public figures.

A break in her testimony allowed Francisca time to consider how her formal statement about the nature of her visions was progressing. When the interrogation resumed on December 2, she explained that it was the physicality of her prayer experiences that attracted attention, as in the case of the judgment vision in her bed, which awoke the entire household. Being in the presence of many of her family members during that time, Francisca herself could not control how they responded to what they had observed. The phys-

---

59. Fol. 188 r: "[E]n esta seguridad que q[ue]dava en su alma podia entender si hera bueno y si hera de parte de nuestro senor . . ."

60. Fol. 188 r: "[S]i fuera cosa del demonio la diera occasion a tener sobervia y presunzion y aborrecer todo lo q[ue] hera fatiga y trabajos."

61. Fol. 188 r: "y no fiandose de si mesma esta confesante lo tratava con miguel Ruíz para satisfacerse mas."

icality of Francisca's prayer experiences must surely have attracted attention at the Chapel of Nuestra Señora del Sagrario in the city's cathedral, but her intent, she argued, was never to become a public spectacle. Interestingly, although embodied experiences of prayer were increasingly suspect during investigations of *alumbradismo* in the 1570s, Valdés did not pursue this as potential evidence of the falsity of her experiences.[62] Finally, Francisca asserted that her prayer experiences had produced in her a kind of zeal she could not hide, a desire that "all creatures love Our Lord and make satisfaction to Him in conformity with what He had shown her." Recalling such feelings, she testified that her conversations with others afterward were intended to communicate some spiritual benefit or induce moral conversion in others.

To summarize, in Francisca's testimony about her religious experience, we see reports of prayer experiences of a majestic God. As Francisca represented herself, she felt called by this God to speak prophetically about the general need for ecclesiastical reform and to respond by personal and communal transformation, particularly in the form of founding a new monastic house of prayer and penance. This same God who encouraged such reforms also empowered her to be someone more than she understood herself to be, a woman of stronger resolve and greater virtue than she had been before such prayer experiences. With these claims of instrumental agency—that is, the implicit and even, at times, explicit claim, to know and embody God's will[63] —Francisca was making an apparently pertinacious affirmation of certainty about the veracity of her revelatory experiences of God.

As Francisca concluded her initial testimony, she most likely thought that she had made an accurate account of her visions and had addressed the inquisitor's concerns about their veracity with a considerable number of proofs. Further, since the conversations toward the end of her interrogation focused more specifically on the effects of her visions, her growth in virtue,

---

62. For some theologians, for example Hernando del Castillo, a Dominican who served as a theological consultant to the Inquisition, the physical elements that accompanied mental prayer were a clear sign that phenomena like visions and levitation were induced by the person herself. In an opinion rendered about 1575 Hernando wrote, "Therefore these feelings which appear with such violence and torment people, leaving them as if they were dead is a sign that they come from the flesh, and there they end." See AHN, Inq., leg. 4443, no. 24, fol. 16r. According to A. Huerga, Hernando de Castillo wrote this *calificación* between 1573 and 1575. Luis Sala Balust attributes this same *calificación* to Alonso de la Fuente. See "En torno al grupo de alumbrados de Llerena," in *Corrientes espirituales en la España del Siglo XVI* (Barcelona: Juan Flors, 1963), 509–23 at 517. For a brief discussion of Inquisitional interpretation of women's embodied prayer, see Weber, "Demonizing Ecstasy," 155–58.

63. For a discussion of instrumental authority in Teresa see Ahlgren, *Teresa of Avila and the Politics of Sanctity*, 180–83.

and her continued willingness to be instructed and guided in discernment, Francisca probably felt she had both a clear conscience and had made a good case for herself as she reviewed and ratified her testimony.

In his *Tratado de la verdadera y falsa prophecia* (Treatise on True and False Prophecy), Juan de Orozco y Covarrubias presents seven rules for the discernment of spirits, four of which have to do with the virtue, lifestyle, and attitude of the recipient. For example, rule 3 is "that one should watch their habits, because from them can be understood whether this is an invention due to greed, vanity or presumption with a desire to be esteemed and honored."[64] And confessors like the Carmelite John of the Cross, who applied such norms in their pastoral work, advocated testing the humility of women who claimed to have had revelatory experiences.[65] Thus virtue, especially humility demonstrated by obedience to one's religious superiors, played a major role in establishing the reliability of religious experience, particularly in women, who, it was claimed, were more easily deceived by the devil. In Francisca's case, however, Inquisitor Valdés could not be convinced of Francisca's virtue except by administering some test of obedience. As a *beata* outside the structures of formal religious orders, there was no established, institutionally sanctioned relationship within which Francisca was operating, no figure other than Miguel Ruíz, her confessor, to whom Francisca could be accountable. In her defense, Francisca makes repeated reference to her consultation with Ruíz and with other male religious, primarily Franciscans and Hieronymites, to be sure that she was proceeding in a morally and spiritually responsible way. However, to a certain extent, once the matter had reached the Inquisition, the dilemma was that at this moment in her religious life Francisca could not prove concretely her humility and obedience to anyone except to the inquisitor himself. Her confessor Ruíz was similarly imprisoned, and Francisca did not belong to a religious order that could administer any kind of penitential discipline. While she might have been placed, as a penitent, under the custodial care of a religious community, the inquisitor ultimately decided instead to have her demonstrate her virtue and humility by her acceptance of an inquisitorial sentence. Her status as a *beata* played a significant, if not definitive, role in her condemnation. But first she would have to be accused formally and make her defense.

On January 5, 1576, the Inquisitional prosecutor presented the formal accusation of 144 charges against Francisca. The charges were extensive; reading them took up the entire afternoon session, probably three to four

---

64. Juan de Orozco y Covarrubias, *Tratado de la verdadera y falsa prophecia Segovia: Juan de la Cuesta,* 1588, fol. 46r: "La tercera regla es, q se mire sus costumbres, porq dellas se puede entender, si es invencion por codicia, o por vanidad, o presuncion, con desseo de estima, y honra."

65. On this issue see Ahlgren, *Teresa of Avila and the Politics of Sanctity,* 98–99.

hours of time. They laid out in exhaustive detail a twisted narrative of Francisca's religious experiences and reform ideals, imputing dubious and even malicious motivations and intentions. The prosecutor had clearly done a thorough job, incorporating testimony from twenty-four witnesses and covering a wide range of issues—from the minute details of personal conversations about her sister's virtue to the socioecclesiastical implications of Francisca's concerns about the effects of Archbishop Carranza's absence, to the prophetic dimensions of Francisca's apocalyptic visions.

A thematic analysis of the accusations shows that they represent both the socioecclesiastical concerns of Francisca's contemporaries (i.e., those of many people outside the Inquisition) and the specific inquisitorial focus on the discernment of spirits. The first theme is Francisca's visionary experience itself (including some potentially dubious revelations) and her recurring references to it to justify her religious authority or her reform efforts. The second theme is spiritual pride, a set of accusations that viewed Francisca's need to establish her authority as a reformer, visionary, and religious woman as a demonstration of singularity and an inappropriate bid for sanctity. The third theme is that of the intercessory role that Francisca claims for herself and the women and men in her reform movement. These themes revolve around the credibility/reliability of charismatic/prophetic power within the life of the church, a problem made even more acute in Toledo in the absence of the archbishop and the "irregular" operation of the archdiocese. Thus, although Francisca's support of Carranza is incorporated only tangentially into the accusations—it forms a part of eight accusations—it highlights the acute tensions in the relationship between prophetic calls for change (i.e., reform) and the need to establish religious authority.

Interestingly, nowhere in the accusations is Francisca portrayed as an *endemoniada*, or a woman possessed by the devil, even though there was ample material to formulate that argument. Her experiences with the devil, as she recounted them, are incorporated into the accusation either as part of her claims to an intercessory role or as part of her prayer experiences, but they do not form an accusation in and of themselves.[66] Further, Francisca is not accused of teaching erroneous doctrine, one of the clearest cases that could be made against the veracity of her visions. Only in accusation 72, where she describes that her visions revealed that Carranza would be released by 1575, is there any hint that the prophetic dimension of her visions is not credible.[67]

---

66. See, for example, accusations 8, 21, 22, 23, 24, 29, 50, and 62.
67. Fols. 202r–v.

The accusations presented against Francisca reflected several levels of inquisitorial concerns from simple haughtiness to deep-seated challenges to contemporary church policy and practice. If, as Francisca claimed, her visions were truly outpourings of the will of God, not only would criticisms of the church have been leveled at a time when it was already embroiled in various crises of authority, but the source of these reforms was a woman of minimal educational background, little credibility, and a fragile support system. There was much at stake in this trial, and Francisca faced a daunting task in responding to the accusations. Any illusion she may have had about having presented herself successfully during her interrogation was certainly dispelled, and the transcript records that at the conclusion of the accusations, Francisca "fainted and remained for a while in a stupor, and she then came back to herself crying and saying that her trial could not end up in this way." In such a state, she asked for time to compose herself before she responded to the accusations at another session.[68]

Francisca spent nearly one month, from January 27 through February 21, 1576, defending herself against the prosecutor's massive accusations. Her defense breaks into three major periods chronologically. For the first two weeks, Francisca responded point by point to the accusations, often challenging imputed motivations of spiritual pride, sometimes calling an accusation untrue, and sometimes acknowledging that the content of an accusation was correct. This fairly open give-and-take between Francisca and the inquisitor continued through the first ninety-nine accusations. Then on February 8, 1576, Valdés broke the rhythm of the interrogation by introducing some pointed inquiries about Francisca's vision of the Last Judgment and her acceptance of tribulations by demons. The inquisitor's questions became more technical and sharp-edged. Francisca's replies lost energy, and by February 14, 1576, she accepted the inquisitor's insistence that his authority in the discernment of the veracity of her visions was superior to her own. From that point on, Francisca was essentially defeated. Her dull response to the rest of the points was flat and formulaic, reflecting her sense of futility: "she has already answered this question."[69]

During these first two weeks of questioning, Francisca focused her defense on objecting to the tone of many of the charges, which often portrayed her as "making public" her visions or even boasting about them.[70] As

---

68. Fols. 207r–v.

69. Francisca's response to accusations 108–44 is virtually the same: "dize lo q[ue] d[ic]ho tiene en esta audiencia." Other variations include, "ya tiene rrespondido a esto y a ello se rrefiere" or "dize lo q[ue] d[ic]ho y confesado tiene."

70. See, for example, accusations 19, 22, and 24.

the accusations moved on to the content and meaning of Francisca's visions, in points 15 through 29 and again in points 44 through 47, she denied any interpretation of them that emphasized her role in the redemptive process or any other implication that she gained charismatic power or authority from her prayer experiences. Francisca also denied that her critiques of the contemporary state of the church were as strong as the accusations portrayed. For example, when she was read accusation 53 regarding the church's need to be reformed and was asked to respond, she replied that "[s]he never said such a thing, nor even thought it, although it is true that she said to those who were there [in the community] that all the prayers they offered were for the exaltation of the Catholic faith and the state of the church, which they said was in great necessity . . ." And she noted that other religious, like the Franciscan friar Juan Bautista, encouraged them in their efforts every time that he visited the *beatas* at the house.[71]

Francisca's answers on these points reveal that she clearly had a public reputation in Toledo as a woman of prayer with access to divine wisdom. She was consulted by outsiders and asked to raise their concerns to God, serving as an instrument for divine guidance. Thus Francisca had most likely achieved a certain not uncontroversial status akin to that of Mari Díaz in Avila, María de Jesús in Alcalá, and others. Yet Francisca denies that she used this position in her community to critique church officials or structures or in any other antiauthoritarian way. Indeed, throughout her trial she implicitly argues that she has attempted to follow divine commands through her visions in the service of God and the church. Inquisitional officials never recognized the element of service in Francisca's reforms nor did they acknowledge that as her intent.[72]

Beginning with accusation 94, the inquisitor had Francisca respond point by point to elements of the judgment vision. These accusations were taken directly from Francisca's own descriptions in her letter to her sister and in her original confessions, and she affirmed each part of the vision. After accusa-

---

71. Fols. 218v–219r.

72. Here Francisca's argument resembles the rhetorical strategy of Hildegard of Bingen, who asserted that ordinarily hierarchical structures of authority in the church would be enough to maintain order and safeguard the sanctity of the church but that, in the absence of genuine and virtuous male leadership, God would raise up "weak women," fortified with divine revelation, to point the way to reform and greater perfection/holiness. See Barbara Newman, *Sister of Wisdom: St. Hildegard's Theology of the Feminine* (Berkeley: University of California Press, 1987); and Gillian T. W. Ahlgren, "Visions and Rhetorical Strategies in the Letters of Hildegard of Bingen," in *Dear Sister: The Letters of Medieval Women*, ed. Karen Cherewatuk and Ulrike Wiethaus (Philadelphia: University of Pennsylvania Press, 1993).

tion 99, which concerned the temptations by devils regarding the sin of pride, the inquisitor began a long detour from the accusations themselves, asking Francisca to give him more details about the experience of possession by demons and why it was that she thought God would lead someone to revelation in this way. For Valdés, this was the most troublesome and dubious aspect of Francisca's religious experiences. In particular, he objected to her characterization of having achieved some kind of "victory" over them, most likely because of the implicit claim that, first, she might be a successful intercessor and, second, she might be immune to sin.

After a lengthy exchange about the experiences themselves, the inquisitor began to ask very specific questions in order to probe her ability to discern between divine and demonic communication. Francisca tried to describe differing internal states that helped her identify whether she was in the company of demonic or divine forces. When she was tormented by devils, "her soul was always plunged into great darkness, with all of her senses and her body tormented," but when the divine light entered her soul, she felt herself freed from this darkness and the torments, and "she felt a very great tenderness and love of Our Lord inside her." In addition to the subjective states she described, Francisca claimed that she grew in knowledge and understanding of God as a result of her experiences.[73]

After Valdés warned her not to have much confidence in her ability to discern these matters because, as he explained, the devil has "so many ways to deceive and entangle souls,"[74] Francisca realized that she was entering dangerous territory. She acknowledged that she was not capable of entering into a highly technical conversation about these matters, protesting that she did not have the ability to respond to such delicate and important issues.[75] She also explained that she knew herself to be "very fragile" and that she could not have borne the struggles she experienced had God not been served to give them to her and "if Our Lord had not favored her for this [task]."[76]

After a few more questions about the specifics of the demonic component of Francisca's experiences, the inquisitor returned with a more ample statement of his concerns. If Francisca's account were true, that demonic torment was given to humans in order for God then to renew the earth, this would amount to "a new way in the world for people to negotiate with God and God with humanity." Further, temptation was an ordinary human expe-

---

73. Fol. 227r.
74. Fol. 227v.
75. Fol. 227v.
76. Fol. 228v.

rience, "something that happens every day to millions of people in the world" without God or the devil asking for people's consent first. The fact that visions and "raptures of spirit" were involved in this kind of procedure only clouded the issue. Thus, he concluded, "this and all the other things she has said are far from credible."[77] For Valdés, Francisca's guilt or innocence was coming down to a question of whether or not she would insist on the veracity of her experiences. Francisca countered that she never would have recounted an experience as true if she had had any doubts about its authenticity.

Using the example of her claiming to have achieved a victory over devils after having been asked by God to be tempted by them—a situation Valdés deemed both novel and incredible—Valdés asked Francisca to account for the discrepancy between the event and its likelihood. Francisca replied that she understood her experiences to have had a pedagogical function, that God had wanted to communicate something to the world through her. But, she acknowledged that "these are secrets of God that she does not grasp, and she did nothing more than have this happen to her."[78]

The inquisitor found even this difficult to believe: why, he asked, would God have chosen her and not someone more well versed and experienced in prayer?[79] Francisca's response had to wait until February 14, 1576. She began by stating that she had been sick to her stomach and with a fever so that she was unable to remember what she might be able to add to her testimony. Further, she looked to the inquisitor for guidance, since he was there precisely to point out her errors and "she was grateful for that because her desire really [was] to serve God in spirit and truth."[80]

Valdés insisted that all of her visions must be from the devil and asked her to state definitively whether or not she believed that her revelations were from God or from the devil. Francisca stalled: "She will not make a determination about whether they were from God or from the devil any more than [to say that] whatever the Lord Inquisitor says and instructs her; that [is what] she will believe." The inquisitor dealt the final blow: "It is a very certain and confirmed thing that none of those revelations was from God, and to believe anything else would be a very great deceit."[81]

Francisca, still sensitive to the implication that she was trying to deceive others, responded that she was willing to defer to Valdés' judgment: "if the

77. Fols. 229v–230r.
78. Fol. 231v.
79. Fol. 232r.
80. Fols. 232v–233r.
81. Fol. 235r.

Lord Inquisitor says to her that this is deceit, she will believe that it is deceit, and thus she believes, but she does not stop believing what she saw."[82] The inquisitor clarified that she did not have to believe that she did not have her experiences but she must believe that the visions and revelations she saw of Mary speaking to Christ about the archbishop and the other one about the cloud of demons and the final one about the majesty of God were actually illusions of the devil or mental illness. "To believe otherwise is a great error and an offense to God, and to speak of it is a thing worthy of great punishment, especially now that she is undeceived about it."[83]

Francisca attempted to regain her credibility and good intentions with her response:

> She believes all that the Lord Inquisitor tells her because he is a person with more light from God to understand those things than she is. And she says that she has not said nor presumed to do anything that is an offense to Our Lord, and if she were to understand that it was, she would not do it for heaven nor earth.[84]

Having assured himself of Francisca's subjection to his judgment, the inquisitor returned to the examination of the remaining forty-four accusations. At this point, however, Francisca realized that her responses would not affect the inquisitor's disposition toward her, and she gave the same flat response for the rest of the day: "she says what she has already said about that."[85] Throughout the rest of the week, Francisca appeared defeated, retreating into a different strategy of self-protection. On February 21, 1576, Francisca said she had nothing to add in her defense, and she ratified it, thus concluding the bulk of her input into her trial. As the trials of her sister Isabel and her confessor Miguel Ruíz continued, no decision was made in her case, and the transcript contains no record of Francisca's voice until March 6, 1577, when the Inquisitional prosecutor brought seven additional accusations against her. These new accusations, which charged Francisca with "dishonest" conduct with another prisoner, could not have helped Francisca's case any, although they do reveal her state of mind and her sense of the probable outcome of her trial.

On the basis of testimony given by another prisoner, the prosecutor presented evidence that Francisca, after representing herself as a holy and vir-

---

82. Fol. 235r.

83. Fol. 235v.

84. Fol. 235v.

85. Her response to accusations 100 through 105, which takes her to the end of the February 14 session, is some variation on "Dize lo que d[ic]ho tiene a que se rrefiere."

tuous woman, had "secretly in these prisons talked with and planned to marry a certain person, and she calls him her husband, and he calls her his wife."[86] In her response, Francisca denied the sexual implications of the new accusations but affirmed that she had corresponded with the fellow prisoner, a man named Hernando Velasco, with the intention that they would marry when both were released from prison. The practical realities of Toledo—and the struggles women faced for social and economic survival within the city— loomed large. Francisca was well aware of the fate that awaited her: her family had most likely been drained by the expenses of her Inquisitional trial, and she herself now faced the stigma of being a discredited religious. Her decision to marry reflects the experiences of many other women threatened by poverty in Toledo. In her defense against the new accusations Francisca wrote, "And seeing myself in the difficulties that this business has put me in and understanding my liberty to be in great danger, I have decided to change my state and marry because perhaps I will save myself better than in this other state."[87] How well she knew her intended, the brother of one of her former neighbors, is difficult to ascertain; they had not met before coming to know each other in the inquisitorial prisons.

Concerned that her conduct with Velasco might reflect on the final verdict of her case, Francisca pleaded for mercy from the inquisitors: ". . . [D]o not do with me what this crime merits but according to the mercy of God and what your graces often use against sinners, and . . . be attentive to the fact that I am a woman and I am almost desperate from having experienced many trials and illnesses in my life. And if your graces understood this . . . encourage the will I have demonstrated in wanting to marry the said man. I ask for the love of Our Lord that I may be favored in all this by your graces since you are in the place of God to help souls."[88] She was granted another audience before Valdés in which she attempted to give him a more accurate picture of what she had intended to accomplish as a religious woman. Although she was a "woman ignorant of matters pertaining to Our Lord and of limited intellectual capacity," she had had religious experiences that compelled her to speak. Because her visions "pertained to the judgment against the world," they "seemed urgent," and because they revealed that God was offended by human sin, she wanted to inspire moral conversion in others. In a final appeal she argued that now that she had been led to understand that her experiences were not of divine origin and renounced them, she should

86. Fol. 243r.
87. Fol. 246r.
88. See fol. 247r.

"be received into the heart of the church and that her penance for her ignorance, insanity and vanity [should be] what she has already suffered in these prisons for the past two years."[89]

The inquisitor responded to Francisca's appeal with a final question. He was perplexed about the origins of Francisca's visions of reform and wanted to know whether or not the entire affair had been of Francisca's own invention. He observed, "This seems to carry little artifice for being an invention of the devil, and even many things contradict each other, giving rise to the suspicion that these [experiences] are simply women's nonsense . . ."[90] Francisca affirmed all of her previous testimony about having received what she understood to be revelations, adding that she could be believed on this point because, for the salvation of her soul, she was very committed to telling the truth in all of her testimony. She returned to her cell to await the verdict.

Francisca appeared in the public auto de fe on April 14, 1578, where she abjured her offenses *de levi*. A lengthy account of her case was read aloud, and she was publicly declared "an arrogant, bold and miserable heretic, blasphemer and perjurer." Afterward, one hundred lashes were administered and she was banished from the city for a period of three years. This form of punishment was characteristic of those given for lesser offenses,[91] but its implications were significant. Francisca had been discredited as a religious visionary and faced poverty and social exclusion. Inquisitorial records end there, and we do not know how she fared in her new role as wife and mother—if, in fact, she ever achieved that status.

SIGNIFICANCE OF FRANCISCA'S STORY

Francisca's case has much to tell us about the role and status of religious women in Counter-Reformation Spain and the challenges they faced. The account of her life provided by the Inquisitional trial gives us a unique view into a number of spheres and realms in which she serves as a point of intersection. First, her case suggests that the reform of religious orders, accomplished gradually and in fits and starts throughout the sixteenth century, was perhaps not as inclusive or as widespread as women's social circumstances required. If Francisca is portraying truthfully the evolution of the community of *beatas* around her, there was clearly a greater demand for opportunities to pursue religious life than there

89. Fols. 283v–284r.

90. Fol. 284v.

91. For a description of the three categories of Inquisitional punishments and a summary of their frequency, see Kamen, *Inquisition and Society*, 183–97.

were convents and other institutional avenues to accommodate women. Following the decrees of the Council of Trent in 1563, increased pressure to enclose women in cloisters made it difficult for female religious to explore their vocations as agents of socioreligious change; for women of lower social classes without dowries, these reforms posed an even more acute problem.

Changes in religious ideals and practices within Catholic Christianity—particularly, in Spain, the increased suspicion of forms of mental prayer—made it difficult for religious women to imitate models of holiness that had previously been promoted by religious reformers in the early part of the century. Even Teresa of Avila, whose mystical experience—not uncontroversial during her lifetime—was eventually enshrined through her canonization process, encountered challenges similar to those of Francisca. Teresa's ability to explain herself theologically and the fact that she could refer to contemporaries with whom she had consulted as spiritual and theological experts set her apart from Francisca, but on some level, both women were trying to move forward an agenda of reform in religious life inspired by the Franciscan revivals of the 1510s and 1520s. On their own, as women, they lacked religious authority, and by the 1570s, the shadow over religious life cast by the 1559 Index of Prohibited Books and the changing shape of what constituted a life of prayer made it difficult for them to invoke textual authorities to justify their religious practices and ideals.

Specifically, women's religious authority as it emanated from embodied, intercessory prayer was subject to intense scrutiny. If in rapture the female body was overcome by the power of God, religious women were vulnerable to suspicions about the power of the devil similarly to possess the body. However, temptation by the devil could be a vehicle to greater holiness, as demonstrated in the hagiographical model of Catherine of Siena. Raymond of Capua's *Life of Catherine of Siena*, which circulated in editions from 1511 and 1569, portrayed Catherine as victorious over temptations from demons that God allowed to assault her body as part of her experiences of intercessory prayer. Francisca referred specifically to this text in her own defense without success, which suggests that Catherine's model of embodied prayer as an expression of holiness had become problematical by the second half of the sixteenth century.

The *Suma de los solicitos engaños de nuestros tiempos*, for example, an anonymous document most likely composed in the mid- to late-1570s, argued that all bodily experiences of prayer and revelation were essentially expressions of spiritual pride in women:

> They take as proof of this holiness these extraordinary feelings and
> visions and revelations, but they also console themselves with these

vexations and desire that they increase, understanding that because of them their holiness is made known, and so they revel in these travails and share them not only with their confessors but also with whoever will listen, and thus they praise themselves publicly, so that they will be perceived to be holy.[92]

It is perhaps less the embodied dimension of the experience than the public space that women appropriated as a result of their experiences that caused offense. Indeed, if Alison Weber is correct in asking us to "reconsider the notion that the ecclesiastical elites were unremittingly hostile to the varied forms of embodied piety in post-Tridentine Spain,"[93] perhaps we should consider more carefully and in more detail the extent to which the religious figures and religious institutions maintained and enforced increasing divisions between religious power and authority and private and public domains. The relative toleration for "cosas de mujeres" disappeared as women sought to exercise influence outside convent walls—and given the socioeconomic structures of monastic life, for most women this was their only religious option.

As religious women appropriated public space, their religious authority was challenged, most often by accusations of *alumbradismo*. At the heart of many such accusations was the charge of spiritual pride, demonstrated when women believed in the visions they experienced and even manifested them publicly in a prophetic role. Spiritual pride occurs in many accusations of *alumbradismo* throughout the 1570s, including what we can reconstruct of the accusations against Teresa of Avila and other *alumbradas* in Seville. It also forms a bridge between one of the earliest *alumbrados*, Isabel de la Cruz,[94] and many of the later ones, providing us with some common ground in the

92. BRAH, MS 9-26-7-D. 185. *Suma de los solícitos engaños de nuestros tiempos*, fol. 82r: "El mal grande que de aquí se sigue es, como por esta falsa doctrina tengan estas vejaciones para ser libres de aquel espíritu y quitar la causa de la posesión, que es la soberbia espiritual, con la cual, engreídas y levantadas, tienen por cosa debida a esta santidad el tener extraordinarios sentimientos y visiones y revelaciones, etc., pero se consuelan con estas vejaciones y desean que vayan en crecimiento, entendiendo que por ellas más se descubre su santidad, y así se glorian de estos trabajos y los cuentan no solamente a sus confesores, sino a cuantos lo quieren oír, y así se huelgan de padecellos públicamente, para que venga su santidad." cf. Alvaro Huerga, *Historia de los alumbrados*, 1: 207. Both Huerga and Sala Balust believe the author of this document to have been Rodrigo Alvarez. See Sala Balust, "En torno al grupo de alumbrados de Llerena," 520. See also Alison Weber's assessment in "Demonizing Ecstasy," 153–58.

93. Weber, "Demonizing Ecstasy," 155

94. The fifteenth section of Inquisitional accusations against Isabel de la Cruz is entitled "On the temerity of this prisoner" and includes five accusations. See Márquez, *Los alumbrados*, 279. See also accusations made against Pedro Ruíz de Alcaraz for "temerity," 259–60.

study of *alumbrados* and, more particularly, *alumbradas*. Charges of spiritual pride (and inquisitorial prosecution on that basis) are manifestations of the assumption that women's charismatic power rooted in experiences of prayer needed to be controlled and regulated.[95] They also reinforce the theory that the role of revelation in theological speculation and rapture as an episte- mological path appropriate for women were roundly rejected in the more catechetical approach to Catholicism reflected in post-Tridentine Spain.

Francisca's case highlights the significant challenges faced by female reformers of religious orders after the Council of Trent. First there was the dif- ficulty of obtaining financial endowments for the initial foundations. Second, reform meant cultivating relations with patrons, requiring both significant diplomatic skills and trustworthy liaisons with men who could represent clois- tered women in face-to-face transactions.[96] Third, there was the need for sup- port from influential religious figures who could advocate on behalf of the women in public arenas or in inner church circles. Religious foundations involved a significant financial commitment, and, unless they were endowed independently, they were a drain on the city's charitable resources. In the absence of the archbishop, Toledan reformers had to negotiate an irregular administrative system that, given its own financially precarious state, would tol- erate no potential risks. The novelty or controversy Francisca and her sister generated perhaps precluded institutional support under such circumstances.[97]

Francisca de los Apóstoles was condemned by the Inquisitional Tribunal of Toledo for reasons that pertained more to the socioreligious climate of the city than to actual heterodoxy or even heteropraxy. The possibility that visions that prophesied Archbishop Carranza's release would encourage reli- gious or political dissent, specifically, the lack of respect for the acting reli- gious authorities, seems to be a primary concern. Once Carranza had died,

---

95. Perhaps the accusation that most epitomizes this issue and the inquisitorial response to women's desire to have influence in the institutional governance of the church is contained in accusation 32.

96. For a study of such issues as they worked themselves out in Teresa of Avila's discalced foun- dations, see Weber, "Saint Teresa's Problematic Patrons."

97. Teresa of Avila encountered similar opposition to many of her religious foundations. See Bilinkoff, *The Avila of Saint Teresa*, 147–50, esp. 147–48: "Ultimately, however, the most impor- tant supporter of Teresa of Jesus and her reform, especially during those critical early years, was the bishop of Avila, Alvaro de Mendoza. Julián de Avila once stated bluntly, 'If the bishop of Avila had not been so disposed towards the Mother, I do not doubt that [city officials] would have closed down [the convent] that very first day.' Bishop Mendoza felt a personal attraction to Teresa of Jesus and her goals but was also much aware of the dignity of his office. In the long run Carmelite reform and other religious movements of the mid-sixteenth-century helped to enhance the prestige and power of the episcopacy, an explicit goal of the Council of Trent."

this potential threat disappeared, and Francisca's apocalyptic visions seemed irrelevant, even absurd and erroneous. The social and religious value of her reform ideals do not seem to have had any mitigating effect on the outcome of her trial, but the critical edge to her visions probably ensured that Francisca's voice for reform would fall silent. Historians and students of this epoch are well advised, however, to take it into account as they recreate this complex moment in the history of early modern Europe, for it reveals an astute observer of contemporary ecclesiastical and social conditions, a creative, reform-minded spirit, and a woman of determination and courage.

NOTE ON THE TEXT

What follows is an excerpted translation of the trial transcript of Francisca de los Apóstoles, contained in Legajo 113, 5 at the Archivo Histórico Nacional in Madrid. The trial transcript is over three hundred folios in length and, like other trials, contains many internal voices, including those of other witnesses and of inquisitorial officials. There is no critical edition or prior study of this manuscript. With the exception of the formal Inquisitional accusations made against Francisca, I have translated only the material in Francisca's own voice, beginning with materials taken from the *beaterio* before her arrest. Next is her initial testimony before the inquisitor, a narrative summary of her religious experience in which the inquisitor allowed Francisca to tell her own story with few interruptions. This testimony is followed by the accusations against her put forth by the prosecutor and her two-month defense. Francisca's testimony is, as far as we can determine, a verbatim transcription of her oral statements recorded in the third person.

After the testimony, I have included more materials in Francisca's own voice, taken from the *beaterio*. This material includes her letters and the vows she wrote out for herself after she had experienced "victory over demons" and committed herself to a life of prayer and reform. Additionally, I have translated Francisca's final statement before the inquisitor, written in her own hand and submitted on March 11, 1577, a poignant appeal for mercy made by a woman determined to survive an ordeal that had clearly drained her spirit.

In all portions of the translation I have tried to strike a balance between faithfulness to the form of the source, a dispassionate trial transcript that records long statements without breaks for sentences, and to Francisca's colloquial, usually frank, and often passionate style.

VOLUME EDITOR'S
BIBLIOGRAPHY

PRIMARY SOURCES

AHN, Inquisición, legajo 3072. *Correspondencia del Tribunal de Toledo a la Suprema*

AHN, Inquisición, libro 578.

Archivo Histórico Nacional, Madrid (AHN). Inquisición, legajo 113, no. 5. *Proceso de Francisca de Avila o de los Apóstoles*

Capua, Raymond of, *Vida de la bienaventurada sancta Catharina de Sena*, trans. and prologue by Antonio de la Peña. Alcalá Alcalá, 1512. Reprint Medina del Campo: Francisco de Canto, 1569.

Castañega, Martín de. *Tratado de las supersticiones y hechicerías*. Madrid: Bibliófilos Españoles, 1946.

Granada, Luis de. *Historia de Sor María de la Visitación y Sermón de las caidas públicas*. Ed. Bernardo Velado Grana. Barcelona: Juan Flors, 1962.

María de Santo Domingo. *The Book of Prayer of Sor María de Santo Domingo*. Ed. Mary E. Giles. Albany: State University of New York Press, 1988.

Orozco y Covarrubias, Juan de. *Tratado de la verdadera y falsa prophecia*. Segovia: Juan de la Cuesta, 1588.

Pérez de Valdivia, Diego. *Aviso de gente recogida* (1585). Madrid: Universidad Pontificia de Salamanca y Fundación Universitaria Española, 1977.

Pisa, Francisco de. *Apuntamientos para la IIa parte de la "Descripción de la Imperial Ciudad de Toledo."* Ed. Jóse Gómez-Menor Fuentes. Toledo: Instituto Provincial de Investigaciones y Estudios Toledanos, 1976.

Suma de los engaños solícitos de nuestros tiempos. BRAH ms. 12-26-7.D 185

Teresa de Jesús. *Obras completas*. Ed. Alberto Barrientos et al. Madrid: Editorial de Espiritualidad, 1984.

Untold Sisters: Hispanic Nuns in Their Own Works. Ed. Electa Arenal and Stacey Schlau. Albuquerque: University of New Mexico Press, 1989.

SECONDARY SOURCES

Ahlgren, Gillian T. W. "Negotiating Sanctity: Holy Women in Sixteenth-Century Spain." *Church History* 64:3 (1995): 373–88.

———. *Teresa of Avila and the Politics of Sanctity*. Ithaca: Cornell University Press, 1996.

Andrés Martín, Melquíades. *El misterio de los alumbrados de Toledo, desvelado por sus contemporáneos, 1523–1560.* Burgos: El Monte Carmelo, 1976.

———. *Los recogidos: Nueva visión de la mística española (1500–1700).* Madrid: Fundación Universitaria Española, 1975.

———. *La teología española en el siglo XVI.* 2 vols. Madrid: Biblioteca de Autores Cristianos, 1976.

Avella Cháfer, Francisco. "Beatas y beaterios en la ciudad y arzobispado de Sevilla." *Archivo Hispalense* 65 (1982): 99–132.

Beltran de Heredia, Vicente. "Los alumbrados de la diócesis de Jaén: Un capítulo inédito de la historia de nuestra espiritualidad." *Revista Española de Teología* 9 (1949): 161–222, 445–88.

———. "Un grupo de visionarios y pseudoprofetas que actúa durante los últimos años de Felipe II: Repercusión de ello sobre la memoria de Santa Teresa." *Revista Española de Teología* 7 (1947): 373–97; 9 (1949): 483–534.

Bennassar, Bartolomé. *L'Inquisition espagnole.* Paris: Hatchette, 1979.

Bilinkoff, Jodi. *The Avila of Saint Teresa: Religious Reform in a Sixteenth-Century City.* Ithaca, NY: Cornell University Press, 1989.

———. "Confessors, Penitents, and the Construction of Identities in Early Modern Avila." In *Culture and Identity in Early Modern Europe (1500–1800): Essays in Honor of Natalie Zemon Davis,* ed. Barbara B. Dierendorf and Carla Hesse. Ann Arbor: University of Michigan Press, 1993.

Blázquez Miguel, Juan. *La Inquisición en Castilla-La Mancha.* Madrid: Librería Anticuaria Jérez, 1986.

———. *Sueños y procesos de Lucrecia de León.* Madrid: Tecnos, 1987.

Bynum, Caroline Walker. *Holy Feast and Holy Fast: The Religious Significance of Food to Medieval Women.* Berkeley, CA: University of California Press, 1987.

Caro Baroja, Julio. *Las formas complejas de la vida religiosa (Siglos XVI y XVII).* Madrid: Sarpe, 1985.

Corrientes espirituales en la España del siglo XVI: Trabajos del II Congreso de Espiritualidad. Barcelona: Juan Flors, 1963.

Cruz, Anne J., and Mary Elizabeth Perry, eds. *Culture and Control in Counter-Reformation Spain.* Minneapolis: University of Minnesota Press, 1992.

Egido, Teófanes, Victor García de la Concha, and Olegario González de Cardedal, eds. *Actas del Congreso Internacional Teresiano (4–7 octubre 1982).* 2 vols. Salamanca: Universidad de Salamanca, 1983.

Eire, Carlos M. N. *From Madrid to Purgatory.* New York: Cambridge University Press, 1995.

Fernández Alvarez, Manuel. "El entorno histórico de Santa Teresa." *Studia Zamorensia* 3 (1982): 357–447.

García Cárcel, Ricardo, ed. *La Iglesia en la España de los siglos XVI.* Barcelona: Península, 1980.

———. *La inquisición.* Madrid: Anaya, 1990.

García Oro, José. *Cisneros y la reforma del clero español en tiempos de los Reyes Católicos.* Madrid: Consejo Superior de Investigaciones Científicas, 1971.

García-Villoslada, Ricardo, ed. *La Iglesia en la España de los siglos XV y XVI.* Vol. 3, pt. 2 of *Historia de la Iglesia en España.* Madrid: Biblioteca de Autores Cristianos, 1980.

Gil Sousa, José-Antonio. *La eclesiología de Bartolomé Carranza de Miranda*. Toledo: Kadmos, 1986.

Giles, Mary, ed. *Women in the Inquisition: Spain and the New World*. Baltimore: Johns Hopkins University Press, 1999.

Haliczer, Stephen, ed. *Inquisition and Society in Early Modern Europe*. London: Croom Helm, 1986.

Hamilton, Alastair. *Heresy and Mysticism in Sixteenth-Century Spain*. Toronto: University of Toronto Press, 1992.

Henningsen, Gustav, and John Tedeschi, eds. *The Inquisition in Early Modern Europe: Studies in Sources and Methods*. De Kalb, IL: Northern Illinois University Press, 1984.

Huerga, Alvaro. *Los alumbrados de Baeza*. Jaén: Instituto de Estudios Giennenses, 1978.

——. *Historia de los alumbrados 1570–1620*. 5 vols. Madrid: Fundación Universitaria Española, 1972–94.

——. *Predicadores, alumbrados e inquisición en el siglo XVI*. Madrid: Fundación Universitaria Española, 1973.

——. "La muerte de Carranza: Informes confidenciales del Cardenal de Como, Secretaria de Estado de Gregorio XIII" in *Cuadernos de investigación histórica* 7 (1981): 15–27.

Imirizaldu, Jesús. *Monjas y beatas embaucadores*. Madrid: Editora Nacional, 1977.

Jiménez Duque, Baldomero. *Maridiaz (La "santa de Avila" en el siglo XVI)*. Avila: Colección Tau, 1989.

Kagan, Richard L. *Lucrecia's Dreams: Politics and Prophecy in Sixteenth-Century Spain*. Berkeley: University of California Press, 1990.

Kamen, Henry. *Inquisition and Society in Spain in the Sixteenth and Seventeenth Centuries*. Bloomington, IN: Indiana University Press, 1985.

——. *The Phoenix and the Flame: Catalonia and the Counter-Reformation*. New Haven: Yale University Press, 1993.

Lisón Tolosana, Carmelo. *La España mental: Demonios y exorcismos en los siglos de oro*. Madrid: Akal, 1990.

Llamas Martínez, Enrique. "Interrogatorio inquisitorial contra los Alumbrados según un ms. del British Museum." *Salamaticensis* 18 (1971): 123–25.

——. *Santa Teresa de Jesús y la Inquisición Española*. Madrid: Consejo Superior de Investigaciones Científicas, 1972.

Llorca, Bernardino. *La Inquisición española y los alumbrados (1509–1667): Según las actas originales de Madrid y de otros archivos*. Salamanca: Universidad Pontificia, 1980.

Márquez, Antonio. *Los Alumbrados. Orígenes y filosofía, 1525–1559*. Madrid: Taurus, 1980.

——. *Literatura e Inquisición en España, 1478–1834*. Madrid: Taurus, 1980.

——. "Origen y caracterización del iluminismo (según un parecer de Melchor Cano)." *Revista de Occidente* 63 (1968): 320–33.

Martz, Linda. *Poverty and Welfare in Habsburg Spain: The Case of Toledo*. New York: Oxford University Press, 1972.

Nalle, Sara T. *God in La Mancha: Religious Reform and the People of Cuenca, 1500–1650*. Baltimore: Johns Hopkins University Press, 1992.

Newman, Barbara. *Sister of Wisdom: St. Hildegard's Theology of the Feminine*. Berkeley: University of California Press, 1987.

Ortega Costa, Milagros. *Proceso de la Inquisición contra María de Cazalla*. Madrid: Fundación Universitaria Española, 1978.

Peers, E. Allison. *Handbook to the Life and Times of Saint Teresa and Saint John of the Cross.* Westminster, MD: Newman Press, 1954.

Pérez Villanueva, Joaquín, ed. *La Inquisición española: Nueva visión, nuevos horizontes.* Madrid: Siglo XXI, 1980.

Perry, Mary Elizabeth. *Crime and Society in Early Modern Seville.* Hanover, NH: University Press of New England, 1980.

———. *Gender and Disorder in Early Modern Seville.* Princeton: Princeton University Press, 1990.

Petroff, Elizabeth Alvilda, ed. *Medieval Women's Visionary Literature.* New York: Oxford University Press, 1986.

Pinero Ramirez, Pedro M. *La Sevilla imposible de Santa Teresa.* Sevilla: Artes Gráficas Salesianas, 1982.

Pinto Crespo, Virgilio. *Inquisición y control ideológico en la España del siglo XVI.* Madrid: Taurus, 1983.

Rossi, Rosa. *Teresa de Avila: Biografía de una escritora.* Trans. Marieta Gargatagli. Barcelona: ICARIA, 1984.

Saint-Saens, Alain. *La nostalgie du désert: l'idéal érémetique en Castille au Siecle d'Or.* San Francisco: Edwin Mellen Press, 1993.

———, ed. *Religion, Body, and Gender in Early Modern Spain.* San Francisco: Mellen Research University Press, 1991.

———. "Thérese d'Avila ou l'Erémitisme Sublimé." *Mélanges de la Casa de Velázquez* 25 (1989): 121–43.

Sala Balust, Luis. "En torno al grupo de alumbrados de Llerena" in *Corrientes espirituales en la España del siglo XVI.* Barcelona: Juan Flors, 1963, 509–23.

Selke de Sánchez, Angela. *El Santo Oficio de la Inquisición: Proceso de fray Francisco Ortiz (1529–1532).* Madrid: Guadarrama, 1968.

Slade, Carole. *St. Teresa of Avila: Author of a Heroic Life.* Berkeley: University of California Press, 1995.

Smet, Joachim. *The Carmelites. A History of the Brothers of Our Lady of Carmel.* Darien, IL: Carmelite Spiritual Center, 1975.

Steggink, Otger. *Arraigo e innovación en Teresa de Jesús.* Madrid: Biblioteca de Autores Cristianos, 1976.

———. *La reforma del Carmelo español: La visita canónica del general Rubeo y su encuentro con Santa Teresa (1566–1567).* Rome: Institutum Carmelitanum, 1965.

Surtz, Ronald E. *The Guitar of God: Gender, Power, and Authority in the Visionary World of Mother Juana de la Cruz (1481–1534).* Philadelphia: University of Pennsylvania Press, 1991.

———. *Writing Women in Late Medieval and Early Modern Spain.* Philadelphia: University of Pennsylvania Press, 1995.

Tapia, Ralph. *The Alumbrados of Toledo: A Study in Sixteenth-Century Spanish Spirituality.* Park Falls, WI: Weber and Sons, 1974.

Tellechea Idigoras, J. I. *El Arzobispo Carranza y su tiempo.* 2 vols. Madrid: Guadarrama, 1968.

———. *Tiempos recios: Inquisición y heterodoxos.* Salamanca: Ediciones Sigueme, 1977.

Vazquez de Prada, V. *Historia económica y social de España.* 5 vols. Madrid: Casa de Socorro, 1978.

Weber, Alison. "Demonizing Ecstasy: Alonso de la Fuente and the *Alumbrados* of Extremadura." In *The Mystical Gesture: Essays on Medieval and Early Modern Spiritual Culture in Honor of Mary E. Giles,* ed. Robert Boenig. Burlington, VT: Ashgate, 2000.

———. *Teresa of Avila and the Rhetoric of Femininity.* Princeton: Princeton University Press, 1990.

———. "Saint Teresa's Problematic Patrons." *Journal of Medieval and Early Modern Studies* 29 (1999): 357–79.

LETTERS AND VOWS

FRANCISCA'S LETTERS[1]

[To her sister Isabel, written on Friday, April 23, 1574][2]

My beloved sister:

It would not be possible to express the great joy that your letter gave us, so I will not try, because God has given me grace to tell you what has been happening. I wrote rather obscurely about the jewel that Our Lady had promised you, and having received from the hand of God a great punishment for not having done this before, I do not want to wait for a greater one, for that is what I have been promised, although God knows I have not done anything out of negligence, but rather because I understood clearly that it was the will of God, since this is what I always want to do even if it costs me my life. And now that I understand that it is truly His holy will that I write you something of the great things Our Lord has given me to understand since you left, I will tell you whatever God has made known to me.

After Our Lord and especially His most holy Mother consoled me for the great loss I felt due to your departure, a few days later, having just received communion, they told me in the interior of my soul that I should make an effort to suffer a great tribulation that they wanted to give me, until the day of the Immaculate Conception of Our Lady [i.e., December 8, 1573], in satisfaction for the ignorance that many had had about this point of the faith, especially the Dominicans. And I, not thinking myself worthy of such a great favor as suffering for such a great satisfaction, offered my soul and body to everything that my God and the most holy Virgin Mary wanted of me with

1. Fols. 149r–157r.

2. All bracketed comments that follow are my own.

such a great desire that I wished I had more bodies to offer up than there are grains of sand in the sea in order to suffer with all of them for the honor of such a great Lord. To say what I suffered during this time is not possible except to say that a human body could not bear nor a hand write of such great torments if it were not favored by this same Lord who ordered it to suffer. And thus with this aid I suffered the greatest darkness of the soul that can be told and torments in the body as well, because these demons, the mayors of God, visibly tormented it so much that if I laid down in bed to rest a little, my rest was to be beaten so hard by them that I could not walk with the pains I felt. My right side turned so black from the beatings that I can't tell it, and this great travail lasted until Easter. God granted me great mercies, which there is no reason to tell you about, and they gave me the chance to endure another similar trial until the Purification of Our Lady. And there was no way to find consolation except on the day that I went to the Chapel of Nuestra Señora del Sagrario. They gave me permission to go and thus it was that I went, but before and after holy communion the pains in my soul were intolerable, although in going to the Sagrario I found great joy. And four days later, a Monday, having just finished communion, they told me in my interior, "Go, my mother wants to speak with you in the Sagrario." And I went immediately, and while I was kneeling down my spirit was enraptured with great sweetness and I saw the Mother of Mercy who was interceding with her Son for the state of the church asking that they charge Archbishop Bartolomé with its reform. For this Our Lady promised great things, and by these things she managed with all the pleas she presented to convince her Son, except when great satisfaction was necessary to appease the Eternal Father.

And the next day, Tuesday, after just having received communion, I heard in my interior that I should go immediately to see great things. So I did go immediately, and my spirit was enraptured again and I heard the Son of God say, "Send out your spirit and renew the face of the earth."[3]

And I saw a great Majesty, who responded, "You ask much of me, Son, that I renew all the earth, because the offenses they have committed against me are great. I have been waiting seventy years, and I only see myself more offended." And His most holy Son showed Him His wounds and all the suffering that the world had cost Him and the prayer that He said on the cross for those who had crucified Him. He told all of this to His Majesty so that He would pardon the world anew. But Our Lady put herself between them, and she offered up two convents, in which people of great spirit would ded-

---

3. Cf. Psalm 104:30.

icate themselves through her hand and which would be enough to satisfy His Majesty for the offenses that the whole world had committed. And the monastic houses would be of the same rule that she had written. I saw how this Majesty turned to my sinful soul and said to me, "What do you think, daughter, for the world has offended me, especially this church because with its words it offends me and it crucifies me with its masses." And with great tears I said nothing more than to beg Him for mercy.

And then I saw how the Son of God took the archbishop by one arm and presented him to His Father saying, "Our Father, you see here Bartolomé, who will be enough to reform the church. Be happy in him, because I am pleased with him and I will represent him; he will lose his life for the honor of Your Majesty and the reformation of Your church." The Eternal Father received him, very pleased with him, and after embracing him, He poured out many blessings upon him, and this happened before her and two other persons. And later I saw in the hands of that great Majesty some large lances with very sharp barbs of four parts, and His Majesty crossed his arms over his chest and said He could not show any greater sign of peace than that. And He turned over everything to Our Lady, and thus she and her blessed Son began to sing, "Cantemus, domine, gloriose" (Let us sing glory to you, Lord). And Saint Hildephons, Saint Jerome, Saint Joseph, Saint John the Evangelist, Saint Gabriel, and Saint Catherine of Siena responded, because they had all been on their knees praying for what I have said, and later I felt how the Archbishop Bartolomé embraced my spirit, exhorting me to great things. And with that, it ended. I have only been able to say the most basic things about this matter, having been entrusted with this great mercy by that great Lord, who gave it to me, a miserable person and helped me understand that His Majesty would be served. Read it in another spirit than my sinful and base one writes it, my sister. To tell you about the great illness that, since this happened to me, God has given me so that I may present great petitions to Our Lord will not be possible until God allows us to see each other. I pray to His Majesty that it may be soon, for His great honor. Amen.

[To Isabel Bautista, undated]

My dear and beloved sister and my consolation:

I cannot tell you the great joy your letters gave all of us, even though it could not be as great as the pain of your absence has been. For it has been like a breach of faith for us to be deprived of you, our goodness and our light. I do not want to speak more of this because I do not have [a strong enough] heart to awaken my pain without bathing the paper with tears. I resign myself to the will of God who has desired it to be thus. I pray that His Majesty be served by our travails.

My sister, in what you wrote about the state of my soul, I wish I could reveal more, but they do not give me permission because letters are so unreliable. I do not dare to entrust something of such importance to paper. But I say in code that I have received such great mercies from Our Lord and with such clarity about our business that I will remain prepared at all times (lit. "with a candle in my hand"), and I have unfailing faith that God will give what He has promised you, especially the jewel that Our Lady of the Sagrario has promised you. Because after we had made many pilgrimages and had many masses said, I was instructed to have two novenas at the Sagrario. In the first one they gave me great reassurances about all our plans, and I saw the jewel they promised you in her hand. With it all the lost would be rescued, in particular the church. In the second novena I suffered great darkness and tribulations up until today, which I have already told you about. But neither faith nor my tongue fails me and complains to God that He show me justice because He has placed us in these present circumstances after we have endured so many illnesses and travails. It consoles me to know that we did not put ourselves in them but rather that His Majesty ordained it, and thus I trust that the one who gave us these hardships will bring us through them with victory.

What your letter says about being left alone and in darkness could not but pain me, even though it is common for God, when He is going to bring about great mercies, to treat people the way He did Abraham: after having made him so many promises through his son Isaac, He then ordered him to cut off his head. May this give us confidence that God will bring about all He has promised us if He be served and if it be His will, because all of us do not want anything more than that His name be sanctified, and may this be in whatever way His Majesty might command me. You say, my sister, that with all this you have rendered sighs and tears before God night after night, having the floor for a bed, and during the day too: so I will do the same until I see God honored and His poor liberated. And so I say to my God with passion that this is my goal.

In other things we are very happy, even with the great pain that what is happening with the confessor has given me. Remember how much Saint Catherine of Siena suffered with the disbelief of her confessors. I don't believe that God asks any less, since he has put tears before you not knowing you. It is clear that if they had spoken with you as we have and had seen you pass so many months fasting on only bread and water with so much spirit and strength, they would have had to take you in hand! What I feel the worst about is how they deny you communion. I trust in God and that He will give you His favor in everything. To recount the mercies He gives us would hardly be possible because we need nothing for our soul or our body that cannot be remedied with the love of the Father.

You already know that fifteen days before Lent, Ribera and his wife came to live in Toledo, sick of Madrid and with the intention never to return there again in their lifetimes. I gave them housing here. And then on Ash Wednesday Cebrián came, and his conversion has been such that it has over-whelmed us. He has made a general confession with Señor Miguel Ruíz, and he is so obedient to his opinion (as I am), and his change of heart so thor-ough, that we cannot but think that you are praying to God to join us all together in one spirit because He has done this. We all go to confession with Señor Miguel Ruíz; Cerezo, Ribera, and their wives receive communion every Sunday; and Cebrián and Mariana go to their mass. Mariana put on a veil on New Years Day, and ever since then she confesses to Señor Miguel Ruíz and with such good intention that no one could stop her. She and Cebrián are like husband and wife, and so we are of one spirit and love, helping one another.

My sister, each one of us wants to write you separately, but Señor Miguel Ruíz did not consent to it in order not to trouble Señor Pedro Gonzalez. Cerezo cried very much at this; now there are no quarrels since they have confessed with our father.

In what you say about the Sagrario you have not been deceived because every day he [i.e., Cerezo] has gone there; he has awakened early each morn-ing with me at the hospital, and after hearing mass he goes to the Sagrario, and now so do Ribera and Cebrián.

Our father came with Ribera and his wife. He spent eight days here with everyone, though he felt your absence deeply. God knows how I felt to see us all together except for you. He wrote me this week that he had sent you a letter by post with a great desire to hear from you. Look around there to see if it arrives. I will tell him later that you wrote. Your letter will not come in time. I will send it to him by another way if God wills, and so I beg you for the love of God, write to us as much as you can because we cannot live any other way, especially because the young men [i.e., Francisca's brothers] are determined to go [to see you] there if you do not write more often. It has been a miracle that we have held them here and they have not gone there; every day they make plans. Although you may be able to live without us, we cannot live without you.

About Luisa de Aguilera and all in her house, I let you know that she is as she usually is and her husband is in Valladolid. It is impossible to put down in particular all the greetings from everyone except to say that we are like

orphans without a mother. May God let us see one another. I do not say anything about Chacón, because he must write himself, except that he has been
a true brother to me.

Your sister, Francisca de los Apóstoles

To my beloved and desired sister Isabel de San Jerónimo.

She is my sister in Rome.

[Dated August 24, 1574]

To my cherished brother Pedro Chacón in the cathedral:

Be sure to respond to me if you receive this letter.

The love I have for you is such that I must at least be happy because of
the sadness you say you have at our absence, and in finding myself paid of
the same debt, I do not want to speak more of it. But I do want to tell you
how we received a letter from our sister Isabel Bautista dated June 29, and it
says that she had already written us three letters and she asked why hadn't
we responded, since it was about time. So we sent someone to the main post
office in Madrid to look for them in case they were detained because they
did not come with Don Pedro. In these most recent letters she says she is
very well and very esteemed in body and soul by Señor Don Pedro González,
and he writes the same thing, that it gives him great happiness to be with her.
Don Pedro highly values the letter I sent him about what I said to you in
secret, and he did not want to give it to my sister until he showed it to the
archbishop, who responded that everything my sister asked him for was quite
fair, and he promised he would give it to her. I tell you that my sister writes
in such a way that leads me to believe that all that we want will be done very
soon, because the pope has told Don Pedro not to come because soon he
[i.e., Archbishop Carranza] will come with the plans for reform. May God
do what we all need. I want so much for your grace to read that letter that
you will not believe it. I cannot send it, but I do send one that she wrote to
my brothers and to your grace, and because in it you will see what she says
to your grace, I do not want to recount more, except that Señor Miguel Ruíz
is pleased to pray a great deal for your grace, and this entire house receives
great contentment with that [unspecified; presumably a letter Chacón sent
to them] of your grace, and we all kiss your hands.

Cebrián works in Madrid in our father's house. It continues to trouble me
that there are no religious orders here. May God be praised for everything,
for this is His to make happen; may His will be done in everything, for this
is what is most fitting for us: to deny ourselves in all things and seek only God
without having any other interest. And I know His Majesty is so just that if

we give Him justly our efforts He will reward us by bringing us all back together for his great glory and our happiness. I hope that this will give me life. May God in His mercy do this as a father. Amen.

        Francisca de los Apóstoles
        On the Day of Saint Bartholomew
        Your grace's sister who desires your greatest well-being

[Dated August 25, 1574]

We received your letters in the octave[4] of Saint Laurence two days after Our Lady in August [i.e., Assumption day, August 15. This would mean that the letters were received on August 17]. We had just finished a fast of forty days, and we were going each day to the crucifix and to the tomb of Saint Bartholomew. We were happy to be able to emerge with the victory because many troubles have presented themselves to us. I spoke of it in detail in a letter we sent a month ago, so I won't say anything here except that our joy was confirmed in hearing from you. It is five months since we have had a letter from you. So how could we feel about your silence when there are no words to make you understand the great pain we were feeling? Glory be to God because in all these travails in which we are embroiled I trust His Majesty to free us from them with victory.

    My sister, it seems that you write like a confused person out of touch with God; your desires are not the same as those you had when you left Toledo, and for this reason your departure seems a dream. But do not believe that it was a dream, because I affirmed on behalf of God that nothing that that His Majesty has promised you will be lacking. Tell me with what wine God could have intoxicated us that we could have so set aside our own will and blinded our understanding, as we did when we let our beloved sister, who was so beneficial to our well-being, leave on those roads, all alone, thinking that it would be for a short time. Just thinking about this so disturbs my brother Cerezo that he said after you left that he must have either been asleep or crazy not to have gone with you. They all talk in this vein every day, and they are all asking God to dull their senses because they do not want to know what could be felt in this matter. I have told you this to take away the pain you have because things are not coming along as quickly as we thought they would. Our Lord has treated us like a mother with her child, who, in order to get him to do what she wants, shows him a jewel but does not give it to

---

4. When used with respect to the Christian liturgical calendar, "octave" refers to the eight days following a feast day during which observance of the feast day continued.

him, not because she doesn't want to give it to him, since it is meant for him, but because he is a child and does not appreciate the value of the jewel. Thus Our Lord has done the same with us because, as you well know my dear sister, His Majesty says, "I am the greatest of things; you must grow and consume me." We must therefore exert ourselves on the path of trials and tribulations to be great in virtue and humble in our own understanding because this is right for us and what we intend to do. It is also not good for us to have spiritual or temporal pleasures, because we do not win victory that way but by continuous pains and torments, and I have chosen these to be my pleasures. For this reason, the trials that I write about and experience give me great delight. One of the greatest mercies Our Lord can give us is to carry our business to its end because affairs that are truly His must go slowly and not hastily. I say this because you are tired, but do not despair of our hope to see the release of our pastor—I tell you for certain that we are experiencing here the same trials that you have written about and even worse—because we are worried about what will happen to you. If the hours became months I would not tire of suffering trials until I saw the Archbishop Bartolomé in his office, and I trust in this because God has given me to understand much about him in all the prayers we engage in. Thus as far as I know, it seems to me that he says, "Take it" with respect to the jewel we desire, because it is certain that God has purified him to reform the church and also Señor Don Pedro Gonzalez, who assures us he will be the first to enter Corpus Christi.

In what you say about not believing what I wrote you about what happened to me in the Sagrario, I will not waste time on it, because we have only one God, blessed may He be, who guides me, and as this is His affair He will make it understood in the souls and spirits as He may be served. This is His business, and my words can do nothing if it is not the will of God, whose spirit comprehends all things.

In what you say of the records and inventory that we ought to do about the young women and widows, I am not going to do this because that is for Señor Miguel Ruíz to do, with the permission of Señor Don Pedro, to whom he remains obedient in everything. I tell you, my sister, if it was necessary to make up the account, I would do it in a single day—of a thousand people if it were necessary—if it would move people. There is a great multitude of people who are in this house since you left with a lady who wanted to found a convent for poor women, for which there is a great need. I have come to understand that a great number of young women and widows have occasion to offend God [i.e., through prostitution] out of necessity. The reason for this is that the prelate [i.e., Carranza] has been gone for so long because of our great sins. As you know, they think all the [economic] needs of these poor women can be remedied with the four *reales* that they give out on Christmas. May God in His mercy remedy evils like this that the long imprisonment of our archbishop causes in the church of God and in the poor. If I did not have the faith I have in God that He will bring him back to remedy all this, I do not know what consolation would be enough for me, because things are so horrible that it seems that God has ordered all the church officials to spend their income amusing themselves. They allow the poor to die and the young women to be lost [i.e., to lose their virtue]. I do not want to speak more of this because I lose my mind when I get to this point, except to tell you what I do with these people I have told you about, which is to sustain their hope that they will not be lost. For this purpose, many upright people have spoken with other people, and they have come to me to pursue the same goals. You would be amazed: very rich people, young women as well as widows, and of such great virtue that they astound me. All tell me they have desired all their lives to enter a convent but that, seeing the decadence there is in the convents, they think it better to stay enclosed in their houses. They have understood that this convent will be a place of great sanctity, and they ask me to receive them into it, to which I respond that I cannot do anything yet but place the matter before God and that if the lady who went away returns with the permission, I will do my part in whatever I can. It's an amazing thing to see that these same people I turn away come back in a few days and tell me about the many prayers they say for it, and in response they hear inside themselves that it will be a convent of such great sanctity and largesse that they cannot stop thinking about it, even when I contradict them to test them and tell them that they must wait until you return and that they must commit their lives and fortunes to such a holy endeavor. Tell me that you do not believe this the way you do not believe about the Sagrario, because I assure you that the faith of this people is so great it seems holy to me and the poorest of these women has 3,000 ducados. If we were to start the convent the response of these people would be great; they would enter with their dowries.

And I trust that God has another way [even better than this to bring about the convent]. For this reason, do not lose hope that Our Lord, who has shown that this holy work will be done, will give us the most suitable way because this is His idea and not ours, for we were content in our house. If God wills, may His Majesty's will always be done. Amen.

My sister, my father and all of us are well, thanks be to God; send him one of your stories. All of my brothers and sisters want to write you individually. Here [in Toledo] they thank you for the beautiful letter you sent. Pedro Chacón is not here, as I wrote you in another letter. He begs you to speak with the chaplain who brought you the letter from the doctor named Andrada, because now he is sending you some papers so that they will give him a chaplaincy. Things cannot be arranged without it, so for the love of God be quick about it so that it may be done shortly.

One thing I have not told you in order not to make you sad is that if it is possible for you, be as reserved as possible and do not tell anyone [about our plans], because a servant of Don Pedro, a young cleric, sent a letter to Alcocer claiming twenty absurdities, such as how you said that the archbishop had to be freed, that he would ask for the reform of the whole world, and that he carried three lists—one on his chest of immoral married women, another on the arm of maidens, and a third on his other arm of bad women. He also said you claimed that a convent had to be founded to gather and enclose all of them. And he wrote other, similar things. Alcocer brought me the letter; he was furious. That cleric asked to be sent information about who this woman [i.e., Isabel] was and what kind of a life she had led and about me too. He responded as was appropriate. God knows the great pain we have all borne until we had news of you.

May God in his mercy let us see you.

Your sister, Francisca de los Apóstoles

[Undated]

My dear sister of my heart:

My desire to see you is so great that I do not know any other way to console myself except to write you, because in doing this it seems that I speak with you, and so I can bear the great solitude your absence causes me. May God be glorified for everything, since His Majesty has ordained everything, and if this were not so, I would not have the patience to see myself separated from my beloved Isabel. Beg God, my sister, to bring us victory over this fight in which His Majesty placed us on the Lord's path.

Don Pedro Gonzalez wrote you about our business and about what happened to me, although without enough detail to describe what really happened; that would be impossible unless I were to go on for a long time. When you read it, confident in God who is being served, it will give you the spirit to understand what God wants in all of this, because these are not matters for here. There is one thing that has happened to me since you left, about which I will write you partially or not at all, and because of it I am very confident that we will see more than what has been promised to us or that we ourselves can desire.

I have wanted to tell you about what happened surrounding your departure. All of those who know you were shocked that such a dainty woman would put herself on such a long journey. You have become famous throughout Toledo, and they all wonder about the great lady who wants to found a convent, whether it is the mother of Don Juan de Austria who went to the cave.[5] I do not contradict this and so they believe it to be true, so much so that the whole city of Toledo is moved and thus every day many young women and widows come to the house telling me of their desires and their great poverty and asking to be admitted.

Times are so hard that my heart aches because of the tremendous necessity here in Toledo; I never thought they would be so bad and all because we lack our pastor. May the Majesty of God give him back or may He take me so that I will not see such a great offense against God and such neglect of the poor. I tell you for certain that since what happened to me in the Sagrario, which I wrote you about, I suffer so many inner trials that I do not know how to tell you. They persuade me in my interior to go to the high mass between the two choirs on all the feast days, and from there I see so many sheep without a pastor and so lost and the throne empty. The anguish I feel is so great that quite often I fear my heart will break. I make a great effort not to cry aloud from these desires that I feel. I know that they have processions, and I see the governor at the head of them, and I say to God with great passion, "My Lord, give us the pastor of these sheep!" and His Majesty gives me great consolation that He will do as He has promised. I have great faith and confidence in this, and nothing will take it from me.

Señor Dr. Mateo López was very pleased that you remembered him and sent for him to ask for his signature, and, since he is writing it, I will not say more about his grace. My brother Cerezo went to Enrique in Madrid upon receiving your first letter so that he could help him with a work [i.e., a painting] that the *corregidor* commissioned from him, and now the whole city is happy, which is no small thing because many people were jealous.

Enrique is here and kisses your hands, and he hopes in God to be able to do a portrait of you, which he cannot do in your absence.

They tell me over and over again how much my father cried with joy to hear from you because he was quite anxious until he received your letter, and so he sends many greetings and he sent you a letter by mail with many greetings and prayers to God; his wife sends greetings as well.

Ribera and his wife are about to write and send their letter along with this one; so much do they want to see you that they want to be the ink on it. Since you left without saying anything to them they felt even more pain than

5. A possible reference to Catalina de Cardona, who left the court of Juan de Austria to become a hermitess. She was famed for her penitence and was written about by Teresa of Avila in her *Foundations* 28.20–36.

all of us, and so they send their best greetings in God. They are doing well—they live in peace without running a shop. They are living well because in the house God provides them with a lot of [commissioned] works.

Cerezo is sleeping while I write this, but because in other letters I have told you about him I do not say more here except that he is doing well, although he has some trouble with his wife who is six months pregnant.

Cibrián is well. Pray to God that he may persevere. And so is Mariana; she wears clothing of Saint Jerome with a long sleeve and is quite happy.

We all live in hope, I even the more, but I do not expect anything to happen until after New Years, because in the year 1575 I have great faith that I will see the Archbishop Bartolomé on his throne. Until then, I will not stop clamoring to God and making pilgrimages, because on the day I write this I have had a mass said to the Holy Spirit; and we walk the houses of Our Lady having nine masses for the nine feasts of Our Lady, each day its own.

Fray Jerónimo de Toledo, our relative, prays for you a great deal and sends greetings. And Fray Prudencio. And the curate continues to wonder about your departure, thinking about how it was with the lady. What he would do if he knew you went alone! He and everyone else would think we were crazy. So I have said nothing to anyone, because everything is wrapped around how you went with the lady, as I have said.

If I start to say something about Pedro Chacón I would not be able to stop. He is very well and in continual prayer for you. He has ordered me to ask you through this letter not to forget what he sent you to do and may you have Señor Don Pedro as your helper.

Señor Miguel Ruíz does not know I am writing, because last night I heard from the doctor that he had to give the letters [for delivery] very early in the morning. So I won't say anything about him, except that he does for us what a father would in everything. And with this I beg the Majesty of God for His great honor that we all see each other again soon. Amen.

Your sister who loves you more than you love her.

Francisca de los Apóstoles

To my beloved sister Isabel de San Jerónimo. They will tell you of her in the *posada* of My Lord Don Pedro Gonzalez de Mendoza because his grace knows where she is in Rome.

[Letter to Isabel dated Sunday, July 18, 1574]

Very beloved sister of my heart:

I cannot possibly tell you how sad we have been not to have had news from you for so long. I have wanted to do this [i.e., write you this letter] every time Señor Don Pedro has written, but Señor Miguel Ruíz has not permitted me, saying that it was more appropriate this way. But when I saw that there were letters from Don Pedro dated July 15 from Toledo and that there was no mention of you, I was very sad and so was Señor Miguel Ruíz, so much so that he could not find it in himself to write you. And while I was receiving communion, I begged Our Lord to show me if He was served by my writing you. I felt with clarity that I should write you what I do now with his favor and say that it does not surprise me that you have not written because this is no time for recreation but only for continual penance, because in what I wrote you in my earlier letter about what happened to me at the Sagrario there is still a cloud remaining between the Eternal Father and the world; and this obstructs the mercies that we were asking from His Majesty. I was shown that that cloud was the sins with which the entire world had offended that great Majesty. I looked past that very dark cloud, and I saw the Archbishop Bartolomé, who was offering himself up as the satisfaction they asked for because of all the world's sins and I saw how God became his advocate. Since then I have had a great thirst to suffer many trials for the satisfaction of the great offenses that I saw had offended that great Majesty.

And Our Lord ordained that we—María de San Jerónimo, Magdalena de San Francisco, Catalina de San Francisco, [and I]—make in one spirit many pilgrimages, and they have not ceased to come to the Sagrario. It's an amazing thing to see that without my saying anything to them Our Lord inspired their hearts to make many prayers on behalf of the apostolic see, the Church, the crown, and the commonwealth. While engaged in these prayers I saw [*sic*] resounding in my soul the voice of the Justice of God, which exhausted me so much that I was faint in bed for many days, as was Señor Miguel Ruíz. Our Lord desired that we feel better at nearly the same time although his illness was worse than mine. Although I was out of bed, I still felt the same fatigue because I didn't see my desire fulfilled, which was to see the Eternal Father satisfied. While I was in this great travail, His Majesty consoled me in some way, because his holiness [i.e., the pope] ordered that the most holy sacrament be taken in all the churches, and having seen that this edict means to promote the same things that we have been taught, my heart has had some contentment. Thus I have tried to pull in all that I am able, to receive some refuge and make satisfaction in some way, in the ways that He is owed.

This rest did not last long, because a few days later the same voice sounded in my heart, which said, "See: I have sufficient reason to execute My justice against the world, for it has been so ungrateful for the passion of My Son." And He showed me how great this ingratitude was and how great was the passion of His Son. One day He had me experience some pains that were so great I had to throw myself down before a crucifix in order to bear them, and I could say nothing but, "Lord, no one can make satisfaction for the least of your pains; so our ingratitude begs your grace." While Our Lord was pleading the case for His justice and I for His mercy, I was told to beg for the Archbishop Bartolomé because at his liberation all would be remedied. So I took heart and asked His Majesty for that, and on the feast day of Saints Peter and Paul, while receiving communion, my spirit was enraptured and I saw how Saint Peter asked Our Lord for the liberation of the archbishop, showing him the great perdition there was in his church and how Bartolomé would remedy these and other great allegations that were made against Saint Peter. Then I saw and heard that he received the answer that more satisfaction than that was necessary in order that what Saint Peter asked be done. And Saint Peter, seeing the great truth in this, asked that he be given some assurance, because there was no other way to make satisfaction. Then I saw the Son of God appear to make this guarantee[6] with his own blood, and the Holy Spirit offered itself to come and inflame hearts. With all these promises they asked for more satisfaction, and Our Lord ordered that during this time we make a fast of forty days and perform penance every third day and that each day, after having received communion, we go barefoot before the cross and the sepulcher to make satisfaction for the ingratitude that we have had for the passion of Our Redeemer. We do this, all four of us, and with such great toil that you cannot imagine. If the same Lord who commanded us to endure this labor did not favor us, we would not suffer one day of it. We have been promised great victories and favors, and thus we are confident that His Majesty will keep his word.

And while fulfilling this pilgrimage, this same voice resounded, in which I was called back into myself with a strong spirit, which was given by that same God, against His justice, reminding Him of his former mercies and our great weakness. I spoke with His Majesty of cases of justice so that He would save the world, because His Majesty had shown me that it was so lost. I did not ask for anything more than what was in me to ask with faith. I came to say that I wanted to make peace and know more about the great protests that impeded the release of the archbishop because in that [i.e., in his trials], so much of our well-being was imprisoned. And so I arranged for a compromise about all the debts that were pled against me, which we owe to the Divine Majesty. The first is great ingratitude. The second is grave pride and conceit in all the estates of the world. The third is the great abominations that are done against the sixth commandment. The fourth is the great sins commit-

6. Literally, to make bail.

ted against the holy faith and worse are those who secretly in their hearts lose their faith in the providence of God and, lacking confidence in this providence, revolt with all the goods given to us by the hand of God and allow the poor to perish, fearing God, who provided all that was necessary for every creature that He created. This complaint was particularly strong against the ecclesiastical officials and learned people in the world and against all those who have more power in it [i.e., the world] in this estate I have mentioned. Our concern is this: we desire to know if God wants things to continue as they are there. Thus, for the love of God, write us as soon as you can, even though our penance is perfected by the absence of your letters. May God be praised in everything and obeyed and reverenced in all the world. And may you, my beloved sister, be favored by the grace of God to do His holy will. And may we always do this holy will, even if it costs us our life. Amen. Amen.

FRANCISCA'S VOWS[7]

In the name of Jesus Christ crucified and the glorious Virgin Mary: I, Francisca, say that I vow each day of my life to pay the great debt that we all owe to the Majesty of God, which is the great love with which Christ descended from the bosom of His Father to pay for the sin that our forefather Adam committed, in which sin humanity remained subjected unto death and to be in continuous war with the devil. This great God, vanquished by love for humanity, left the bosom of His Father and threw Himself down to drink the bitterness that sin had caused in order to make satisfaction for sin to His Father. Furthermore, so that humanity would not lose its inheritance as children of heaven, He bore our sins and had a continual war with hell, which crushed his strength. He covered himself in the sin of Adam, so that He lived in continual poverty and subjection, persecutions, affronts, burdens, defamation, lashes, and finally death on the cross in order to give humanity a clear path upon which it would be able to defeat its enemies, whom it allows to defeat it each time it flees from these pathways of Jesus Christ crucified.

Therefore I, Francisca, say that I oblige myself to live the passion of this great God with all the powers of my will, and I will do all that is in me to instill this passion in all the souls with whom I come into contact and even more so in the convent of the Holy Encarnación, which commits itself to paying these debts of sin, which I have described, in order to make satisfaction for the great ingratitude we have all had for all the benefits that Our Lord

7. Fols. 158r–162v.

created for humanity. And for the satisfaction of [this ingratitude], the will of the Holy Trinity and the glorious Virgin Mary is that all people who enter Corpus Christi and the Encarnación have the intent to imitate and to follow Jesus Christ. Because the one who leaves the world to enter into these holy religious houses will have this as her first task: that she leave behind all the delights of the world to pay Christ for those that he left in the breast of His Father when He humbled Himself to clothe Himself with our flesh and to call us to be children of His Father and His own brothers and sisters, so that we could be inheritors of His kingdom, which we will most certainly be if we imitate His beloved Son. And to that imitation I call all people, especially those who will enter these religious houses, because this is their vocation: to awaken the passion of Christ, because it has been frozen by continual sin and by our desire to flee from troubles and by our love of the body.

In the name of Jesus Christ crucified and the glorious Virgin Mary: I, Francisca, say that I oblige myself all the days of my life to live in subjection and humility and poverty for the satisfaction of the whole world, which has opposed the humility and poverty of Jesus Christ crucified, trying with all its might to live in pride and riches, even though those same riches have led them to the worst possible ends.

In the name of Jesus Christ crucified and the glorious Virgin Mary: I, Francisca, say that I oblige myself to live all the days of my life in the true knowledge of who God is and of His true pathways, which are humility and poverty and gentleness and mildness and mercy, which I propose to have with all my neighbors in satisfaction for the blindness that all the world has had with respect to knowing and following those true pathways of Jesus Christ, who was crucified for us sinners and ungrateful ones in the great passion that He suffered for us. And I call all peoples to this knowledge with tears in my heart.

In the name of Jesus Christ crucified and the glorious Virgin Mary: I, Francisca, say that I oblige myself all the days of my life to sanctify the most holy name of God with continual praises and with a loving will, persuading all creatures as much as I can that they do the same in satisfaction for the ways in which we have all offended this great God with blasphemies and curses and all types of oaths through which we have deprecated this great Lord and His holy name and the glorious Virgin Mary and all the saints. And I call all peoples to this knowledge that they may come to know and sanctify this strong and powerful and terrible and gentle and merciful and benign and friendly and loving God, that sinners may be converted to know this Lord before the gates of His mercy are closed.

In the name of Jesus Christ crucified and the glorious Virgin Mary: I, Francisca de los Apóstoles, say that I oblige myself to live in perpetual righteousness of spirit all the days of my life, basing all of my works in only pleasing God and mortifying myself for the satisfaction of sins that we have committed, particularly churchmen, who serve and love God with hypocrisy, pretending to be holy with our half-hearted works, not to give honor to God but instead to gain honor and authority, crucifying Jesus Christ again with each of our works. Come priests, come to the righteousness of this spirit of God who descended from heaven to earth in your hands. May your works be worthy of the great office that you have been given in perpetuity, living in perpetual purity of soul and body, so that this Lord may be reverenced and served for His own sake and not for any other interest. Because to Him should be given all the honor and glory of all of our works. Amen.

In the name of Jesus Christ crucified and of the glorious Virgin Mary: I, Francisca de los Apóstoles, say that I oblige myself to live all the days of my life in perpetual chastity and abstinence and scorn toward the clothing of the world that demonstrate its pomp and vanity for the satisfaction of these three things [i.e., sexual license, gluttony, and vanity], through which the world has offended the Majesty of God, particularly married people, who are obliged to live the gospel, fulfilling it as they promised in holy baptism when they renounced Satan and the world and its vanities. But having forgotten this, they have lived and live according to the laws that they renounced, living according to the sensual appetites of their flesh and creating children of wrath and condemnation because of the bad habits that they have in raising them. It is a sad dream in which you live, because you did not choose the Justice of God in such a state and it is so little known in you. Come, widows, to the frequent reception of the most holy sacrament where the salve of God is found; receive it, and you will abandon your old and present ways and live in continuous righteousness and justice, having only God as the recipient of your works. Come young women, whose understandings and wills wander wherever they happen to find themselves at the time; do not seek your joy in creatures, because you will not find it there, or in sensual delights, because they are our perdition. You will only find it in God and His pathways, so come, come: how can you be without knowledge of such a great God? Even the ass and the donkey knew him at the manger, and yet we do not know Him when He is cooked and roasted to be made into our food.[8] And thus we

8. "Cocido y asado en la cruz por hacerse nuestro mantenimiento." Francisca's colorful language has a Eucharistic dimension, suggesting that Christians feed upon Christ. "Mantenimiento" here can be understood as food or sustenance.

arrive at the altar to receive Him like beasts at the manger to eat straw, and with such disgust and boredom as if He were our enemy because we do not know God. It is as if a genteel gentleman passing by a mule was disgusted by the smell and tried to pass by it quickly. So we, who do not know His way of life, cover our senses, since we do not understand the greatness of His ways and what He asks of us in His great love. We will not leave behind our pleasures, and we follow all our conquerable sensual appetites. When I consider this, great pain threatens to split open my poor heart, because I see how my Lord and Creator and Savior and Glorifier is scorned and hated and crucified each hour. I ask Him, out of the great love with which He descended from heaven to earth, to send us His cross, that we might know His Majesty for who he is and love and serve and revere only Him. Glory be to the Father, Son, and Holy Spirit. Amen.

O great Justice of God, whose complaints against the world and the poor sinner are understandably great, for we have been truly ungrateful for all the benefits of Jesus Christ crucified! I, a sinner, seeing the reason [for your complaints] and seeing humanity abandoning the end for which it was created, vow to you, Divine Justice, to pay these debts, if the Creator favors me, under whose wings I flee from my enemies. And if I do not do this, may you unleash upon me your wrath.

And I take for my patroness the glorious Virgin Mary, remedy and mediatrix of all sinners.

Francisca de los Apóstoles

And I take for my fathers Saint Jerome and Saint Francis and Saint Joseph and Saint Dominic and Saint Hildephons and John the Evangelist and Saint Gabriel, and I take for my mother Saint Catherine of Siena.

TRANSCRIPT
OF THE INQUISITIONAL TRIAL
OF FRANCISCA DE LOS APÓSTOLES

INITIAL INQUISITORIAL EXAMINATION OF FRANCISCA DE LOS APÓSTOLES, OCTOBER 5 TO DECEMBER 5, 1575[1]

At the afternoon session of the Holy Inquisition of the city of Toledo on October 5, 1575, the Lord Inquisitor Dr. Juan de Llano de Valdés ordered a woman to be brought from her cell. She was sworn in, and under oath she vowed to tell the truth in this session as in all the others that they would have with her until a judgment was rendered in her case, and she said her name was Francisca de Avila, or Francisca de los Apóstoles, born in the town of Novés, and now a resident of this city of Toledo, and she said she was 36 years of age, more or less, and she declared her genealogy in the following way:

Parents:

Cebrián de Avila, a painter, who lives in Madrid by la Victoria

Juana Diez, now dead, who was born in Camarena and whose father was from Cabañas

Paternal grandparents:

She said she did not know them or what their names were.

Maternal grandparents:

Alberto Cerezo, deceased; she does not know where he was from nor does she remember her grandmother's name.

Her siblings:

Andrés Cerezo, a painter of retables, from Toledo who lives near the mayor of the city

Blas de Ribera, a rope maker from Toledo who lives with Andrés Cerezo

Cebrián de Avila, a painter who lives with the defendant

Isabel Bautista, a *beata*

Mariana, a *beata*

Her children:

She said she did not have any children nor has she been married because she was a religious.

When asked of what caste and race the defendant was and her parents and grandparents and the others she has named, and if they or any one of them had been imprisoned and punished by this Holy Office, she said that they are old Christians and she had always heard that and that her maternal grandfather is a relative of Mateo López, the inspector (*visitador*), who resides in that city, and that she does not know that any of them has been punished by the Holy Office of the Inquisition.

When asked to say her prayers, she made the sign of the cross and blessed herself and said the Our Father, Hail Mary, Creed, and Salve Regina.

When asked whether she knows how to read and write and whether she has had any formal studies, she said that she knows how to read and write and has not studied formally.

When asked whether she is a baptized and confirmed Christian and whether she attends mass and confesses and receives communion at the times required by the Holy Mother Church, she said that she is a baptized and confirmed Christian and that she was confirmed in Novés by a bishop whose name she does not remember; that she goes to confession and receives communion at all the times that the Holy Mother Church requires and even more; that she last confessed with the cleric Miguel Ruíz on the afternoon before the feast day of Saint Jerome; and that she received communion at the church of La Sisla on the feast day of Saint Jerome.

When asked if she has traveled outside these kingdoms she said no, that since they brought her from Novés to this city she has always lived here. This was when she was a child, and she has only left it twice for Madrid.

When asked to give an account of herself, she said that she was born in Novés in her parents' house and that she grew up with them and with Doña Francisca Sarmiento, a noblewoman of Novés, until she was 16, when they [i.e., her family][2] brought her to this city and placed her in the Church of Santa María la Blanca where she lived for eight years. Her father took her out of there, and she stayed here in Toledo with her sisters where she has resided until now; most of this time she has lived in the parish of Santo Tomé.

When asked if she knows or presumes or suspects the reason why she has been imprisoned in this Holy Office, she says she does not know why,

2. All bracketed comments that follow are my own.

except that a year ago or more she heard it said that the defendant[3] and her sister Isabel Bautista and Miguel Ruíz were all denounced to the Inquisition and that no one should talk with them because things would not go well for them. She said that if she had understood herself to have done anything wrong, then she would have come to accuse herself before this Holy Office; that her sister and Miguel Ruíz would have done the same, because all three of them discussed it; that a cleric named Porras who lives in Fonseca said to the defendant and to her sister that they should come to this Holy Office if they were troubled by anything because that way they would receive a lighter punishment and they [i.e., the Inquisition] would punish those who went about Toledo saying things about them. But since they had no reason to do so, they did not come. The defendant went to the prior of the Monastery of La Sisla who is there now and spoke with him about some of these things that might cause her conscience to have a scruple. The prior reassured her about it, and because of the assurance that he gave her in these things and with this conversation, she understood that she should feel the same way about other things that she did not communicate to him.

When asked what the reason was that they gave them for saying they were accused to the Holy Office, she said that they gave her a reason but she does not remember it; that she will tell everything that occurs to her to say; and that, in order to do that, it is necessary for her to have some letters and papers that her sister Isabel Bautista sent her from Rome and those that the defendant and Miguel Ruíz wrote to her sister in response to her sister's letters, as well as some papers and obligations that the defendant has made to Our Lord. When the vicar went to the house of the defendant, they stored them away and then gave them to Miguel Ruíz so that he would keep them, and he took them and said there was no reason to hide them he put them on a table in his room. When they gave him the papers, Miguel Ruíz said he would throw them in the street so that whoever wanted to see them could.

And what she remembers is that, after having left Santa María la Blanca about eleven years ago, as she has mentioned, and having understood the way in which many young girls and women lost their virtue, she gathered some of them together and taught them needlework, which she knew how to do.

During this time, about five years ago, her sister Isabel Bautista fell ill and was almost paralyzed for a year, and once she was relieved of this illness,

---

3. Throughout the first half of her trial, prior to the presentation of a formal accusation by the inquisitorial prosecutor, Francisca is technically a *confesante*, a person making a confession. (The transcript itself is not completely consistent in this regard, however, at times calling Francisca a witness, or *testigo*.) After her accusation, she becomes a defendant. I have used the word "defendant" throughout the entire trial, to improve the flow of the text.

they advised her [i.e., Francisca] to take her sister to Alonso Hernández, a cleric who cures those afflicted by demons. And once she had been taken to Alonso Hernández, he said that the sickness she had was from spirits that were hidden behind that sickness. And the archbishop's council gave permission for Alonso Hernández and a priest from the chapel of San Pedro to exorcise her, and thus they exorcised her many times in the five months that she was in that state. One night during the Christmas season they exorcised her in the presence of the archbishop's council, and Alonso Hernández made a test case of her so that the men of the council would believe that she was possessed. The defendant would go with her sister when they exorcised her, and she felt great anguish to see it. She said as much to Alonso Hernández, who said to her that the defendant [i.e., Francisca] suffered from this sickness too, because she herself had been plagued by illnesses for twelve years. Alonso Hernández said that many times Our Lord sent those kinds of illnesses to control a body so that it would serve God. Because of this fear, the defendant stopped going with her sister when they were going to exorcize her, and a lady named Doña Isabel de Mesa, who has gone to the Americas, took her. Because many people saw her sister in this anguished state and with her judgment [i.e., mental state, *juicio*] such that she left the house and wandered around the streets and to the river, they advised the defendant not to take her to be exorcized, but to take her instead to Miguel Ruíz, because he was a man who led people by way of prayer and communion. So they asked him to help her, and he did not want to do it because he said that he did not have the permission (*licencia*) to do it. But, persuaded by others, he did it.

And then Miguel Ruíz told her [i.e., Isabel] that she went about all dressed up and that she should enclose herself and not dress like other women and instead devote herself to prayer and communion and then she would get well. And so she enclosed herself and did all that Miguel Ruíz told her, and within eight days she was fine and had her good judgment back and did her needlework and worked as before. From then on she began to fast a lot and do penance and persuade the defendant to do more than she had been doing for the state of the church and for the growth of the Catholic faith. In the space of two years Isabel Bautista would go many times barefoot to San Jerónimo, and she fasted and did not sleep in her bed; and she took communion frequently and persuaded the defendant and her sisters and brothers to enclose themselves and take communion very often, all for the growth of the Catholic faith and the state of the church. And when the defendant saw her sister doing all this, even though she was younger than the defendant, she began to do the same.

And about two years ago, Isabel Bautista wanted to go to Rome. And when the defendant asked her why, she said she wanted to go with a lady and that she wanted to go to Madrid to talk with her, and she went. And, having come back from Madrid, she completed a seventy-day fast of bread and water and wrote a monastic rule, and while she was writing it the defendant asked her why she was writing that and hiding herself from the defendant, and Isabel Bautista said, "You should know that a lady and I want to go to Rome to see about founding a religious house for women."[4] When she left for Rome on All Saints Day, she said that that woman was waiting for her on the way. On the day she left and on the day before in front of a few friends, who also went to confession with Miguel Ruíz, she said that she was going to Rome to see about founding a religious house. She did not say anything more that the defendant heard other than that they should commend her [i.e., Isabel] to God. And so she departed. And the defendant and these friends, to whom she said all this, prayed for this religious house and for her and that the house would be founded. Before she left, Isabel Bautista gave the rule she took with her to the defendant, and she read it. Since then, the defendant has taken Miguel Ruíz as her confessor, because before this she did not confess with him except to reconcile herself on occasion.[5] She began to spend time with the women who confessed with Miguel Ruíz, and they all got together to fast and say prayers and receive communion for their intention [i.e., religious house]. To offer these prayers, they went many times to say novenas at Nuestra Señora del Sagrario and San Agustín and the Churches of Nuestra Señora del Camino and La Vitoria and Nuestra Señora del Estrella and Nuestra Señora de San Ceprián and Santa María la Blanca and La Trinidad and La Madre de Dios.

Having been to all these churches and making many prayers and fasts for the state of the church and begging Our Lord to provide saintly prelates for his church, one Monday after having just received communion the defendant heard it said in her interior that she must go to the Sagrario.[6] She went

---

4. The word here is *monasterio*, not *convento*, which implies Isabel's intention to found a religious community where women could live apart from the world but not necessarily in the strictest form of enclosure. Because Isabel apparently wrote her own rule and the idea to align the house with the Hieronymite order evolved later, I chose to use the term "religious house for women" rather than "convent." Similarly, given that the word "monastery" often implies a community of men, a community that Francisca and Isabel decided to found after Francisca's visionary experiences, I have not used the word "monastery" either.

5. That is, observe formally the sacrament of confession. After several experiences of Miguel Ruíz as a confessor, Francisca apparently took him as a spiritual director, making a regular account of the state of her soul.

6. The chapel of Nuestra Señora del Sagrario was located in the city cathedral; the statue of Our Lady there was a major pilgrimage site. Thus the prayer experiences Francisca is about to describe were quite public.

immediately after receiving communion, and arriving at the Sagrario, she went into a state of prayer and felt her spirit enraptured and taken out of herself. She saw in that enraptured state how Our Lady interceded before her Son on behalf of the state of the church and that He would give them Archbishop Bartolomé Carranza who is imprisoned in Rome. Then she saw how Our Lord was very moved and overcome by the pleas of his mother. On the following Tuesday, she returned to receive communion with Miguel Ruíz, and after receiving communion she felt the same thing, that she should go to the Sagrario and that there she would see many things. Later she went, and when she arrived and began to recollect herself[7] she saw the same thing as the day before, and while in a state of rapture she heard a voice say to Our Lord, "Emite spiritum tuum et reabuntur et renobabis facien terre" (Send out your spirit and renew the face of the earth). Then she saw a great Majesty [i.e., what she calls the "Majesty of God," a God sitting in judgment of the world on the Last Day] on a throne become unveiled and say, "You ask much of me, daughter, that I renew all the earth; for seventy years I have been waiting for them and they offend me all the more." Many other things were revealed to her, and things happened there that she saw, and they are written in a letter the defendant sent to her sister in Rome and in others that are in an envelope she gave to Miguel Ruíz for him to safeguard. In this rapture she also saw in her spirit the whole world entangled with demons and all the cities darkened, and Our Lord asked the defendant if she could bear that those demons come into her in order to render an account of what they had made creation do to offend Him. The defendant waited for the space of six months to accept this request, and during this time Our Lord showed her many things that had offended Him. These are written in another letter in the envelope with the other letter in Miguel Ruíz's hand because when the defendant wrote it to her sister in Rome Miguel Ruíz made a copy of it.

During this time that she had this doubt and was in this conflict about accepting what Our Lord was asking of her, she happened to come across in the book of Saint Catherine of Siena[8] a chapter that treats of how she saw similar demons and asked them to come upon her, and she was thus very tormented by them on behalf of the church of God. Because of that the defen-

---

7. By "recollecting herself," Francisca means recollecting herself in prayer; it is likely an implicit reference to the practice of *recogimiento*, meditative techniques used in mental prayer.

8. This would be Raymond of Capua, *Vida de la bienaventurada sancta Catharina de Sena*, trans. and prólogo Antonio de la Peña. Alcalá Alcalá, 1512, or perhaps more likely a 1569 edition (Medina del Campo: Francisco de Canto, 1569).

dant was emboldened and dared to do it, and she said to Our Lord that whatever was most becoming to His honor and His church she would accept with good will, whatever His Majesty wanted to do, as long as He gave her the favor of His grace so that she would never offend Him. And right after this protestation, which would be a month or so, around the Octave of the Holy Sacrament [i.e., the eight days following Corpus Christi] of last year,[9] the defendant felt within her new tribulations and torments in which demons came to her to make a declaration to Miguel Ruíz, and they told her that they were the ones who had possessed all the world with pride. The defendant, being very wearied by them, went to give an account to Miguel Ruíz, and while she was doing so, the devil spoke, through the mouth of the defendant, to Miguel Ruíz, saying that they were the devils of pride who came to her to weary her. Thus Miguel Ruíz understood that demons were wearying her then and that demons would come to weary her again and that she should have patience because Our Lord would take them away. After this, other demons came from another sin and others from another until they finished tormenting her, which would be from the Octave of the Sacrament until ten days before All Saints Day.[10] And in those ten days before All Saints Day, one day, after receiving communion, the defendant was asked in her interior to suffer again all these troubles because Our Lord wanted them to make an account to Miguel Ruíz, through her mouth, of the way they had made all the creatures in the world live. Thus when the time came for the devils to give their account, which was five days before All Saints Day, the defendant was finishing her communion, because in order to be able to bear these things she had no other moment of refuge than when she took communion, and thus she was receiving communion every day. After receiving communion she felt a great peace and relief in her soul, and here in the interior of her soul she was given to understand that she should oblige herself to serve God in the opposite way to the way that those demons had made creatures sin. Thus the defendant, in her own hand and in her own words, wrote the obligation as if we were to say that she wrote, "I oblige myself all my life to keep righteousness in the act of humility." On that same day the demons of that sin [i.e., a specific type of sin, for example, pride] freed themselves, and they were explaining to Miguel Ruíz how they had made people sin in that way, which they did by entering the defendant and through her mouth telling the way they had made the whole world live in that sin. All of this he has written in some papers that, as she has said, are in his hands. He himself wrote it down,

9. The feast day of Corpus Christi is observed on May 30.
10. This would be approximately June 1 through approximately October 21.

and what is written in the hand of the defendant, such as those vows, he himself copied with the other things. And, it being late, the session ended.

OCTOBER 8, 1575

After being sworn in, she said that around this past All Saints Day, the one that just passed, these events and fights with demons ended in the defendant and she achieved victory over them and felt a great peace and contentment in her soul. Because the defendant had seen and understood the things she has said and explained, she was anxious to engage in more prayer and fasting and communion, asking Our Lord to supply a means by which she could make satisfaction to His Majesty for the offenses that had been committed against him. On the Monday before the Conception of Our Lady[11] in the evening, the defendant was indisposed in bed, and her brothers and sisters-in-law were with her and two maids—one belonging to Andrés Cerezo whose name is Quiteria and the other belonging to Blas de Ribera whose name is María; she went back to say that María is the maid of Cerezo and Quiteria of Ribera, her brothers—and another male servant of Ribera whose name she did not remember, although later she said he was named Antonio de Morales, and also her sister Mariana. And Isabel Bautista was at that time in Rome.

The defendant fell asleep and then woke up very disoriented, crying out loud, and she felt transported out of herself without knowing how and was as if put on a cross with her arms extended. In this transported state she saw a great Majesty very irate like a terrible judge, and the defendant cried out loudly saying, "Heaven and earth fear to see God made into our judge." Then she saw Our Lord on the cross asking for justice for His wounds to that Majesty. Then she saw Him at the pillar asking for justice for His lashes and for the ingratitude people had for His passion. At this, the defendant began to cry out to Our Lady telling her to favor sinners, and then she saw her with her Son in her arms having just been taken down off the cross,[12] pleading to that Majesty for the same justice, saying how ungrateful we had been at her Transfixion. At this, the defendant cried out to the saints to defend sinners, since in all parts of the world they were helpless. Then she saw Saint Peter come forward, saying to that Majesty, "Eternal Father, may there be a harsh punishment for the priests who have followed You so poorly, because, naked, I followed the naked one, but they go about weighed down by their incomes and vices." At this she saw many hosts, with Christ cruci-

11. That is, December 8, 1574.
12. That is, in the position of a pietà.

fied on each one, flying over her bed, each one asking for justice from that Majesty. The defendant cried out to Our Lord because she saw that God would hand down a great sentence against all the world because of his legitimate complaint against all the estates of humankind. Many other things happened to the defendant in this regard that she does not remember right now, except that she was occupied in this vision from eight o'clock at night until eleven o'clock.

When she came to, her brother Andrés Cerezo arrived to cover her because she was completely covered with water, and she was unable to come to until the following Thursday. And on the next Friday night at the same hour of eight o'clock, after having spent more than four hours in agony, she felt as if her soul were pulled out of her body, and she remained transported more than ever before. She saw the same Majesty whom she had already seen and Our Lord and Our Lady and many saints and Saint Peter, and all of them were praying to that Majesty on behalf of the entire human race, asking Him to show how He wanted to be satisfied, and then that vision ended.

Then she saw Our Lord at the Last Supper on his knees, washing the feet of his apostles, and although the defendant did not understand or see who said it, except to hear it said, "Who could make satisfaction for the humility of the Son of God, which has been offended by all the pride of the world?" They (she does not know who) said to the defendant, "Say that the same humility of the Son of God will make satisfaction to the Justice of God and the humility that must be practiced and carried out in the religious houses that are to be founded." Then she saw Our Lord when He instituted the sacrament [of communion; i.e., at the Last Supper], and they said to the defendant, although she does not know who, "What will make satisfaction for the great love with which Our Lord consecrated himself for sinners and the election of priests?" Then they said to her, although she does not know who, "Say it is the great frequency with which they will receive the sacraments and the purity of the priests in these monasteries."

Then she saw Our Lord in the garden of Gethsemane when He was praying, and they said to her, although she does not know who, "Who will make satisfaction for the righteousness of this prayer of the Son of God, who has been offended by the falsity with which all creatures serve God?" Then someone said to her (she does not know who), "Say that that same prayer from the Son of God will make satisfaction to the Justice of God, and the righteousness of spirit that there will be in these monasteries."

Then she saw Our Lord at the pillar, and they said to her (she does not know who), "Who will make satisfaction for this delicate flesh which has been beaten and has been offended by the indecency of all the world?" And they said to her without her knowing who, "Say that this same Lord at that pillar and the chastity that will be observed in the monasteries will make satisfaction."

Then she saw Our Lord on the cross and they said to her, "Who will make satisfaction for all the manners of torment that Our Lord suffered?" And they said to her (without her knowing who it was), "Say that all will be satisfied in the same way that His Majesty has been offended." Then she saw Our Lord with a crown of thorns on his head, and for that and for the mouth and feet and hands and side and clothing of Our Lord they wagered over, for all this they said to her, "Who will make satisfaction for each of these things?" And they said to her (without her knowing who), "Respond that the satisfaction for the crown of thorns will be made by the religious of these monasteries who will always be occupied in recognizing His Majesty."[13] And she should say that the mouth about which the complaint had been lodged—that it had been offended with blasphemies and oaths—would be satisfied with the continual praises these religious would offer. And regarding the gambled clothing, they told her, "Say that the chaste clothing of the priests will make satisfaction."

After this they showed her a procession in which she saw priests dressed in coarse, woolen cloth and black bonnets and another procession of nuns all dressed in coarse white wool with white capes of the same width that the canons of the Cathedral of Toledo wear. And then Our Lord said to the defendant, "These are the religious whom I want to make satisfaction to me in the same way that you have vowed. I want them to celebrate each Thursday the feast of the Most Holy Sacrament and I want it to remain in the monstrance until the next Friday. I want the priests and nuns to remain there throughout the entire night, meditating on the torments I suffered that night and forgetting all else in the world. And all day Friday they should occupy themselves in this and on Saturday on the Transfixion of Our Lady. After all these things and other similar ones had passed, she returned to herself and this entire vision summed itself up in the fact that Our Lord wanted, for the reformation of the entire world and satisfaction of those offenses, that these religious houses be made in all of the dioceses and that there be seminaries for the prelates from which priests could leave to serve the churches; that they have a common income in the apostolic life, without possessing anything of their own; that their occupation consist entirely in uprooting evil and encouraging virtues and attending to the needs of others; and that they have a school

---

13. That is, in meditating upon the passion of Christ.

for young men to train them in serving the church, because Our Lord wanted to be honored and revered by his priests, as His Majesty deserves.

Then she said that after all this had happened Isabel Bautista, her sister who had gone to Rome as she has said, came home with a Portuguese woman. And Isabel Bautista said that she did not bring back an order (*rrecaudo*) to found the convent that they wanted to found. The defendant did not know the reason her sister went to Rome any more than that she said she went with the intent to bring back permission to found a convent, but she did not tell her what convent it was or what order it would be or what caused her to want to go to Rome, any more than she showed her the rule she had written that would be followed in the convent. After Isabel Bautista came back from Rome with the Portuguese woman, she said that the Portuguese woman was very rich, that she had left Rome with a legal matter, and that she was going to Portugal to get her property and come back to the defendant and her sister in order to found the convent. And the same Portuguese woman said as much to many poor young women who were coming to the defendant's house, and then the Portuguese woman left and has never returned.

Then she said that while Isabel Bautista was in Rome, she sent word by letters to the defendant about the convent, telling her that she had spoken with Don Pedro González de Mendoza, that she was glad to see him because he was from Toledo, that she had given him an account of her intention about the convent, and that Don Pedro González told her that if the archbishop was released as they all expected, he would see to it that he would grant what she asked for and favor her intention, and this is what she always wrote and nothing else.

Then she said that after Isabel Bautista came from Rome with the Portuguese woman, everyone thought that she was the lady that she had dreamed went with her, and thus many women and men came to visit. Thus she and her sister were persuaded by many women who showed themselves to be rich and desirous of the rule of Saint Jerome to found a convent of that order. So they begged Don Pedro González de Mendoza to ask permission from the governor that twelve women who had dowries be under obedience to the governor according to the rule of Saint Jerome as he wrote it to Saint Eustochium. The said Don Pedro González asked the governor. Several days went by between the request and the governor's response. In the interim, Isabel Bautista went to Madrid to speak with Doña Isabel Osorio because she learned that she intended to found a convent and she wanted to move her to found it in Toledo under this rule. The said Doña Isabel Osorio told her that she could not because it had to be where she had her subjects [lit. *vasallos*, or vassals], but that she would help her with the house and the church and she would seek the favor of the king. And thus she gave her a letter for the king's confessor and another for Doña Catalina Laso. After she spoke with Doña Isabel, Isabel Bautista came back from Madrid and gave a petition to the king, asking him to order the governor to give them this permission (*licencia*). The king handed it over to the Council and the Royal Council gave it to the governor. Because there was already a scandal over this matter in this city, they did not grant the license to the governor. Since Isabel Bautista gave the petition to the king, she came back afterward because she thought the act was accomplished [i.e., permission would be granted], and they rented a house and there they gathered some women they were acquainted with, and being late the session ended . . .

OCTOBER 13, 1575 (AFTERNOON)

She said that after they had rented the house, the defendant along with her sisters Isabel Bautista and Mariana and a poor woman they had had with them there for about two months because she was poor and blind moved into it. Because the license for the foundation that the governor was supposed to give was delayed, they did not receive anyone into the house, even though many came there. During that time, a woman named Juana Ximénez came with her young niece named María de Jesús, and she begged them many times to let them enter. The defendant and her sister Bautista told her that it was not yet a convent, and she [i.e., Juana Ximénez] said that since she had that niece in the neighborhood, could they not take her in, that she would pay whatever needed to be paid so that she [i.e., her niece] could be enclosed. During this time, the defendant and her sister Isabel Bautista spoke with Fray Juan Bautista, the discalced Franciscan. They told him almost all the things that had happened between them and Our Lord and how Our Lord had caused them to understand that these religious houses would be founded for the satisfaction of sin because His Majesty had been offended and that they did not know to whom to turn because the governor clearly would not give them the license and everything was on hold. Fray Juan Bautista responded to them that they should be enclosed and that they should not go to court or talk with anyone, but rather close their door and give themselves over completely to prayer according to the rule of Saint Jerome that they wanted to keep. After that they recollected themselves in their house and kept their door closed.

One day Fray Juan Bautista came to see them, and he saw that María de San Jerónimo and Francisca de Santiago and Inés de la Concepción and others who were friends of hers [i.e., Francisca's] and her sister were with them— she does not remember their names. All of them wanted to be in the defendant and her sister's company. To all of them gathered there, Fray Juan Bautista said that since all of them desired that recollected way of life, they should keep it and observe the rule of Saint Jerome and that he would talk with a priest he knew who was named Porras who resides in Fonseca and who went to Rome frequently. Since he was a man who liked to do such good works, he would ask him to go to Rome and would himself ask permission of his prelate to go to Rome with him; and they would ask the pope to confirm this rule of Saint Jerome, and he would ask a lady that he knew in Madrid, who was quite wealthy, and one of her brothers who intended to found a convent to give money for the project, and she could join her [i.e., Francisca] and her sister. He said to the defendant that, since she had already been in a convent, knew about religious life, and was older than her sister, she should teach them how to keep that rule. With this, the discalced friar told María de San Jerónimo and Inés de la Concepción and her aunt, who is named Francisca de Santiago, and Juana Ximénez and her niece and Luisa de los Angeles, whom the same Fray Juan Bautista had brought, to stay with the defendant and her sister. Thus they all began to keep the rule of Saint Jerome as it is contained in the letters of Saint Jerome, and they read it every day. After that, María de Jesús, whose mother lives in this city and is the sister of the wife of Martín Hernández, the one who killed the horse, came to them. After that came María de la Paz, servant of Doña Leonor de Mendoza, and all of them together devoted themselves to keeping the Rule of Saint Jerome.

The defendant said to them, "Sisters, now that we have gathered ourselves here, our mission must be to be grateful to the mystery of the Incarnation, because the name of the house, if God allows it to be founded, will be that [i.e., the Incarnation], and we will dedicate ourselves to showing gratitude for the most Holy Sacrament each Thursday, and on Friday we will give thanks for the Passion, and on Saturdays the Transfixion of Our Lady. And to inspire them to do this, the defendant, on two or three Thursdays, made them do what nuns do on Holy Thursday, although without as many formalities. And on Friday evenings she read them the Passion and on Saturday the Transfixion of Our Lady. And then all those who could, stayed to pray through the night.

The defendant did all this and made the others who were with her do this because the judgment vision she has already discussed told her to do this. In that judgment she saw that they ordered her to do things this way in these religious houses that were to be founded for the satisfaction of the sins of the world, and because of this Our Lord asked the defendant in that judgment vision to say that things would be done that way and to declare all that she had seen in that judgment, and the defendant promised to do this that way, and thus she tried to do her part in everything. Most nights they got up to pray matins at midnight, and in the morning, as it became light, they said primes, and then they all made a procession in the patio of the house and said the litany for the state of the church.[14] They carried in the procession a small, clothed image of Our Lady and one of the Angel Gabriel and a large Agnus Dei they had on the altar and other images.[15] They did this until the time that the vicar [i.e., the archdiocesan official in charge of religious orders] came to visit them and they knew that they should not go forward because the governor was not giving them permission. So they stopped doing everything except reciting the divine office, which they have always prayed.

During this time the curate from Navahermosa,[16] who is the brother of Becerra, chaplain of the Capilla de los Reyes, came to the house to see Juana Ximénez whom he knew or who was from the same town, and in speaking with the defendant and all of them in the house, the curate told them how, many years earlier, one night when he was sitting in a chair half-asleep, he had been shown in a field many things, among which he had seen two religious orders, one of priests and another of women. The one of women was the one that the defendant wanted to found, and they were dressed in the same way as these women. Since then, he had come to Toledo because although he lived far from there, he had been told that these religious orders had to come about in Toledo. For this reason, she [i.e., Francisca] and her sis-

14. According to the testimony of Francisca de Aguilar, who had spent four months in the *beaterio*, the women had masses said and made processions specifically for the release of Carranza, which they understood would happen only by some miracle of Our Lady. See fol. 87v.

15. These processions may well have been based on similar processions performed by members of confraternities. In his account of the Hospital of San Ildefonso, for example, Francisco de Pisa describes the following practice: "Also in this district is the chapel and hospital of San Ildefonso where hospitality and lodging is given to women pilgrims or beggars, and where the prostitutes are gathered up during the weeks of Lent, when they hear sermons and spiritual talks [given] by religious and learned persons, and some of them are converted to God and leave their bad way of life and either marry or join a house of reclusion. From this hospital a solemn procession leaves on the day of St. Ildefonso with the confraternity and confreres of that name, [on their way] to the hermitage of that same St. Hildefons which is beyond the [city] walls." See Francisco de Pisa, p. 62: "También en este distrito es la capilla y hospital de San Ildefonso, donde se hace hospitalidad y se acojen peregrinas mujeres o mendigas, y se recojen las mujeres públicas en las semanas de Cuaresma, donde se les hacen sermones y pláticas espirituales por personas religiosas y doctas, con que algunas de ellas se convierten a Dios, y salen de su mal vivir, y las casan o ponen en un recogimiento. De este hospital sale una solemn procesión el proprio día de san Ildefonso con la cofradía y cofrades de este título, a la hermita del mismo san Ildefonso que es extramuros."

16. Alonso López de la Cuadra, the curate from Navahermosa, testified against the women on July 23, 1575. Although at first favorably impressed by their devotion and supportive of the community, he grew troubled by their association with Juan de Dios, whom he considered "the devil in person" (see fol. 43v: "le tenia por demonio en cuerpo [h]umano").

ter Isabel Bautista told him many of the things that had happened to them regarding what Our Lord told them, just as she has already declared, and the curate offered himself for the journey to Rome for the confirmation of the rule. And for this purpose, on the eve of this past year's feast of Saint Peter,[17] the curate and the cleric Porras and Miguel Ruíz gathered together in the house of the defendant. With her sister Isabel Bautista, they all talked about how their entire project came down to the fact that it was the will of Our Lord to found a college of priests who would live the apostolic life and would renounce all their property and the income they got from the college and another community of women of the order of Saint Jerome, with the same renunciation, and that they would be subject to the ordinary. The defendant told them that Our Lord wanted the priests to take care that any income that went over what they needed should provide for the necessities of the poor. The said Porras said that this was not a new thing, because in Milan and in other places he had seen things done this way, and from there the priests left to serve all the churches and others to attend to the needs of the poor. Thus they decided that Porras and the curate from Navahermosa would leave for Rome to ask for the confirmation of the rule.

OCTOBER 15, 1575

She said that while the curate of Navahermosa and Porras were talking about going to Rome, Juan de Dios came in and entered the conversation and said that he too was going to Rome and that he would be happy to accompany them and serve them. And the curate of Navahermosa said to the defendant and to her sister Isabel Bautista, so that Juan de Dios did not hear him, that he had to go to Our Lady of Guadalupe first and that he would take him [i.e., Juan de Dios] with him in order to see what kind of a person he was. So he went and took him with him. After he returned, the curate of Navahermosa said to the defendant and her sister that Juan de Dios was not the man to take with them to Rome because he was a scandalous person, and the defendant and her sister said not to take him. After this on another day the curate of Navahermosa came to the defendant's house and said to the defendant that he had been with his brother Becerra, who said he was very concerned about how he was spending time with this woman and her sister because they were women who were very vexed by demons. He [i.e., Becerra] gave other similar reasons for his concerns, and the defendant and her sister told him that he had already seen their will, that he should do what he wanted as a priest,

17. That is, June 28, 1575.

and that he and Porras together had planned to go to Rome [i.e., on their own initiative]. Then the curate went to the house of Becerra, his brother, and on another day he sent for Juana Ximénez, who was in the house with the defendant, and she left; and when she returned she said that the curate had told her that she should leave the defendant and her sister and not stay with them and that she had responded that she did not want to leave because she had not seen them do anything they were not supposed to, and thus Juana Ximénez stayed with her and her sister for more than two more weeks until the curate of Navahermosa grew very angry with her. Then the defendant and her sister said to Juana Ximénez that she should go because she said that she wanted to bring a lawsuit against the curate about some property that he had, and they made her go because in staying at the house Juana Ximénez was involving her and her sister in a scandal. So she left, and after she left Juana Ximénez and the curate became friends.

On another day after that, Juana Ximénez came to her house and told her how the curate said that the defendant and her sister had filed a case against him and had made the defendant's brothers witnesses in it, which the defendant and her sister had not done or had any reason to do. Because of this scandal, Doña Leonor de Mendoza sent for her servant who was there, who was named María de la Paz, and because she learned that someone [Birviesca? difficult to decipher] from the Archbishop's Council was going about gathering evidence against them, nearly all of them left. When the defendant and her sister saw this and saw how much scandal was growing, both of them went to speak with the vicar,[18] and they told him that since the time he had visited them and seen the way of life they observed, a great scandal had now arisen over them. His honor might tell them what they ought to do and whether he wanted the four religious who were still with them to remain in their company and they would do whatever he ordered. The said vicar said that they should not worry but should remain calm because all that people were saying about them was just storytelling, and thus they have been in their house until they were apprehended by this Holy Office. With her were Francisca de Santiago and Inés de la Concepción, her niece, and María de Jesús and Marina de la Cruz.

She has nothing more to say except that in regard to what she said about the demons who entered her to give an account of what was happening in the world, another legion of devils entered on the day of the Incarnation and gave an account of the way in which they had made creatures live. Thus the

18. El Licenciado Serrano, the vicar of religious orders in the archdiocese of Toledo, came to visit the *beaterio* and made inquiries about the women's religious practices on May 27, 1575. The information he gathered was eventually transmitted to the Inquisitional Tribunal of Toledo.

defendant, after receiving communion, made a vow to live according to the way Our Lord inspired her soul, which was to make satisfaction for the vices that caused people to sin in that way. On the day of Saint Barnabas[19] another legion of demons came and made an account of the way they made people sin, and to this legion that came to the defendant she did not make a vow. She has nothing more to say than what she has already said, and if she has erred and been deceived by their sins when the demons possessed her understanding, she asks pardon from God our Lord and penance with mercy from the Lord Inquisitor.

She was told that she has the obligation to say anything she might know about herself and any others and about things she knows that would pertain to this Holy Office. And if in these things that she has said and confessed about herself there have been other persons who have counseled her in something or have said something to her or taught her what she should do in these matters or if she knows of others who have experienced these things or if she has done anything under the influence of the devil she should confess them, so that in all things the truth can be understood in what has happened and what Our Lord has done to her and why she has been brought before this Holy Office, so that they can put everything in order and so that her conscience can remain free and clean. So she is admonished that, out of reverence to God Our Lord, in whose service she says she has done all these things that she has confessed, she say and declare the truth. This having been read to her and having been made to understand, she said that she does not know that she has anything more to say except that she has communicated all these things that she has declared to Miguel Ruíz.

OCTOBER 17, 1575

She was told that the warden has informed them that she asks for an audience. She should say if this is true and for what reason she wants one, saying the truth in everything under the oath she has made.

It is true that she asked for it in order to say that she has thought about what the Lord Inquisitor said to her and that she cannot think of anything that she has spoken about with others that might have offended Our Lord or that pertains to this Holy Office. And what more she has to say is that Isabel Bautista, her sister, never spoke with the defendant before she went to Rome about revelations or about any other thing because before she went to Rome she went to Madrid, as she has said. There she spoke with their father, and

19. That is, June 11.

returning from Madrid she prepared to go to Rome and the defendant understood that she had permission from their father to go to Rome; for this reason she did not speak of anything else to the defendant, but rather let her do
her own will. Afterward she learned how their father had not known anything about her departure, and thus she did not know anything more about
her other than the rule she took with her that she read to the defendant. After
Isabel Bautista departed to Rome, she wrote a letter to Miguel Ruíz at the first
stop on her way telling him of a vision she had on the way. The defendant
does not remember the way she described it, but it will appear in the letter
that Isabel wrote, which is with others that the defendant wrote to Isabel
Bautista, all of which are in the hands of Miguel Ruíz. After this, being further along on the road, she wrote another letter, although she does not
remember whether it was for Miguel Ruíz or for the defendant, in which she
told the defendant and their friends who could to make pilgrimages to Our
Lady; this letter is with the others in the hands of Miguel Ruíz or so she thinks.
The defendant spoke with María de San Jerónimo—she does not know whose
daughter she is, but she is the one who lives with her mother (she does not
know the mother's name either) on the Adarve del Sordo—and with
Magdalena de San Francisco, who lives with her mother (but she does not
know the mother's name) on the street opposite that of Doctor de la Fuente,
and with Catalina de San Francisco, who lives with her sisters across from
San Román. She told them how her sister Isabel Bautista had written her to
go to pray at the houses of Our Lady and asked whether they wanted to help
her in that, and they did. So the four of them went into the houses of Our
Lady as she has said in previous sessions. The defendant spoke with these
women about the things her sister Isabel Bautista wrote from Rome, and she
also spoke with them about the convent they wanted to found, even though
the defendant always told them that her sister had gone to Rome with a lady.
These three women she has spoken of went to confession with Miguel Ruíz
because all three were vexed by the devil. She saw many times that when the
above-mentioned women went to receive communion with Miguel Ruíz in
the Hospital de la Misericordia, they could not go to the altar to receive the
host. Catalina de San Francisco would become as stiff as a board and
Magdalena de San Francisco would remain seated and could not move if they
did not move her, and the defendant helped her to stand up many times and
led her by the hand. The said Miguel Ruíz, holding the sacrament in his hands,
conjured the devil so that he would leave them and immediately he gave them
the sacrament. A good while after having given it [the sacrament] to them,
Miguel Ruíz spoke to them, and what the defendant understood was that he
spoke to them to get them to understand that we have two spirits, one from

God and the other from the devil. He told them that they should not believe the temptations of the devil, that the spirit of God persuaded them to do all that was good, and that just because they were told things in their interior they did not have to believe them unless they were consistent with the gospel, because even though an angel came to tell them something, if it were contrary to the gospel, they should not believe it. Once the defendant saw that Miguel Ruíz told Magdalena de San Francisco, who was the most tormented by the devil and whom the devils permitted to esteem the least what Miguel Ruíz told them, that for her own good she should depart with the blessing of God, because they could not believe anything she said, and thus she left. After the sisters of Catalina de San Francisco saw that Magdalena de San Francisco had left the company of Miguel Ruíz, they brought her sister Catalina de San Francisco.

[At this point Francisca's entire testimony up to this point was read to her and she ratified it.]

NOVEMBER 28, 1575

She said that she has nothing more to say than what she has said except to beg the Lord Inquisitor to give her some company because she has been ill for many days with pains in her liver and her heart suffers greatly and she cannot live in such solitude without it being a great detriment to her soul. During the previous night and on other nights she has suffered many frightening things from the demons and she cannot bear to be alone.

She was told to go through her memory again and to think about her case and tell the truth. She said that she had nothing more to say and that she will think about it. Thus admonished, she was ordered back to her cell.

DECEMBER 1, 1575

She said that she has asked for an audience to say that she has thought about what she was asked the other day about whether or not she has more to declare, and she remembered that she had not declared what she will now say, the bulk of which is contained in a letter that is in the bunch of letters she has already mentioned that were in the possession of Miguel Ruíz, in which everything else she has declared is written.

The first thing is that one day, after having just received communion in the Hospital de la Misericordia at the hands of Miguel Ruíz, she felt that she was asked in the interior of her soul to make a fast of thirty-three days in honor of the life of Our Redeemer Jesus Christ and another of sixty-three days in honor of Our Lady. During those days she received communion frequently and fasted and did penance, and she had many masses said in honor of those most holy lives, offering everything to the Eternal Father and asking him by the merit of His Son and the most holy Virgin to pardon the world for how it had provoked all of the wrath He had shown to the defendant, of which she has already spoken. And she felt, while praying in this way, that in the interior of her soul she was told to make another fast in honor of all the saints, Saint Peter with the apostles and Saint Michael with the angels. And in this way, on All Saints Day, she would see the reason why she was ordered to do all of this. She finished all this fasting and masses on the very same day of All Saints Day of last year, having had a mass said for each order of saints. On that day, the last mass was offered on behalf of all the saints. And on this day, when the defendant was finishing communion in the mass that Miguel Ruíz said, she was taken out of her senses and enraptured in her spirit, and she saw the Justice of God in heaven, which took an upright, white form, and many angels came out around it with drawn swords in their hands. The Justice carried in its hands a decree that was shown to the defendant and that had the power to make a general punishment against the entire world. The punishment consisted of five things: great wars, floods, fire, famine, and pestilence, and the pestilence was going to begin in Toledo. Then she saw Our Lady coming out to this encounter saying that she would not consent to such a thing because she was the patron of this city and that it [i.e., the Justice of God] should contain its fury because Our Lady extended privileges to this city because of many people pleasing to God, who would be enough to make satisfaction for its complaints, and that where the Justice wanted to start the punishment, Our Lady would have commenced instead the satisfaction that was owed for offenses committed against the Majesty of God. Then the defendant saw how the entire court of Heaven, to whom the masses had been said and the fasts made, made haste to present themselves before the Justice with similar pleas, as Our Lady had. All those saints and Our Lady, along with the defendant, begged the Justice of God and made the defendant promise that she would make known all that she had seen and whatever else she might be shown and all the terms by which satisfaction could be made for the complaints. With this and with other things that happened, all that she has described ended.

Then she says that she saw later a very long procession of priests dressed in coarse, woolen cloth and that many angels received them, singing a psalm that begins "His foundations upon the holy mountains";[20] and the procession

---

20. "fundamenta ejus [sic] in montibus sanctis" (Ps 87:1).

of priests lasted until the psalm was over. And then she saw Our Lord on the cross saying, "O world! See how you have offended me: how long must they swear your evils against me?" And later the defendant saw Our Lady who was offering Him all those priests she has spoken of, saying, "Our Lord, look at the worthy gentlemen I present to you from this city of Toledo of which I am patron. They will be enough to conquer the world and assure that you are satisfied." Later she saw how Our Lord called out to all the priests with great love, saying, "Come, come, my priests and let it be seen what my church has cost me and how it has offended me." And she saw that He allowed those who were the oldest to enter into the wound in His side, showing them the great love with which He had redeemed the world. To the younger ones He showed all the symbols of His passion. He had those who were quite young retire from this scene, for they did not dare approach. To all of them He said, "You have seen what my church has cost me. Go out to all the world and preach penance to them, that they might abandon the mistaken paths they tread, because if they do not, a great punishment against the world has been decided upon." Then she saw how they scattered themselves throughout the world, at which point this vision ended. Then Our Lady ordered the defendant to say what she had seen, and she [i.e., Francisca] asked whom His Majesty ordered her to tell. She was told not to worry about that, because He had decided when and to whom all these things she had been shown should be manifested and that was to the prelates of His church, because His great mercy ordained that a punishment should not be sent against the world without first giving a warning so that people might do penance. After this, the defendant says that she returned to herself[21] and that there were many people in the chapel who had seen her because she had experienced a great rending of her body while she experienced this and while all this happened. In order not to raise her voice and reveal what she was feeling, her heart and head broke open,[22] and she was ill for many days afterward. And this is what she said in the letter regarding All Saints Day and how the Justice of God came with the decree.

Then she says that there is one more thing she remembers from that letter, which is that as she has said that she experienced victory over those demons and that Our Lord had favored her with so many gifts, so she vowed to make satisfaction for the many sins as she has explained. One day, a few days after what she has described in this session, having just received communion at the Hospital de la Misericordia from Miguel Ruíz, she felt within

21. I.e., returned to her senses, "tornó en si."
22. "se la abrió el corazón y la cabeza."

herself a deep knowledge of her own lowliness and a new light [i.e., understanding] about who Our Lord was. An internal voice made her recognize that in herself she was nothing and unable to make satisfaction for the smallest fault, even though she had vowed to do so, unless His Majesty, because of the great love that He has for the world, wanted to set up in this experience of hers a model so that other people who also wanted to satisfy His justice would understand how to do so. So she was made to understand her own vileness for many days, and this is what she understands now. All of this happened about ten or twelve days after All Saints; the victory over the demons was five or six days before All Saints; and the vision of the decree was the same day of All Saints. And what she has said about the judgment was the Monday before the Conception of Our Lady and the Friday after the Conception. This is when everything she was shown stopped, and this coming Monday is a full year after her experience of the judgment.

She was asked to say how she knows that what appeared to her was Our Lord and Our Lady and the saints and how she saw it all.

She said, "Lord, that I do not know how to say, because then the soul is so outside itself that it cannot really understand, nor is there any feeling left in the body until it returns to itself. And it marvels at how that could have been, because she and whatever other creature this might happen to remain well aware of their own misery and of the fact that they do not merit such things."

She was told that according to what she says this could well have been a dream and perhaps she did not see any of what she has said. This happens every day when people sleep and dream many things that are not true and that are nothing more than dreams.

She said she does not know what to say to this, except that she renders herself subject to what she is told and what they teach her about where she has erred, so that she might better serve God in truth. Because in all these things that she has said and confessed that she saw, she does not believe them nor does she depend upon seeing them nor does she take from them anything more than what helps her to walk the right path and serve Our Lord and guard His precepts and gospel. And in what she says she neither believed nor disbelieved, because she leaves this up to the judgment of the Lord Inquisitor, and whatever he orders she will turn around and believe and hold as certainly as the commandments of Our Lord.

She was told that in order to be taught it is necessary that she say all that she had believed and understood about these matters and others, if there had been any other experiences. And after she has fully unburdened her conscience she will be told in detail where she has erred and the path she must follow in order to be on the road to God. So she must say all there is to say without respect whatsoever to fear or shame, since she says that she is only trying to save her soul. Therefore she should unabashedly attempt to let go of anything that might be an offense to God and to hold fast to what is in God's service.

She said that she will think about what she has been asked and in the afternoon she will speak more.

AFTERNOON SESSION OF DECEMBER 1, 1575

[After reading aloud the end of the morning's transcript, the inquisitor asked Francisca to describe further her experience of rapture.]

She said she has already responded to the question.

She was told that she would be read what she had responded earlier today because she had not completely answered the question. Then she was read the question and what she responded, and having read all of it word for word she said she had heard and understood it.

She said that a person is enraptured at the time and that she cannot say more about it than what she has said. If this were a case of seeing with one's bodily eyes it might be possible to say more.

She was told that she has not understood the question well and to pay attention to this explanation: she says that this revelation of what she calls a rapture is impressed [or established; lit. seated, *asentado*] in her memory and that in it she saw Our Lord and Our Lady and the celestial court and all the rest that she has recounted and that she was ordered to make public to the world all of what she saw. Now she is asked whether or not she holds for certain that she saw that or not.

She said that she holds it as true that she saw that vision and that it was not a dream because it happened in the moment just after she had communion. And all the other things she saw were in the same moment [i.e., just after communion], except for the vision of the judgment, which she saw while sick in bed. Thus she takes as true what she has seen, and that she truly saw it and that it really happened as she has recounted it in all of the past hearings.

She was told to declare how she saw and understood that the upright white thing that she saw was the Justice of God.

She said that when she is enraptured the meaning of each thing is also impressed in the soul, so much so that it is as if she were to see a known person and someone were to tell her, "That is this person.'"

She was asked to declare more about this.

She said that she does not know how to say more, because when a soul is in this state, each thing is declared to it with such clarity, as if to help the defendant know more than what she herself could.

She was told to say what that decree was that she says that the Justice of God brought in his hand.

She said that it was a piece of paper folded over many times and that he carried it in his hand.

She was told to say how she saw the decree on that paper since it was folded over: was there writing on the outside or how did she understand that it was a decree?

She said that the same Justice of God told her soul what it was.

She was asked to declare who this Justice of God was who carried the decree.

She said that she could not say except that she saw the form of a person white and upright and it was made known to her that this was the Justice of God.

She was told to say and declare what clothing he wore.

She said that everything was white.

She was asked if his face was ferocious or gentle.

She said that the whole form showed ferocity against the world and that she could not say anything about his face because one cannot look at it with too much attention.

She was asked about the angels who came with the Justice of God and who carried the swords in their hands; she was asked what kind of clothes they wore and how they looked and if they came armed or unarmed and how they came.

She said that they were dressed in white and that the faces were handsome and the clothing they wore was like albs.

When asked about how Our Lady appeared, she said she would not know how to say it in words because she was resplendent and in her splendor she saw a lady of great majesty.

She was told that in all of her discourse she should be able to say something about Our Lady's appearance and her clothing and how she wore her hair and what she wore on her head, whether it was a crown or what it was.

She said she did not know how to say.

She was told to declare what the other saints wore or what they looked like.

She said that she could not say anything more than that she saw a great multitude of people in great splendor.

She was told to say and declare the manner in which the Majesty of the divine Justice told her that he brought a decree against the world to destroy it and about those five ways that were flood and fire and war and famine and pestilence.

She said that she cannot say anything about this because in that rapture one is given to understand things much more clearly than that light, and she pointed to a candle that was in the room. And if they were like meaningful words that a person speaks to another in the physical world, she might be able to say more, but these are words that pass between the soul and that which appears to it, and these things are clearer than if they were said in words and are understood immediately in this way, more than if many words were used to actually say the thing. It is as if a person were walking around and seeing many things flying through the air and as if that person were a creature who could in a very short time understand all the things and their meanings that have been given to its soul to understand. And thus the soul remains very satisfied to see each of those things more than if it saw them with its bodily eyes or if they were spoken to it. And she cannot explain this in any other way.

She was told that with all that she has just said, she has not explained how she knows that what she saw were things from God and not a dream or some imaginary thing. She should say and declare more because what she has said does not make this certain. Just because these things happened after receiving communion is not enough because in that time and before it and even during that same communion and in all times the devil is always seeking an opportunity to deceive people. She should say if there is any other reason [i.e., to believe her experiences are from God].

She said that this was seen to be something from God and not the devil first of all because her spirit would be enraptured with great tenderness, and in that time the senses do not feel any corporal thing nor is the soul perturbed. Instead, everything is gentleness, and the soul is given a very great light and great knowledge of its own vileness and of what has just happened in what it has seen. And the person returns to herself and finds in herself great humility and great subjection in all that pertains to the service of Our Lord, so that, with great ease, she can perform works of virtue. It [i.e., the experience] bestows a great loathing for all that is sinful, and she embraces with great efficacy all things that are difficult and tedious for love of Our Lord. And in this security that remained in her soul, she can understand if it [i.e., its experience] was good and from Our Lord. Furthermore, not trusting herself, the defendant spoke with Miguel Ruíz about it in order to reassure herself,

and Miguel Ruíz told her that, because they had imprinted in her soul the
desire to follow with righteousness the paths of Our Lord and to keep the
commandments, she could feel confident that this was not from the devil and
that she should remember her vileness because she was obliged to loathe
whatever was an offense against Our Lord and to love all labors for the love
of Our Lord and that all the rest she should leave to the ordination of Our
Lord and not worry about this. And so the defendant tried to reassure herself in this and do everything Miguel Ruíz had taught her for this purpose,
as she has said, because if this were something from the devil, it would give
occasion to be prideful and presumptuous and to detest anything that was
wearisome or difficult.

She was told that what she has said in this hearing and in others are things
that we hardly know God has shared with the most perfect saints after having spent many years in great solitude and penance and with a lot of fasting,
disciplines, and other penances. And even after all this they do not believe
or suggest that God has been so merciful to them or that they merit this. But
rather they are very circumspect, knowing that it is common for the devil to
appear as an angel of light and that he looks for these means and others to
deceive them. So when they see such things they increase their penance,
knowing as they do, that even as great as their works may be, they in no way
merit such favors. Thus the defendant ought to look at her own insignificance
in the same way and consider that it is more likely that these things are matters of the devil, not favors and gifts from the Lord, particularly because she
and her sisters have been possessed by the devil and also because the saints
themselves never made public favors they received from God, and with good
reason, since they ought to have feared that the evil angel might use their
own vanity against them. Instead, they were very humble. She was told that
this vanity has completely possessed her because she has said and made public to many people what she has confessed and declared in this inquiry. Thus
it is clear that the accused knows well that all that she has said is something
from the devil, not from God, and thus she is admonished to say and declare
what is really going on and what truth there is in it [i.e., in what she has said].

She said that this was a lot to have to respond to, but that in what pertains to our Lord having granted her these favors because of her own merits,
it is not her understanding that she merits them but rather that she merits
hell. But she says that God is powerful and our absolute Lord and can grant
those favors and other greater ones because she does not understand that any
single one of these things that happened to her was related to any merit on
her part. Instead, she has understood that it has happened in order to put her
squarely on the path of His law. She recognizes this, that she has been made

to go by the straightest path, because she has never been very fond of bodily penance. She says that she has given as good an example as she could in her life at this time and ever since she was sixteen years old and that this example has moved all those who have been close to her . . .

DECEMBER 2, 1575

[The next morning, December 2, the audience continued. After reading over the transcript from the previous day, which Francisca asked to hear, she continued.]

She said that if she has given some wrong impression about the favors that Our Lord showed, it has not been out of pride because she does not have any pride, always recognizing her insignificance and that she merits nothing, even if she were to do more penance than the saints. She said that the reason that some of what had happened to her has become known about the city was because during the time of the judgment vision she has described, her sisters and brothers and their wives and their servants were in her chamber and, having so many people present, it could not help but be known because they told other people about it when they were away from her. Also, her soul was possessed for more than a year by a great love of our Lord and also by the love of souls, and in this great love that possessed her soul, she desired that all creatures love Our Lord and that they make satisfaction to Him in conformity with what He has shown her. Since she felt such a great desire to see Our Lord satisfied for the offenses that His creatures had committed against Him, all that she had seen and been shown was for the cause of justice against the souls [of sinful humanity], although she had conceived such a love for them. The passions she felt and held in her heart about this were so great because, on the one hand, she saw herself united in a great bond of love for our Lord and because, on the other, she found herself united in another bond of love for all humanity. With this union and desire for the salvation of souls, she felt a great contrition for all the sins that she had seen and knew had offended Our Lord, and thus in all this time she cried out with great insistence and tears to Our Lord in pain from all those sins. And she says that her desire regarding what she has described about our Lord being satisfied and souls not losing the end for which they had been created is so great that it is not surprising that at that time she told something of what had happened to her to some people she thought would benefit, because she acted out of zeal and not pride. Because when a soul is possessed by this love that she has described, it does not look for anything for itself but only for the glory and honor of God and the good of souls. And she says that this desire she has described and the love of Our Lord were so strong that she fell ill twice from the debilitation she felt. The first time was a year ago this past summer, and her brothers called a doctor and he said that she wasn't sick with something that could be treated, and thus she wasn't treated because she says that the illness she had wasn't a bodily illness but rather the great longing she had in her heart. And the other time that she was sick over this was about a year ago around this very time because that is when what she has said about the judgment happened to her. Thus, she was not sick of an illness but of the longing that she had that our Lord be satisfied.

As far as having been possessed by the devil, that has not distressed her in what pertains to the service of Our Lord; rather, during all the time in which these things have happened, her soul has possessed and possesses an inner peace with great calm, and all of hell or the calumnies of all the people who have risen up against her or any trial has not been sufficient to distress her or to turn her away from what she must do in the service of Our Lord, because even though she feels these things very much on a human level, upon entering into her interior she finds and has always found a great conformity with the will of Our Lord in all the things that have come to pass. She has not been disturbed in her interior by any trial, and because of this fact she recognizes and has recognized by way of this internal peace that she has described that God possesses her soul and not the devil—since the devil does not give peace and tranquility, but rather war and rancor and all that is evil. Also, all the disturbances that the demons have caused in her have been corporeal and do not in any way pertain to her soul. And that is all she has to say.

She was told to return to see if she persists in what she has said and explained to them because these things of God are of such weight and importance that she should not dare to treat them so palpably, even if what she has said were the truth, but especially since it bears no resemblance to the truth.

She says it had not been made clear to her nor does she understand what she could add to what she had said because it is something that moves her soul to serve Our Lord, to pain and contrition for her sins and what they do to His Majesty, and to love Our Lord with all the strength of our soul—which she can do because His Majesty gives her grace to do it, for without it [i.e., grace] she can do nothing. She does not understand how there can be error in this because if she were to understand this she would not do it or any of the other things she has described.

She was told that the error is not in loving God and desiring the salvation of one's neighbor because this is a very holy and virtuous work and in it is based all our good but that what is reprehensible is her vanity, the inappropriate things she recounts that she has seen and sees and the security with which she speaks of them and that she wants them to be understood as true.

She said that everything she has said she says not out of vanity or to make any point about herself, but rather to say truthfully what has happened to her and to bear witness to what she is obliged to bear witness to, in conformity with what they are talking about, because she understands that she should not become vain on account of it. And in everything she is attempting to give an account to the Lord Inquisitor as she would to God in heaven.

She was told that what she says would be fine if it were so and if she had not spoken of it to other people, but that the entire city is full of her ideas, and from her own mouth, by which it is seen that all is vanity.

She said that she herself has not said things so publicly unless it was something and said to some particular person with whom she spoke as a friend, and this would be with the end that she has said before, desiring for the benefit of souls.

She was told that in yesterday's audience in the morning she said that she was instructed in her interior to engage in some fasts and other things she described there and she was told to say who instructed her to do that.

She said that she did not understand who said it to her within her interior. She understood it to be the inspiration of Our Lord, and because it was something good, she did it, because if it were something bad, she would not consider that it could be an inspiration from Our Lord.

She was told to consider this well because at the beginning of that audience it [i.e., the record] says that in the interior of her soul, they told her to engage in a fast to all the orders of the Saints, to Saint Peter with the apostles, and to Saint Michael with the angels, and in this way with all the other orders, and that on All Saints Day she would see the end for which they ordered her to do all that, which implies that there was a voice that really spoke to her.

She said that that is the way it is: in her soul she felt a spirit and a very light and sweet voice that told her to fast and everything else that she has said.

She was told that what she now says and what she said before when they asked her this question appear to contradict each other because now she says that they spoke very lightly and sweetly and before this she said that the voice was an inspiration of Our Lord, which shows that it was an inspiration, not a voice.

She said that she has already said that it was an inner voice and a gentleness of spirit that she understood could be an inspiration from our Lord.

She was told that we should not go into what it could be because it could also be something from the devil and she speaks of it as something very certain and true . . .[23] after the decree she has spoken of.

She said that she held this to be certain and true because she felt in her spirit that great gentleness and that sweetness that the devil never causes in anyone and also because what they ordered her to do was good and she did not do it out of hope for what they promised her she would see because she did not remember or pay attention to that or to any other thing except doing what she saw was good.

She was told that in the revelation about the decree of the Justice of God she says that Our Lady and all the saints and the whole court of heaven to whom she had said masses and made fasts had appeared suddenly to detain the Justice of God and that Our Lady and all those saints arrived with the Justice of God. She was told to say and tell how this happened.

DECEMBER 3, 1575

[After reading Francisca the question again, she responded:]

She said that she has no words to be able to say what she has been asked because in the rapture that she felt at that time in her soul, her spirit was absorbed in an incomprehensible light. In that light they showed her soul all of those things, and she cannot say with any words anything about how she then understood them. She does not know the manner in which these things were engraved in her understanding in order to be able to say what she saw. She cannot find any words other than those she already used because the soul well understands at that time and with great clarity that the meaning that the Justice of God signifies is not really that form; it understands with clarity that it is not paper that he carries in his hand because it really is not. Likewise, the Justice carried in His other hand a rod that she had forgotten to describe, and the defendant understood clearly that it was not a rod. She understood that the meaning of that upright and white form was that it was the righteousness of the Justice of God. The bar symbolized his great power to execute anyone for the offenses they had committed against His Majesty, and the same was signified by the folded piece of paper. The great ferocity she saw was the punishments she has said, and she has no other words besides these to declare more about this.

She was told that in the response she has given she has not answered what she was asked, and so, in order that she might understand better, the

23. An illegible word makes the end of this sentence unclear.

question was read to her again and then she was admonished to say how she could say that.

She said that she had no words to explain the state of her soul in the rapture she has spoken of or to explain how such a union could be effected in her. She has already said that in that incomprehensible light in which the spirit is absorbed what is understood is what she has already said, which she cannot say in any words, and she does not know how that power that came to her as the Justice of God remains imprinted in the understanding nor does she know how to say anything else about it.

She was told that if she cannot say more about that then she should say how it occurred that Our Lady and all the saints made the defendant make a promise to the Justice of God and to them that she would say all that she had seen and what more she had to be shown and all the terms by which their complaints would be satisfied.

She said that she has already responded that in that great light in which her spirit was absorbed she was given to understand by Our Lord all the things that His Majesty wanted her soul to understand. And for that reason the defendant cannot say how this happens, because all these things that she has spoken of, her soul understood while in this light and there are no more reasons that she can offer because these are things that one cannot say in words how they are understood then.

She was told that what she says is not a good answer because in this way she can say as many things as she wants if she does not have to give any reason for them or any more clarity. And for Our Lord and the saints to have spoken with her so that she would make the promise she has described, it is clear that they would have had to speak some words to her and that she would have to respond in the same way, since the defendant is not a spirit and therefore cannot comprehend and speak of things only in her understanding.

She said that she cannot say anything more than what she has said because at that time she did not feel herself to be a corporeal being because she was not really herself,[24] but rather her spirit was enraptured in what she saw and they showed it to her within, in the light that she has spoken of. And since they were not saying corporeal things to the defendant, she could not respond through her mouth. And she cannot say more than she has said.

She was told that since she wants people simply to take her word about what she has said, without giving any real reason for sustaining its truth, that she at least has to say and declare how she saw or knew that those who accompanied the majesty of God were Our Lady and the apostles and angels and

---

24. "no estava en si."

other saints and the celestial court. What sign did they bring so that they could be recognized or what proof does the defendant have so that what she has said can be believed without any other reason or proof or testimony? Because no one, as respected as he might be, can be believed without proof.

She said that she repeats what she has already said, that in that state of absorption that the soul is in and in that incomprehensible light that she has described, our Lord gave the defendant to understand what she has described in such a way that the defendant cannot say the form that the saints or Our Lady took. She can in no way describe it because she did not see there what they were wearing nor what they had on their heads nor did she see anything more than that in that light they showed her all that she has described, in such a way that now she cannot explain it in any words; and she has nothing more to say about this.

She was told that in this business she is demonstrating her blindness because she is not giving any information regarding what she has been asked or in the case against her in order to create a belief that all that she has recounted and these revelations are from God and not dreams or deceit by the devil. To prevent her from showing her blindness she should leave aside her reasons and leave everything to the understanding. If it is really true that everything proceeds from God, she must give some evidence for how she has understood that or she must demonstrate a miracle so that she can be believed or some works to prove what she says or some proof that would give us to understand that her raptures are from God. Because she ought to know that there are many people who have been deceived by the devil with such vanities and that they have been given to understand many things, sometimes teaching them while already knowing that they were a lie, but they stuck by them for vanity or other reasons. So she must say what is really happening here.

She said that she does not find in that anything more to say than what she has already said. It is up to God only to perform miracles, and the defendant remains in the belief that what she has said is true and not nonsense or spoken out of vanity, but that the defendant understood it to be from God. If she had understood it to be from the devil she would not go about allowing her soul to be deceived in offense to God because she has always desired to serve and please God and to work toward her salvation, and she has nothing more to say.

DECEMBER 5, 1575

She said that in addition to what she has already said, she cannot think of anything more to say or any reason for her to have understood that what she experienced was from the devil because in all the time that what she has described happened and always and even now she did not follow him and nothing remained of him afterward nor did she abandon prayer or follow the other exercises that she understood were contrary to the law of God. And in all this time she did nothing more than ask for masses to be said and fast and other similar things, and for this reason she cannot believe that it could be from the devil and she has nothing else to say.

She was told that from what she has just said and from what she has testified in other audiences, she clearly intends to give the impression that she is very advanced in her journey with God—and so favored as to be confirmed in a state of grace because her soul is so prayerful. And she lives in such security that the things that happen to her are from God. She was told to say and declare if this is so.

She said that she does not understand that she is confirmed in grace with God because she holds herself to be what she is, which is a true sinner, and the cause of her security in regard to those things that she just said is because when these things happened, she said, "If this is from God, I accept it. If this if from the devil, I deny it." And after this she went around with much perplexity for many weeks and even months asking our Lord with all her might that His Majesty enable her to understand if these were deceits of the devil, greatly begging His Majesty that He in no way allow her to be deceived since she wanted so much to serve Him and she did not intend any other thing. And many times while in prayer in which her heart was on fire with Our Lord and she felt great love on behalf of His Majesty, she was emboldened to beg His Majesty again to give her true guidance as to whether this was from the devil. An interior voice answered that they were not deceits of the devil, and for what she has said and for the works of virtue she was forced to do—which could not proceed from her own bad inclination because she is rude and sinful—she understood that it was from God and not from the devil, even though she did not pay much attention to the things she saw except to do the things that were good. Except for this, she has nothing more to say.

She was told that it has never been clear what her internal voices are. If it is a voice it is not an inspiration, and if it is an inspiration it is not a voice, because the voice presupposes something in the exterior and an inspiration is an interior thing. The Lord Inquisitor asked if she had understood, and she said no, that he should explain. So the Lord Inquisitor explained it to her and used examples, and after she had understood she was told to explain what has happened to her.

She said that while being in a state of mental prayer the person sees her interior and that she does not feel anything in this great prayer except some great tenderness from God with a very inflamed fervor of love so that she seems to leave herself. And there the soul senses an interior voice of great sweetness, which emboldens the soul to ask what it wants of Our Lord, and it is given a great sweetness; and then the creature feels its great lowness and has knowledge of the love God has for it. This is what the defendant means by "inner voice" and nothing else.

She was told that what she says seems like a kind of fiction because even if the soul in prayer is more inflamed to speak with God in some interior way, it does not seem that that desire should be responded to in that way, because speaking and responding correspond with the people who are speaking or responding.

She said she does not have any more to respond than what she has said, and that she understands that God responds to the soul with that sweetness and tenderness that He shows it.

She was told to say if it is true that God responds to the soul through what it sees; she was told to speak about and clarify this because the devil can also do the same to fool her and to cause vanity in her.

She said that the reason is that the soul is left with peace and deep humility.

She was told that those two things can also be from the devil because once the devil has won over a man and a woman who are engaged in sin, they cannot combat their sin. That they are left in peace and humility is not enough of a sign because many times behind the cross rests the devil: he knows these tricks and many others.

She said that she does not understand herself to be in sin, by the grace of God, because mortal sins cause us to lose the favor and gifts that God gives the soul and sometimes those joys and gifts that God gives us through signs are even lost.

She was told that since she has said that God responds to the soul, she should say how she understands that, either giving a reason or telling whether God appears to her there. It could be the response of the devil and thus given with sweetness, because if the devil were to enter the soul with force one would realize who he was and then run away from him and for this reason he comes with gentleness.

She said that God does not appear there and that one does not see anything, but rather she does not know the way in which the soul is sure of what she has said except that it feels there great pledges of the love of Our Lord, which it does not understand that the devil is capable of giving; she has nothing more to respond.

She was told that since she cannot see who is speaking, with the other indications that exist in her history, it seems that these are works of the devil, either because she understands them to be such or because he is deceiving her, which is very easy for him to do because of the vast experience he has in such things and the long time he has been doing these things and because it is so easy for us to be persuaded to be esteemed and to have our works held in good repute.

She said that she does not understand what the Lord Inquisitor has said and for him to explain, and the Lord Inquisitor explained with examples, and having understood it and having said she understood it, she said that she cannot think how to respond to this except for what she has said because his reasoning is subtle, and she desires, if she is living in deceit, to be free of the deceit in which she finds herself.

She was told that in the sessions they have had with her, up until this present month of December, they have discussed diverse matters, and since then she has not ratified them. It will now be well to review them in her mind so that she can say how she has testified and so that she can ratify it [i.e., her statement] and think about what she has said in them and about her affair in such a way that she completely unload her conscience. And thus she was read all the sessions, word for word, and after they were read to her she said that all that was read to her was written the way she has said and declared and that there is nothing in them that should be amended or added or deleted, but that everything was true and that she believes it. And she affirmed and ratified it and if necessary she would say it all over again. And with this admonition she was ordered back to her cell.

JANUARY 25, 1576

At the afternoon session of the Holy Inquisition of the city of Toledo on January 25, 1576, being present the Lord Inquisitor Dr. Juan de Llano de Valdés, by his command Francisca de los Apóstoles was brought in and being present she was asked if she has remembered any other thing in her case about which she must tell the truth under the oath she has sworn.

She said that she has nothing more to say than what she has said and declared . . .

She was told that the prosecutor of the Holy Office wanted to make a formal accusation against her and that before he made it, it would be better for her conscience and for the brief and good handling of her case to say and declare the truth about what she feels she is guilty of before she is told and hears what the prosecutor says so that justice may be done.

She said that she has nothing more to say than what she has said.

OFFICIAL ACCUSATION AGAINST FRANCISCA, JANUARY 5, 1576[25]

And then the Licenciado Soto Cameno appeared in chambers and presented an accusation in his name against Francisca de los Apóstoles and swore that he did not make it out of malice. The Lord Inquisitor accepted it and ordered that it be read and Francisca de los Apóstoles be notified, and the contents of it are what follows:

1. First, she has said that her sister had great revelations of Our Lord and many inspirations that all the law would become one and that before long many marvels would occur.

2. In addition, she has said that a prophet [i.e., Juan de Dios] has come to this city; he is now imprisoned in jail, and the aforesaid Francisca greatly longed to talk with him and she asked a certain person to go talk with him on her behalf.

3. In addition, that the man whom she calls and esteems a prophet of God was in her house and had described great things that had happened with the inquisitors; and that important educated people had come to talk with him; and that he had told them what would happen in the year 1575. He was approved by the inquisitors because they later let him go.

4. In addition, she said many other things that the prophet had foretold would happen and they were simply untrue and contrary to the gospel and Christian doctrine, even though she held them to be very Catholic and true. And she said that those things that that man said agreed with what her sister had said [i.e., foretold].

5. In addition, she said that it all comes to this, that anyone who did not want to heed what that man said would see that all that he said was true. And what he had said was that they had to found great monasteries and convents; and that one would have to be founded outside Toledo called the Conception and in Toledo they would found two, one for widows and virgins and the other for the Blood of Christ, which was Corpus Christi; and that this project would involve women with only one man working with them.

6. In addition, she has said that those convents and monasteries were the calling of these women and that thus one could see the spirit of prophecy of that man and that God had revealed it to him because she had never seen him in her life.

7. In addition, she said that when her sister was born she had seven guardian angels.

25. Fols. 196r–208v.

8. In addition, she said that her sister had experienced demons for the glory of God and was holier than many in heaven, and she named some of the holy martyrs, and when a certain person chastised her for saying that she grew angry with her because she had been contradicted.

9. In addition, she said that when a certain person died he had to spend a year in the chamber of desire, which Francisca de los Apóstoles said was a chamber next to the door of heaven that was there to purge the person of the little desire he had had while living to see God, all this being after he had spent a year in purgatory.

10. In addition, she has said that when the dead person saw that they were not letting him enter heaven, he asked Our Lord to grant the mercy of letting his soul spend that year in the chamber of Francisca de los Apóstoles and that she saw him there and expected to see him glorified or his banishment ended. And the dead person did not get along well with Francisca de los Apóstoles during his lifetime.

11. In addition, she told a certain person to prepare to go to Guadalupe because either while a certain person was saying mass or before, God had ordered that he and Apóstoles and others should go to receive the Archbishop of Toledo, who is imprisoned, and her sister, who had both left Rome, to have novenas there. And that Our Lady or her Son had told her the way that the church and the city and the poor would have to receive them and many other things.

12. In addition, she said to a nun of a certain convent that, while receiving communion one day in a certain place, she was ordered or received a revelation to go to the Chapel of Nuestra Señora del Sagrario and that, obeying the order, she was enraptured in spirit; and that God had revealed great things to her; and that she had seen her sister Bautista who was in Rome and her face was mortified and resplendent, which seemed like a heavenly thing; and that she had said many things that she declared [i.e., that Francisca had already declared in her testimony]; and that it had seemed like a revelation.

13. In addition, she has said that the Archbishop of Toledo is imprisoned without being guilty and is purging the sins of his religious order.

14. In addition, she said to certain persons that soon it would be the will of God that she atone for the sins of the archbishop and his order, and that at times she was so tormented in spirit that much of the time she could not even stand up and that her body was black and bruised and that she suffered great interior afflictions.

15. In addition, she has said and says and confesses that one day as she finished receiving communion they [unspecified] ordered her to go to the Chapel of Nuestra Señora del Sagrario and that, entering it, she was

enraptured; and that a very sweet spirit appeared to her and said to her, "Francisca, give me your heart to clothe me because I cannot cry"; and that the spirit was Our Lady, who was clothed in her heart and then she began to weep and moan before the Majesty of the Father. And the Son and the Holy Spirit were also there, and Our Lady was asking the Majesty of the Father to pardon sinners, and she offered for this the passion of her Son.

16. In addition, she has said that she saw that the Father was so indignant holding in his hand a bunch of very big arrows with barbs of four points and he said, "Leave me alone, lady; eighty [sic; this should be seventy years] years have I suffered with these canons of the cathedral and the sinners." And then the Virgin knelt down and offered to make a convent and a college where He would always be served and that Apóstoles promised the same. And that later God embraced her and threw away the arrows and crossed His arms and said, "What more can I do?" Then a great chorus of voices was heard singing, "Send out your spirit" and another psalm, "Let us sing to the Lord."

17. In addition, she said and has said that another day after that she had another revelation and spiritual rapture; and that Our Lord was clothed in the heart of Apóstoles as His mother had clothed herself before; and that she does not know what the Son meant when he winked at the Father or the Holy Spirit, making a sign for them to be quiet because she was there; and that when the Father came to make peace, He embraced the defendant and three other people whom she named.

18. In addition, she said about a certain person in her house that she was holier and was esteemed to be holier than many martyrs because they had suffered for one moment and the person had suffered for many years.

19. In addition, she has said and said publicly and confesses that, while in prayer in the Sagrario in this city, Our Lord gave her to understand and she felt in her heart that the Justice of God complained greatly against the world and wanted to destroy it. And Our Lady begged her Son not to destroy the world and told him that she would give him four people to make satisfaction for the sins of the world, who were Bartolomé, the imprisoned archbishop, and Miguel and Isabel Bautista and Francisca, her sister, who is the defendant. Later she saw that the Eternal Father threw some arrows with some four-pointed barbs and He crossed his arms and said, "I relent if that is done."

20. In addition, she said that she saw clearly the above vision in spirit and that behind this she saw something like a very dark cloud that signified the sins of the world. And she felt that when this cloud dissipated that God would be appeased.

21. In addition, she said that when she begged Our Lord to remedy the many evils there were in His church and especially in the state of the priests,

Our Lord responded to her that, if she wanted, all the demons who had obscured the paths of virtue could come over her and torment her and make amends for those evils, and she said that she accepted that.

22. In addition, she boasted and said that while she was saying her prayers and fasting for the sins of pride in the world, she felt many legions of demons come over her of the kind who tempt people in this sin and that they tempted her to be very prideful and, while she was suffering these temptations, those demons came into her and through her mouth confessed to a certain person, whom she named, that they would let go of their stranglehold on humanity. And thus she made satisfaction for the sins of the world.

23. In addition, she said and affirmed that among the demons there was great discord about whether it was wrong to release their stranglehold on people and that she heard them asking Our Lord for permission to tempt her while she was sick and unable to avail herself of the sacraments and telling him that if she resisted them while being sick like that, they would surrender. And this happened on another day when she had fallen ill in her bed and had pains in her chest, and while in this state she felt that they were telling her to send for a certain person and that person was a witness to the agony in which she found herself.

24. In addition, she said publicly that she was taught in spirit that she had to be the abbess of that convent; and that God would give her so much holiness that she would create anew the apostolic life; and that she would go about taking the power away from the demons who have darkened the state of humanity; and that this was a tremendous undertaking.

25. In addition, she has said that Our Lord said that if she obligated herself to make satisfaction for the sins of humanity and if she did indeed do it, He would let go of His wrath; and that she had said to Him that she would obligate herself to do this through His divine favor; and that then she felt within herself fear and Our Lady appeared to her and had said, "Do not fear; I will be your helpmate, and I will gain the favor for you so that you can do it."

26. In addition, that in fulfillment and satisfaction of the aforementioned, she made many and diverse vows in which she promised to live in virtue and contrary to the vice for which she wanted to make satisfaction, and for that end she has made many vows.

27. In addition, having understood that Our Lord had chosen her to be abbess of that convent that was to be founded, she said that God instructed her to ask that they [i.e., the earliest women in the convent] be taught the names of the twelve women who would first be chosen for that convent. And having prayed about this, the defendant spoke as if in the person of God and named four of them who were there, calling one Peter and another Paul,

and she told her to imitate Saint Paul, and another she called Saint Andrew and another she called Saint John the Evangelist. Thus the women went about speaking in the name of those saints as if they [i.e., the saints] themselves spoke through them.

28. In addition, she said publicly that one of those nights when she was sick she saw in her spirit that God complained about the sins of the world and wanted to destroy it; and that He wanted to conclude the trial that He was conducting before he destroyed the world; and that He was notably indignant about the priests. And she saw Him on the cross, and she saw a great multitude of hosts fly over the bed, which meant that the priests were crucifying Him with their sacrifices of the mass.

29. In addition, she has levitated in the air with only the points of her toes on the floor and her body levitating in the air. And while in the form of a cross she said that she had seen Our Lord asking for justice against the world and Our Lady and Saint Peter and Mary Magdalene and many saints and that she said to Saint Peter, "Be quiet, you old man; Our Lord says to His Father that He died for humanity." And she said that if God had died that she also would die. And the demons shrieked or raised their voices and said to the defendant that the world and sinners would be turned over to them and thus that they had planned that at the beginning of the new year all the sinners would die and that only the saints would remain.

30. In addition, she has said that she saw Our Lady come in mourning with her Son in her arms as when they gave Him to her after they took Him down from the cross; and that Francisca de los Apóstoles had begged the saints who were there who had been sinners to intercede with Our Lord that He not end the trial of the world; and that He did end the trial.

31. In addition, she said publicly that her sister Isabel Bautista had gone to Madrid; and that being at some novenas in a certain convent Our Lord had taught her there the rule and habit that the convent they were trying to found should have; and that Our Lord had taught her the rule; and they had it written down and read it.

32. In addition, she has walked about saying that her sister Isabel Bautista had to go to Rome to be received by the pope; and that the pope had to take her advice about how to rule the church; and that the matters of the church would be governed on the advice of five women who were to collaborate on these things; and that they would have to take the advice of these women, consulting them so that they would pray about things and be taught about God by them.

33. In addition, she has said to many people that Our Lord had said to her that she give Him the tributaries and then He would give her what He

had promised her, and by tributaries was understood those who would be nuns in the convent.

34. In addition, she said that her sister Isabel Bautista suffered more than many saints in heaven who had not suffered as much for the love of God as her sister. And when another person said that Saint Ines and other saints had been martyrs and she ought not compare her sister with them, she responded that they had had a knife put to their neck in one day and then died but that her sister had suffered much more.

35. In addition, she has said and recounted that the angel Saint Michael or Saint Gabriel, one of the two, had spoken with a certain person and had told him or her about the life of her sister Isabel Bautista; and that he [i.e., the angel] told him or her that she had been created in the divine mind; and that God had created her beautiful and full of grace and pleasing to God and to people; and that she had six or seven angels to guard her; and that God would give her a gift [lit. *joya*, "jewel"], who was the Archbishop of Toledo.

36. In addition, she has said that while certain people were in a room, her sister Bautista was transported or enraptured in such a way that she had risen in the air and one of the people had grabbed her by the robe. And she said that while she was transported certain people in the room were saints and that God wanted them to confess to a certain person. And when she returned to herself a certain person asked her, "Isabel, what was that?" and she responded, "God wants that house very much," pointing to a certain house.

37. In addition, she said that her sister Isabel Bautista had already worn for three hours the habit that the nuns of the convent they would found had to wear; and that Our Lady had clothed her in it; and that Isabel Bautista had risen up to heaven so that she could be clothed in it or that Our Lady had come down to earth to clothe her in it.

38. In addition, she has said that when the points of her feet were on the floor and her body in the air Saint Peter had come; and that God had taken her as a spouse; and that He had sent him [i.e., Peter] to ask her father for permission to marry her; and that in her He had found a just and holy soul and she would make satisfaction for the world and sinners; and that she had asked for the dowry for her betrothal to God and she was given virtue to be holy or to resist temptation.

39. In addition, while talking about the convents and the hospital she would found she said, "This is not a fabrication but faith and because faith is like the creed, one has to believe it."

40. In addition, she has said and affirmed that a certain man was a prophet of God; and that all that he said could be believed like the creed and the faith; and that he had told her and her sister many things that had happened to

them during their lives without having seen them or talked with them; and that what that man said could be believed and was like the faith and the creed.

41. In addition, she has said and believed that her sister Isabel Bautista, on her way to Rome, had seen three people, one of whom was a Nazarene and was Our Lord; and that He was mounted on an ass; and that it had begun to run and she was following behind Him and then He disappeared.

42. In addition, she said that on a certain Christmas past she had seen Our Lord recently born and His mother with Him; and that her sister Isabel Bautista had received communion with the Archbishop of Toledo (who is imprisoned in Rome) in the pope's mass; and that she had known or seen it; and that she had known that the archbishop's trials were over and he was in Guadalupe.

43. In addition, she said that her sister could do miracles in Rome.[26]

44. In addition, she said and recounted that while she was sick her chest rose up and her feet were placed one on top of the other, and she took the form of the cross with her arms extended. And while in the air her spirit soared to heaven and she saw Our Lord, who was very irate with the world and wanted to destroy it; and she begged Him not to destroy it. And Mary Magdalene said to destroy it because the poor were dying of hunger and Francisca had said to Mary Magdalene that she had been a loose woman and a sinner.

45. In addition, she said that Saint Peter also said to Our Lord that He should destroy the world because people were liars and blasphemers, and she had said to Saint Peter, "Be quiet, old man; you too denied Our Lord." And Our Lady said to Our Lord that He should destroy it because each day people were worse and they did not take refuge in the fruits of His passion. And the defendant said to God that if He had died she also wanted to die and suffer trials and that He should not destroy the world.

46. In addition, she said that it was arranged with Our Lord that He would send a very great pestilence and that only the saints would survive it, and after she came back to herself she found her bed full of bleeding hosts.

47. In addition, she said publicly that when her spirit had arisen to heaven, Our Lord had said to her, "Do not go, Francisca; for it is my delight to speak with the sons of men and even more with you, for you please me greatly."

48. In addition, when a certain person died she said that the spirit of the dead person had been with her for a certain time because the soul had asked that favor of Our Lord.

26. "Yten [h]a dicho q[ue] no estuvo en un canto de un real de a quatro de hazer su hermana milagros en rroma."

49. In addition, she has said many times before many people, "What could I ask from God that He would not give me?" since she had served God so well.

50. In addition, she said that God ordered her to recount these things to a certain person and when she did not tell them to him the devils tormented her until she went to him to tell him.

51. In addition, she has said that her sister was holier than many saints in heaven, more than Saint Catherine and others, and that God had taken her in order to have her help in the rescue of the world, confirming this with a specific revelation that they said she had, which, besides being great pride and blasphemy, is an error, because it is known that the sister has many imperfections that are not fitting in any glorious saint.

52. In addition, after admitting and receiving as a nun in her convent a certain person, she told her that she would please Our Lord with four mysteries, which would be fasting and prayer, because discipline was a punishment or penance for commoners.

53. In addition, in the house where she lives she told and taught many people that the Catholic Church was in need of being rebuilt; and that it would be rebuilt by the order of clerics and nuns that she would institute; and that a great punishment over all Christianity would have to come; and that this was prophesied.

54. In addition, as prioress and abbess, which she pretended to be, in front of those who were in her congregation and company she said her faults and ordered the rest to say them and they said them. And afterward she gave them a long talk saying that they had to eat the bread of the wedding; and that she and her sister had to suffer trials and that the others would be blessed; and that they had been chosen to be stones in the foundation.

55. In addition, she placed great fears in the women who were in her company if they did not observe well the rule that she had invented, and she ordered the one who was the most well established of them, as the oldest in the community, to urge them not to talk during hours of silence and if they did not obey to tell her.

56. In addition, one day coming back from receiving communion she said publicly that she had asked Our Lord how to oversee these women who were with her, and she was told in her mind that "the olive branch who was not dead should be thrown out," and she said this many times. She ruled them as her mind told her, and she taught them that they had to do those things that had been inspired in her interior.

57. In addition, while reading in a certain book about a saint and a certain revelation that Francisca de los Apóstoles had in her mind, Francisca de

los Apóstoles said that it meant and taught that God reveals things in the understanding. And she told of a nun who was with her in whom God had once revealed some things, and she later went to look in some books to see if some other person had had that same revelation and if she found it she said, "You see here: one things accords with another," referring to the revelations that had come to her.

58. In addition, she said and affirmed that through the revelation of God certain people had joined together in this city and in her house who she said also had revelations and she said that she also had revelations all the time and she wrote down her revelations and placed them on the altars.

59. In addition, she said that the Chapel of Nuestra Señora del Sagrario had told her twice that the Archbishop of Toledo who is imprisoned would confirm the rule and reform Christianity and that they would free him by Christmas, and four Christmases have passed since she says that Our Lady told her that.

60. In addition, she said publicly that Our Lady had told her to enclose herself and the others who were in her company, and thus they had cloistered themselves, and that the ordinary would not accept that she retained people in this congregation.

61. In addition, she has said before many people that while she was sick she levitated from her bed and she saw the last judgment of God; and that she had seen all the saints of heaven asking Him for mercy; and that Saint Peter had been called and she saw him come; and that Saint Peter asked justice of Our Lord against the priests because they did not live or uphold his rule[27] as he had upheld them in his time, and later the defendant saw that her bed was full of white hosts.

62. In addition, after she saw the abovementioned, many demons entered her body and some were prideful and others brought riches like silk bedding and others were more humble; and they gave her many torments. And after she returned to herself she remained very tormented, and many times they blew out a candle that had been lit and they put something very heavy over top of her that seemed to suffocate her.

63. In addition, Apóstoles had some writings in a box, and she said that they were about when she had seen the judgment, and that God had insisted that she write it all down and so she had written it. And she did not want anyone to see it, and she hid it from all who were with her. And when the vicar of this city went to her house, she took it out of the box and hid it in the base-

27. Here, "rule" (*regla*) could refer to Christian morality more generally, as in the Ten Commandments, rather than "rule" in the sense of a monastic rule.

ment underneath a mound of dirt, and after he left she took it back and wrapped it in cloth and burned certain letters, saying that she was burning them so that the vicar, if he were to return to her house, would not find them.

64. In addition, the abovementioned Francisca has a servant in her house about whom she said to certain persons that she had observed that in the very short time since she had entered this house that this woman, meaning the servant, had been granted many favors by God; and that she had seen in heaven a chair for Apóstoles and another for Isabel Bautista, her sister; and that God had said, "I have these two chairs for my servants Apóstoles and Bautista."

65. In addition, the defendant, while seated on a chair as abbess as she claimed to be, ordered all who were in her company to throw themselves on the floor before her to tell her their faults, and this they did, and she gave everyone their penance.

66. In addition, the abovementioned Francisca asked those who were with her in her house to make a vow of chastity and poverty and religion and humility, which they actually did, and the defendant said that in her interior she was given a great desire for that to be done.

67. In addition, after they had made the aforementioned vows she asked those who had dowries and possessions to give them over to her since they ought not have or control anything but rather follow her will.

68. In addition, she said and said publicly that her interior was afflicted and that she felt in her body a voice that told her to do what she did.

69. In addition, when the vicar of this city went to her house asking for certain papers on which was written what they had to pray, the defendant and another person hid the papers. When a certain person saw them worry about where to hide them, she asked them what papers they were and if she would feel bad if they were torn or burned, to which Apóstoles responded that they would not do that because these were things that she had felt in her interior and that she wanted to keep until God delivered them, and so she hid them underneath a certain thing and later took them out and put them somewhere else.

70. In addition, the defendant said that a certain person who was in her house had felt in her interior many things about the convent that they had been instructed to found, and before they were revealed to her they were revealed to the defendant in her interior. They told her in her interior that the person would come to tell her about them. And the person did come and tell Apóstoles all that she had felt in her interior about the convent and in her interior she had been ordered to give her an account of it.

71. In addition, she described how she had seen the judgment of God; and that Our Lord was very irate with the priests who were living in sin; and

that she and her sister and the others who were together in their house wanted to appease Our Lord with prayers; and that she had seen Saint Peter and other saints in the judgment.

72. In addition, she has said that in her interior had been revealed to her and to her sister and to another person that in the past year 1575 that there would be great marvels and a great destruction; and that the Archbishop of Toledo who is imprisoned in Rome would be liberated in the year of 1575 by the person; and that for that reason he went to Rome; and that the person was a holy prophet of God; and that the aforementioned Francisca and the others believed all that the man said; and that they hoped that he would do great things. For that reason he went to Rome, and to the king he revealed what was to happen in Granada and other things before they occurred.

73. In addition, she has said that Saint John the Evangelist had clothed himself in her spirit and, through her spirit, had impelled her to say a certain thing that she had told a nun.

74. In addition, she said that one day while her sister was in prayer she saw her levitating from the floor and her face was like that of a seraph, and she was saying to a person who was there, "blessed are you and blessed are those who come to you."

75. In addition, she said that during a mass that a certain person said in a certain place, Saints Gabriel and Joseph and Hildephons were present at the mass and that she had seen them.

76. In addition, she said that when the convent was founded and the nuns were inside it, when a nun did something that she ought not, the devils would punish her and that Our Lady would be very pleased with the convent and would accompany them each step of the way.

77. In addition, she said that she had been at the judgment of God; and that the demons were accusing her of the gravity of her sins; and that she had made a promise to change her ways; and that Our Lady had come forward to support her.

78. In addition, when a certain person said to others that she go hear mass and give thanks to Our Lord for the mercies he had given them Apóstoles went to the person who had said that and told her, "This woman who is speaking is not so-and-so—naming her by her name—but the angel Saint Gabriel." And she said that the spirit of her sister who was in Rome was inside the person.

79. In addition, while her sister was in Rome the defendant said that she had been here in Toledo embracing her, implying that her sister had come from Rome in spirit.

80. In addition, she told many people that Our Lord had revealed to her that in addition to the convent that would be founded for orphaned young

women, they would have to found another convent so that erring women might enter it and that Our Lord had given her to understand that a nun who was in a certain convent would have to enter her convent.

81. In addition, she said that in the convent that she was to found, twelve nuns without dowries would enter and that they would live the apostolic life; and to each of those who were in her company already and to those who would enter she gave the name of an apostle.

82. In addition, she said publicly that Our Lord inspired her in her interior and that she was following the calls that Our Lord was making in her interior.

83. In addition, she said publicly that while she was in prayer she had seen visibly a procession of virgins; and that she had seen the procession many times; and that seeing the virgins was a sign of the convent and religious order that she wanted to found so that she would understand and know that the nuns who would enter into the convent that would be founded would wear the same habit that those virgins wore; and she affirmed that in that procession she had seen Our Lady.

84. In addition, she has said, says, and confesses that, because of callings that Our Lord has made in her interior, she has made certain obligations to suffer on behalf of the church of God as many torments as God might be served to grant her in order that His Majesty might be satisfied for so many offenses as have been committed against Him and that this is what the nuns who would be in her convent must commit themselves to doing.

85. In addition, she said that the vows that she made because of the callings were made because she had seen a judgment that Our Lord had shown her while she was ill and that in the judgment Our Lord had taught her how He was very offended by many types of people; and she said that all of this she had written down in her own hand.

86. In addition, she said to those who were in her company that no nun ought to have anything to herself but all should be held in common; and that whoever had something had to renounce it and turn it over to the house; and that she had offered herself to Our Lord as the servant of all. And if anyone told any part of this to anyone when she went out of the house, she would be damned. She read the vows that she had made and had written down so that all the women would make the same vows.

87. In addition, when Francisca de los Apóstoles was reading the rule that the nuns in her convent had to follow, she stopped reading and said they were suffocating her and she cried as if she were a small creature and she appeared for a while to be unable to talk. And when she came back to herself many of the people who were there thought she had experienced torment

from the devil and that he suffocated her so that she would not be able to move forward what she had started.

88. In addition, she read a paper and said they were the vows that she had made, and she said to those who were there that they should make them as she had, saying that she vowed to live in perfect chastity, poverty, and righteousness and all those with her said the same.

89. In addition, she said and recounted that in a vision she had seen, Our Lord had taught her that she had to be in charge of all the nuns who had been shown to her in the vision; and that Our Lord would be served by bringing another nun so that she and the others would obey her [i.e., the other nun]; and that Our Lord had shown her that she had to be the abbess and patroness of that religious order that she wanted to found. Thus the person who was in charge of those nuns would have little work to do and that this business would not be done by letters but by the spirit.

90. In addition, she described how in another vision she had seen, Our Lord had shown her that the Archbishop of Toledo who is imprisoned would leave prison not by ordinary means but by a miracle.

91. In addition, she said that she had seen purgatory and that in it she had seen many souls, among whom she had seen one who was crying out to her, asking her to have a mass said and that later he would leave purgatory, and she had had the mass said.

92. In addition, she said that on the day of the Incarnation she did not observe it the way she should have, because there would come a time when it was celebrated every day of the week, and that on that day they ought not eat meat, and so she and other people did not eat meat on a certain day [i.e., out of observance of the feast day]

93. In addition, she has said and says that she had written a rule that had to be followed by those who were in the convent that would be founded; and that while she was writing it she had had many battles with the devil; and that in the battles that she had had with him she had defeated him; and that in the rule she wrote nothing more than what Our Lord had taught her in her interior.

94. In addition, she says and confesses that she went to certain churches and made many prayers and fasts for the state of the church, begging Our Lord to provide the church with holy prelates and that once on a Monday after receiving communion she heard a voice say in her interior that she should go to the Sagrario, and thus she had gone. And upon arriving there, she recollected herself and felt her spirit enraptured and was pulled outside of herself.

95. In addition, she confesses and affirms that she saw in that rapture how Our Lady interceded with her Son for the state of the church saying that

she would give him the Archbishop Bartolomé who is imprisoned in Rome. And she saw that Our Lord was moved by the entreaties of His mother and was vanquished by the prayers of His mother.

96. In addition, she confesses that on the following Tuesday she returned for communion and she felt the same thing in her interior, that she should go to the Sagrario because she would see many things. And then she went and upon arriving she recollected herself again, and she says she saw the same thing as she had the day before. And that while she was in that rapture she heard Our Lord say, "Send out your spirit and they are created, and you renew the face of the earth,"[28] and then she saw a great Majesty on a throne reveal Himself, and He said, "You ask much of me, Son, that I renew all the earth because I have waited seventy years and they offend me more," and many other things were revealed to her there.

97. In addition, she affirms that in that rapture she saw in spirit the whole world enveloped by demons with all the truths obscured and that Our Lord had asked her if she would allow all those demons to come into her to give an account of what they had done in the world to make all creatures offend Him, and she deliberated for six months about whether or not to accept this task.

98. She confesses that in the time Our Lord showed her many things that had offended Him and, still being in doubt as to whether or not to accept the task that Our Lady had asked her to take on, she had come upon a chapter in the book about Saint Catherine of Siena that talked about how she saw similar demons. She had asked that they come over her and she had been very tormented by them on behalf of the church of God, and thus Apóstoles had the nerve and boldness to decide, and she told Our Lord that it was right for her to accept in good faith whatever His Majesty wanted her to do for His honor and that of the church, as long as He gave her the grace not to offend Him.

99. In addition, she says that after this decision, which would be about a month later more or less, she felt within herself new stirrings and tribulations and torments in which the demons came into her to declare things to Miguel Ruíz, and they said they were the ones who had possessed the world through pride.

100. In addition, she confesses that, seeing herself worn out from them, she went to give an account of it to Miguel Ruíz, and while she was doing so, the devil said through her mouth to Miguel Ruíz that they were the devils of pride who had come to tire her out. And thus he understood which devils tormented her then and which devils would come to torment her.

---

28. "emite spiritum tuum et creabuntur et renobabis faciem terre" (Ps 104:30).

101. In addition, she says and confesses that afterward other demons of another sin came to her and others of another until they stopped tormenting her.

102. In addition, she confesses and says that after that, one day having just received communion, she was asked in her interior to suffer these torments all over again because Our Lord wanted all the demons through her mouth to give an account to Miguel Ruíz of the way they had made all the creatures live in the world.

103. In addition, she says and affirms that when the time had come for the devils to give their account, just as she was finishing receiving communion as she did every day, they gave her to understand in her interior that she should make a vow in which she committed herself to serve God through acts contrary to those through which those demons had made people sin, and in her own hand and writing she wrote down the vow. And later that same day the demons made her break the vow and then gave an account to Miguel Ruíz of how they had made people commit that particular form of sin that she says was done by way of entering into her and saying through her mouth the way that they had made everyone live in that sin.

104. In addition, she says and confesses that these encounters and fights with demons ended and that she experienced a victory over them and felt a great peace and tranquility in her soul. And because she felt and understood these things she wanted to make urgent prayers and fasts and have communion, asking Our Lord how she might make satisfaction to His Majesty for the offenses that had been done to Him.

105. In addition, that while she was sick she says she fell asleep and then woke up very frightened, and she cried out and found herself transported out of herself without knowing how, being placed in the form of a cross with her arms extended. And in that transported state she saw a Majesty very irate, like a terrible fearsome judge, and she screamed aloud, saying, "May you fear, heavens and earth, to see God made your judge."

106. In addition, she confesses that later she saw Our Lord on the cross asking for justice for that Majesty for His wounds and that later she saw Him at the pillar asking for justice for His lashes and for the ingratitude for His passion.

107. In addition, she says that she began to cry aloud to Our Lady asking her to grant favor to the sinners, and she confesses that later she saw her come with her Son in her arms having just come down from the cross, asking for the same justice before that Majesty and saying how ungrateful we had been at her Transfixion.

108. In addition, she says that while in this state the defendant cried out to the saints to return for the sinners because she saw them forsaken in all parts, and later she saw Saint Peter coming and saying before that Majesty, "Eternal Father, may there be a harsh punishment for the priests who have followed you so poorly, for naked I followed the naked one and they go about weighed down by their incomes and vices."

109. In addition, she affirms that she saw many hosts with Christ crucified on each one flying over her bed, asking for justice before that Majesty, and that she then had cried out to Our Lord because she saw him give a great sentence against the world. The complaint was against all the estates [i.e., religious and lay], and many things happened to her there.

110. In addition, she says that another night at eight o'clock after having spent over four hours in agony she felt how her soul was being yanked from her body and she remained transported [i.e., enraptured] more than at any other time and she saw that same Majesty she had seen before, and Our Lord and Our Lady and many saints and Saint Peter, and all of them were begging that Majesty on behalf of the whole human race, and He showed how His justice wanted satisfaction.

111. In addition, she says, confesses and affirms that that vision she saw threw her into confusion and later she saw Our Lord in the cenacle on His knees washing the disciples' feet, and she says and affirms that she heard it said, although she did not see nor understand who said it, "Who will make satisfaction for the humility of the Son of God, which has been offended by all the pride of the world?" And they told her (she does not know who) to say that the works and way of life of those in the religious order she would found would make satisfaction to the Justice of God for the same humility of the Son of God.

112. In addition, she says and affirms that later she saw Our Lord when He instituted the sacrament, and they said to her (she does not know who), "Who will make satisfaction for the great love with which Our Lord consecrated himself for sinners and the election of priests?" And later someone told her (although she does not know who) to reply, "the frequency of reception of those sacraments and the purity of the priests in those monasteries."

113. In addition, she says that later she saw Our Lord in the garden as He was praying and they said to her (she does not know who except to affirm that she heard the voice), "Who will make satisfaction for the righteousness of this prayer of the Son of God offended by the falseness with which all creatures serve God?" And she confesses that they said to her, without her knowing who, that she say that that same prayer of the Son of God would

make satisfaction for the justice and the righteousness of spirit that would be in those monasteries.

114. In addition, she affirms that later she saw Our Lord at the pillar and they said to her (she does not know who), "Who will make satisfaction for this most delicate beaten flesh offended by the dishonesty [i.e., sexual licentiousness] of the world?" And she said she was told to say, "This same Lord on that pillar would make satisfaction and the chastity that would be upheld in the convents."

115. In addition, she says that later she saw Our Lord on a cross and they said to her, "Who will make satisfaction for all these torments that Our Lord suffered?" And they told her, without her knowing who, to say that He would be satisfied on the same terms as those by which His Majesty had been offended.

116. In addition, she affirms and says that later she saw Our Lord with a crown of thorns on His head and they said for this and for Our Lord's mouth and feet and hands and side and His clothing that was gambled over—for all these things they asked her who would make satisfaction for each thing, and she was told without knowing by whom to respond that regarding the crown of thorns, the religious of those monasteries who would occupy their thoughts always in recognizing His Majesty, and regarding the mouth that complained that it had been offended by blasphemies and oaths, it would be satisfied with the continuous praises that these religious would make, and regarding the clothing, it would be satisfied with the modesty of the robes of the priests.

117. In addition, she says that after this she was shown a procession and that she saw in it priests dressed in coarse cloth and black capes and another procession of nuns all dressed in white wool with white capes, of the same type as those that the canons of Toledo wear.

118. In addition, she affirms that then Our Lord said to her, "These are the religious orders that I want to make satisfaction to me in the same way that you have committed yourself, and I want the feast of the Most Holy Sacrament observed every Thursday and for it to remain in the monstrance until the following Friday, and that night all the priests and nuns, each in his or her own state, will remain there and reflect on the torments I suffered, which is required but which the whole world has forgotten." And each Friday they should spend in this reflection and Saturday they should spend in reflection on the Transfixion of Our Lady.

119. In addition, she says and affirms that in its entirety, this vision conveyed that, for the reformation of the whole world and the satisfaction of those offenses, Our Lord wanted monasteries to be founded in all of the archbishoprics and bishoprics; and that there be seminaries so that from these, people would go out who would serve all the churches; and that they might have a

common income and live the apostolic life without anyone possessing anything of his own; and that their purpose would be to uproot evil and plant virtues and provide all the necessities, and thus they would have a school for young boys who would accompany them to serve the churches because Our Lord wanted to be honored and reverenced by his priests, as His Majesty deserves.

120. In addition, that because of the vision and revelation, the above-mentioned gathered around her many women and she taught them how to observe the rule of Saint Jerome as it is contained in his letters, and they read it each day; and she told them that since they had come together there their job was to please the mystery of the Incarnation because the advocation of the house had to be that and the observance of the Most Holy Sacrament each Thursday and on Fridays the Passion and on Saturdays the Transfixion of Our Lady.

121. In addition, that to encourage them in this the defendant read them a book about the Passion on two or three Thursdays, as is done by the nuns on Holy Thursday and Friday night, and they all stayed the rest of the night in prayer. And all this the defendant says and confesses that she does and the others who are with her do because of the vision she had in which she saw that judgment and because she says she was ordered in that judgment vision to have this done in the religious order and that it had to be done to make satisfaction for the sins of the world.

122. In addition, she says and confesses that Our Lord asked her in that judgment that she tell others to do this and that she declare all that she had seen in the judgment, and she promised to do this, and thus she tried to do what she could in this matter. She got up most nights to say matins at midnight, and in the morning she said primes, and later she and the others made a procession in the patio of their house and said the litany for the state of the church, and they carried in the procession an image of Our Lady and the angel Saint Gabriel and a Lamb of God and other symbols and images, and they did this until the vicar came to visit them.

123. In addition, she confesses and says that in what she has said about the demons who entered into her to give an account of what was happening in the world, she says another legion of demons entered her on the day of the Incarnation and gave an account of the way they had made people live, and so, as she finished receiving communion, she made a vow in the way that Our Lord had inspired her soul for the satisfaction of the vices that men were engaging in.

124. In addition, she says that on the day of Saint Barnabas another legion of demons came and they gave an account of the way they made men sin through that sin and that after this legion came the defendant made no vow.

125. In addition, she confesses and affirms that one day after having received communion from the hand of Miguel Ruíz in the Hospital de la Misericordia she felt that she was being asked inside her soul to fast for thirty-three days for the life of Our Lord Jesus Christ and another sixty-three for the life of Our Lady, during which days she made many communions and fasts and disciplines and had many masses said in reverence for those holy lives, offering everything up to the Eternal Father and asking Him, for the merits of His Son and the most holy Virgin, to pardon the world for all the manners of ire that He had showed the defendant He had against the world. And she says she felt, in making this prayer inside her soul, that she was being told to make another fast to all the saints and to Saint Peter with the apostles and to Saint Michael with the angels and in this way with all the rest of the saints and that on the day of All Saints she would see the reason why she had been ordered to do that.

126. In addition, she says that all of the aforementioned fasts and masses ended on the actual day of All Saints this past year, after she had had a mass said to each saint. And that day was the last mass, and it was said to all the saints; and that day, after receiving communion in the mass that Miguel Ruíz said, the defendant remained outside of her senses, enraptured in her spirit, and she saw the Justice of God come from heaven. She says that the Justice of God was in a very upright and white form and that it came with many angels with drawn swords in their hands; and the Justice brought in its hands a decree that she says they showed her that had the power to give a general punishment against the whole world with five things, namely, great wars, water, fire, famines, and pestilence and that the pestilence would begin in Toledo.

127. In addition, she affirms that as this happened, she saw how Our Lady had come to this encounter saying she would not consent to that because she was the patroness of this city and that He should relent in His anger because Our Lady had granted this city privileges on account of many people who were pleasing to God who would be enough to make satisfaction for His complaints and that where the Justice of God wanted the punishment to begin Our Lady would begin the satisfaction for the offenses that had been made against the Majesty of God.

128. In addition, she says and affirms that later she saw how the entire court of heaven, to whom those masses had been said and to whom those fasts had been made, devoted themselves to detaining the Justice with similar reasons as Our Lady. And she confesses that all those saints and Our Lady came together with her to the Justice of God, and they made her promise that she would say all that she had seen and whatever else she might be shown

and all the terms by which they had to make satisfaction for all His complaints. And with this and other things that happened she says this vision ended.

129. In addition, she affirms that later she saw a very great procession of priests clothed in sackcloth, and they were received by many angels singing a psalm that begins "His foundation upon the holy mountains." And she says that the procession of priests lasted until the psalm was over. Then she saw Our Lord on the cross saying, "Oh, world, how you have offended me! How long must your evil deeds against me last?"

130. In addition, she says that later she saw Our Lady who offered all those abovementioned priests saying, "Lord, look at these worthy gentlemen I present to you. They are from this city of Toledo of which I am the patron, and they will be enough to conquer the world and be sure that you are satisfied."

131. In addition, she affirms that later she saw how Our Lord called all the priests with great love saying, "Come, come, my priests, and I will show you what my church has cost me and how it has offended me."

132. In addition, she says that she saw that those who were older He let enter His side, showing them the great love with which He had redeemed the world, and to others who were not so old He showed the signs of His passion, and to others who were younger He collected them outside because they did not dare approach. And to all of them He said, "You have seen what my church has cost me. Go out throughout the world and preach penance that they may leave the error of their ways, because if they do not, I have decided upon a great punishment against the world." And then she saw that they all went out throughout the world, at which point this vision ended.

133. In addition, she says and confesses that later Our Lord ordered her to tell all she had seen and she asked Our Lord who His Majesty was ordering her to tell this to, and she says that she was answered that she should not worry about this, because He would determine when and to whom she should make manifest all that she had been shown, which was to the prelates of His church, because it was an ordination of His great mercy that He not punish the world without first giving a warning that they do penance. And after this she says she returned to herself, and there were many there in the chapel who had seen this because she had experienced great tremors in her body while she saw all the abovementioned happen.

134. In addition, she affirms that because she was silent and did not speak of what she was feeling there, her heart burst open and so did her head, and she was sick from this for many days.

135. In addition, she says that, as she has confessed, there was a victory over those demons and that Our Lord had favored her with so many mercies

and that she had committed herself to make satisfaction for many sins in the way that she has said. After several days had passed, one day in the same hospital, as she finished receiving communion from Miguel Ruíz, she says she felt within her a great knowledge of her lowness and a new light about who Our Lord was. And through an internal voice she was given to know that she was nothing, not enough to make satisfaction for the least sin, although she had vowed to do so, but that His Majesty for the great love He had for the world had wanted to make out of her a model for other people so that His justice would be satisfied, and so she was left with this knowledge of her lowness for many days.

136. In addition, she says and affirms that the abovementioned happened to her ten or twelve days after All Saints Day and that the victory over the demons was five or six days before All Saints and that of the execution of judgment was on the same day of All Saints and that of the judgment she saw was Monday before the Conception of Our Lady and the Friday after the Conception.

137. In addition, she confesses, says, and affirms that all of the above-mentioned was clearly a thing [i.e., gift] from God and not the devil, first because her spirit was enraptured with great sweetness and that during that time her senses did not feel a single corporal thing nor was her soul perturbed, but rather she felt a very great light and a deep knowledge of her own lowness; and after it was over and she returned to herself she found in herself a great humility and great subjection in everything having to do with the service of Our Lord, so that with great ease she could do all things that normally cause pain and fatigue for the love of Our Lord; and in that security in which her soul rested she understood that it was good and from Our Lord.

138. In addition, she confesses that she in her soul was possessed for more than one year by a very great love of Our Lord and of love for other souls and that in that great love her soul possessed she desired that all creatures love Our Lord and make satisfaction to Him in the way that had been shown to her.

139. In addition, she says that although she was possessed by the devil, it did not disturb her in what pertained to the service of Our Lord, but instead, before the abovementioned things happened that she has confessed have happened to her, she affirms that her soul has possessed and possesses an inner peace with a great tranquility. And neither all of hell and the calumnies of all the creatures who have arisen against her nor any other trial is enough to rattle her or detain her from what she owes in service to Our Lord, because she says that although she feels things very humanly, when she enters inside herself she finds and has always found a great conformity with the will of Our

Lord in all things that appear, so that they do not give her any disturbance or inner trial.

140. In addition, she says that through this interior peace she described she knows and has known that God possesses her soul and not the devil because the devil does not give peace and tranquility but war and rancor and all that is evil and that in all of this the demons have perturbed her only with corporal pains and not in anything concerning her soul.

141. In addition, she says and affirms that in the interior of her soul she felt a spirit and a very gentle and sweet voice that told her to fast and do the other works she has described and that it was an inner voice with a gentleness of spirit that she understood to be the inspiration of Our Lord and that it was certain and true and she now believes and affirms it to be so.

142. In addition, she says that many times while in prayer in which she says her heart is on fire with Our Lord, she feels great love for His Majesty, and then she becomes bold and begs His Majesty to give her true light to tell her if that is from the devil, and she affirms that in her interior she received the reply that these were not tricks of the devil.

143. In addition, she spoke about this inner voice and was asked what it is, and she said that when a person is engaged in mental prayer inside oneself, she does not feel anything more than a great devotion centered in the place where one feels great tenderness for God, with a fervor so ardent that it seems to burst out of one; and there the soul feels an internal voice of great sweetness that gives the soul the boldness to ask Our Lord what He wants of it, and it is answered with great sweetness. And then the creature feels its own great lowness and an understanding of the love that God has for it.

144. In addition, that in all of the aforesaid and many other things, she says and affirms under oath that these things actually happened and that she saw them and believes them to be true and as such has talked about them publicly with many people. And in addition to that, it is presumable that Francisca de Avila or de los Apóstoles has said, done, and believed many other things more and less grave and that she has said and done them to other persons and that she has been quiet about them and covered them up maliciously so that they do not come to the attention of Your Honor. So under this pretext I accuse her of each thing and when something else comes to my attention I will come forward and if necessary add to this accusation. For now I accuse her of this and find good reason that for all that has happened that she should be given a sentence of excommunication, accepting as I accept the confession of the prisoner as I interpret it. Thus I beg Your Grace to order it declared and to declare her a heretic and to order her to be turned over

relaxed to the justice of the secular arm [i.e., for execution], and if not, to order her condemned to the greatest and gravest punishments the law provides as an example for other similar delinquents.

Another thing I ask is that if it is necessary to put this matter to the question of torture, that it may be given to her and repeated as many times as necessary.

El Licenciado Soto Cameno

Once the said accusation had been presented and was read word for word and Francisca de los Apóstoles was notified of it, she was overcome by a fainting spell and was a bit disoriented. Then she came to, crying, and she said that these things should not have come to this and she said that she was not in any shape now to be able to respond to the accusation and she asked the Lord Inquisitor to leave her response to another session. And she also said that torturing her would not be necessary for her to tell the truth, that without torture she would tell the truth. So she was admonished and ordered to return to her cell.

Then she asked the Lord Inquisitor to have a lawyer appointed for her to respond to this accusation because she would not be able to respond without a lawyer to so many points as there are here.

The Lord Inquisitor said that first she had to respond to the accusation, confessing what was the truth and denying what was not in such a way that she tell the truth and there is no other possibility for her.

Then Francisca de los Apóstoles said that she is a woman of little strength and the Lord Inquisitor is a person of great rigor in his questions and in other ways and that she does not have enough strength to respond to such terrible impugnations. And she asked again to be given a lawyer in order to feel some support.

She was told that there is nothing more to do than to respond to the accusation and all of its points, that the impugnations are there so that the truth can be known and not for any other reason, and he said that in telling the truth she had no reason to fear anything.

The said Francisca de los Apóstoles said that if she responds to all those things without a lawyer, afterward one will not be necessary, that after passing through that storm why would she want a lawyer? For the mercy of God please give her one, she is as frightened of the Lord Inquisitor as if he were Jesus Christ coming to judge her and he were judging her and that fear does not allow her to say things the way she would like because she has already experienced this in the past in the confessions she has made up to now.

The audience ended at this point.

FRANCISCA'S RESPONSE TO THE ACCUSATIONS[29]

[On January 27, 1576 (morning session), the entire accusation was reread so that Francisca could respond to it.]

At the beginning of the accusation that was read to her, she said that she was a baptized Christian and understands herself to be one and that she is not a heretic and that she has already said that they should give her a lawyer to respond to this accusation and that she will not know how to respond without one.

She was told that she had already been informed that she would not be given a lawyer in order to respond to the accusation, that she must respond to the accusation, telling the truth under the oath she has sworn.

She said that they should give her a lawyer because this is the way they do things in trials outside and that she will tell the truth because they accuse her of things she has never done.

She was told that she was already informed that she would not be given what she asks for but that she must respond to the accusation and afterward she will be given a lawyer.

She said why would she want a lawyer afterward when she needs one now in order not to condemn herself because she is a woman, and even though she will tell the truth she needs a lawyer to give her advice about what she has to say.

She was told not to talk about this anymore because there was nothing more to be done beyond what had been said to her already and that she should respond to the accusation telling the truth and if she does not want to do it then she should return to her cell.

She said that she asked for justice before God and before humanity that they might give her a lawyer in order to respond because, since she is a woman and without counsel, she cannot respond to such important things like these that they have put to her and because she cannot confess to what she did not do without the advice of a lawyer and because she does not dare represent herself in this inquiry without a lawyer.

She was told that if she does not want to respond she should return to her cell and that she should realize that until she has responded to the accusation she will not be able to speak to a lawyer.

She said that since the Lord Inquisitor was accusing her of things that she does not understand, how will she be able to exonerate herself when she is ignorant about such things? She said that she will respond but that she does not dare to respond to the Lord Inquisitor because she is very fearful of him

29. Fols. 208v–239v.

and that because of this fear she will not be able to explain things as they should be explained and that this is why she asks for a lawyer, not because she does not want to tell the truth.

She was told that what her lawyer would tell and counsel her if he were present would be only to advise her to tell the truth and that this is what in fact the Lord Inquisitor is advising her and also that she should not fear any person.

She said that she will respond to everything as well as she can and that she asks for mercy because she does not know how to exonerate herself without a lawyer.

To the first point of accusation that was read to her:

She said that she had not said what the point contains but that she has praised her [i.e., her sister Isabel Bautista] because she was very virtuous. And she said that she heard Juan de Dios say that all the law would become one and that they would gain the holy house and that all would have to be Christians. And he showed her some writings that said that he had notified the king, and this the defendant heard from Juan de Dios after the aforesaid left the Inquisition. And she also heard him say many things that she will say he said publicly and that what she heard him say she then said to other people.

She was asked if she talked much with Juan de Dios. She said that many times he came there to her house, as many times as he wanted.

She was asked what she thought of him. She said that in many things she thought he was crazy and that in other things that seemed to sound right, it seemed that they couldn't be the words of a crazy man.

To the second point that was read to her, she said that what happened in this case is that a man was in her house who is a shopkeeper who sells dresses, and he said that a man who was said to be a prophet of God was in prison and that he knew how the holy house would be won and many other things. She does not remember what this merchant's name was. And all the things that the merchant said to the defendant, she told to Miguel Ruíz, saying, "Lord, they say there is a man here in prison saying many things," telling him what the merchant had said. And Miguel Ruíz said later to the defendant that he had gone to the prison to see a young woman who was said to have been with some witches and that he had spoken with Juan de Dios, but that he had not been impressed because he spoke about many things that seemed to be nonsense. They brought Juan de Dios from the Royal Prison to the Holy Office, and after he left this Holy Office he went to stay at the Hospital de la Misericordia, and the defendant came to know him there and talk with him as all the others did. But the defendant never had enough desire to talk with him that she sent another person to jail to talk with him on her behalf, but since everyone wanted to see and talk with him because they said he was a prophet of God, the defendant also wanted to see and talk to him. And Juan de Dios said that he had never studied but had learned through knavery and that he had spent much of the inheritance from his father on horses and women and that he had spoken of this before the Inquisition and that he had debated with learned persons and thus had he done in the Inquisition. He said that he had made prophecies about all that would happen in the year 1580 and that he had given the king a prophecy about Granada and what would happen, and he said that he was a prophet of God in disguise. And the defendant did not believe that he was a prophet of God, but when she saw him leave the Inquisition a free man it seemed to her he was a man with whom she could converse.

To the third point that was read to her, she said that before she spoke with Juan de Dios she had spoken about him saying that a prophet of God was here, but she never affirmed that he was a prophet; and that after speaking with Juan de Dios the defendant was taken aback because while speaking of other things he said to the defendant, "Do you think that I do not know that a convent of the blood of Jesus Christ will be founded here and another called the Incarnation and another for lost women?" And when the defendant heard this she said to herself and to others with whom she had conversed that this is the same matter that my sister went to Rome about, to found the two convents. And she also said to some people, "Truly this man confuses me because he says some lofty things about the future and he has told me about how my sister has gone about the business of the two convents, yet on the other hand I see him going about at odds with everyone." And the defendant even said to him, "Juan de Dios, you say you are a prophet of God and so holy and so good and God has chosen you for many things; how is it that you are very impatient with everyone? Because where Our Lord is, there is always humility and much patience." And he responded that in God there was mercy and justice and that he would serve those who served God and that he would shun those who offended Him.

AFTERNOON SESSION OF JANUARY 27, 1576

To the fourth point that was read to her, she said that in this business she has remembered that one morning when she went to mass at the Hospital de la Misericordia of this city she found in the hospital Juan de Dios, who had slept there, and as she had heard so much about his holiness and that he was a prophet of God and seeing that the Inquisition had let him go free, she took him to be a prophet. And thus that day her brothers invited him to eat, thinking that it would be a good thing. And the defendant told a few of her friends and others who were in her house about that prophet, and others knew about it because word was getting around, and in front of all those who came Juan de Dios said that he was a hidden prophet of God and he had been approved as such by the Inquisition; and he told many things about what was to happen and how there would be pestilence during the past Lent or this next one to come. And he spoke of many other things. And as the defendant and her brothers saw that he said he had been freed by the Inquisition, they got to know him there [i.e., at the Hospital de la Misericordia], even though he went other times to their house. They let him in and believed him in some things, mostly when sometimes in the mornings they would ask him where he was going and he would say that he was going to eat lunch with the Lord Inquisitors. And the more they saw of him the less the defendant liked what he said, and she began not to believe he was a prophet, and she made them deny him entrance to the house in order not to see him. And what bothered the defendant most was that he talked a lot and that he said he told the truth like Saints Peter and Paul and many other things like these. And that she never heard a thing that went against the faith except for what she has said, and these were not things of great sanctity. And in what pertains to this point about her sister, she has already said this morning what she said about that and that was about the convents.

To the fifth point that was read to her, she said that she did not say what the accusation claims except to say that she was very confused, seeing that he clearly said that her sister had gone to Rome.

To the sixth point that was read to her, she said that she docs not remember if she said it in the way that the accusation says, except that she said, "My God, if this man says this about the convents, which is not possible for him to know, then God must have revealed things to him," or something like this.

To the seventh point that was read to her, she said that she never said that nor did she imagine it and no part of it is true and that she does not know how many guardian angels God has given her, but one guards each person.

To the eighth point that was read to her, she said she certainly never said that nor does she remember hearing that.

To the ninth point that was read to her, she said that they should read the next point after this because both are about the same thing and that she will talk about them both together.

The Lord Inquisitor ordered it read and after it was read,

She said that none of this pertains to her, and what happened is that one day Isabel Bautista, her sister, said to her that they should go to have some masses said that were much needed. And the defendant asked her what they were for, and Isabel Bautista told her that because she did not want to trouble her she had not told her what had happened to her, which was that one night while sleeping in bed between dreams she had seen a priest come who was already dead and who had been the confessor of the defendant for a long time. And he had asked her if she would have thirty masses said, and the defendant felt great pain and confusion over this and at the time she did not give credence to it and did not want to do it. And after seeing that the masses were not said, she decided to have them said so that thirty masses were said among the monasteries and she discharged the duty that the dead man had asked of Isabel Bautista. And because she was troubled, the defendant went to Santa María la Blanca and said to the nuns that she knew best that they commend to God the soul of a dead man in need of prayers, and they said to the defendant, "Why are you so troubled about the dead man? He must be your teacher," meaning the person whom she was commending to their prayers. And as the defendant understood whom they meant, in order not to disclose his identity she said that one could be detained in purgatory for few things, because she had heard it said that after souls left purgatory they still had to be detained in the chamber of desire to be purged of their lack of desire to see God; and that she had heard Miguel Ruíz say the same thing; and that it was said in a book by a saint; and that is what she can say to respond to these two points.

To the eleventh accusation that was read to her, she said that she does not remember that what it says there actually happened, but what she can say is that she had a very sick woman in her house who was named Luisa de Aguilera and that she had committed herself to go to Our Lady of Guadalupe and that her husband did not let her go and did not take her. And one day the defendant was speaking with Luisa de Aguilera about this, and Luisa de Aguilera was expressing the hope that she would later be well if they took her to Our Lady of Guadalupe. To please her, the defendant brought her one day a letter from her sister Isabel Bautista from Rome in which Isabel Bautista said that on the day of the Incarnation two years ago coming up it was said in Rome with certainty that the pope would free the Archbishop of Toledo and take him to eat with him, and this same news came from Rome in other letters that came to other people. The defendant was so delighted by this that she went to Luisa de Aguilera and said to her, "Get up! They have written us this happy news!" And she read it to her and said, "If this is so, my sister will go to the archbishop and ask him to confirm the rule that she took to Rome and she will come back with him, and we will all go from here to Guadalupe to receive him," saying this because she believed that the road went through Guadalupe. Later, she understood from her sister that this was not the way. And she has nothing more to say about what is in this accusation. And with respect to the poor, she did not say that but said that if the archbishop returned, many poor would be helped. And Luisa de Aguilera said, "Even if he returns, don't take me, because I am sick." And the defendant said that she and Miguel Ruíz would take her and that they would go slowly for she too was sick.

To accusation 12 that was read to her, she said she did not remember either of the things contained in it.

To accusation 13 that was read to her, she said that she had never said that nor had it ever passed through her imagination.

To accusation 14, she said that she never said that about the archbishop, but that what happened is found in a letter that she wrote to her sister Isabel Bautista in Rome in which she had said many things. She was shown a letter that had as its title "Very beloved sister of mine" and at the beginning it said, "The great delight that your letter gave us . . ." and it ends "may it be soon for His great honor. Amen," and it is two pages long. And having shown it to her she was asked if that was the letter in which she says that many things are found pertaining to the fourteenth accusation just read to her and she saw the letter and read it.

She said that it is true that the letter that was shown to her is hers and that she wrote it and sent it to her sister and it responds to what she was asked in this accusation.

She was shown another letter that is addressed "Very dear and beloved sister and my consolation" and begins "It would not be possible to express the great joy that your letter gave us . . ." which she acknowledged was written in her handwriting.

JANUARY 28, 1576

To accusation 15 that was read to her, she said that that had never happened to her nor does she remember having said it, but that what did happen in it is what she has confessed in her confessions and what is written in her hand in the first letter that she recognized as hers, which begins "The great joy. . ." And it is on the second page of it at the beginning where it says "One Monday after having received communion, it was said to me in my interior, 'Go, because my mother wants to speak with you in the Sagrario,'" and that is what it refers to.

To accusation 16 that was read to her, she said that what the accusation says did not happen in that way and that the truth of what happened is written in the first letter and that what is written there is the truth and she defers to that.

To accusation 17 that was read to her, she said that what happened in what the accusation says is written as it happened in the first letter and what is written in it is true and she refers to it. And the only other thing left to say about it is in another letter that the defendant wrote to her sister in her writing and that was then copied by Miguel Ruíz in his writing so that she had a copy of it. That letter was shown to her and read, and its addressee says, "Very beloved sister of my heart," and it begins, "I cannot tell you with any words the sadness we have had . . ." and ends "May we always do this even if it costs us our life. Amen." And having been shown this and seen it, she said that it is true that the letter is the one she wrote to her sister and that Miguel Ruíz copied it afterward and that what is said in it is what happened her. And what is written in the first letter is what happened at the Sagrario and after that the torments and the demons came to give their account of human temptation and the victory over them [i.e., the demons], because what she has said in her confessions happened to her in the Sagrario and is contained in the first and second letters.

To accusation 18, she said that she does not remember such a person or having said that.

To accusation 19, she said that what the accusation says did not happen that way, but as it is described in the first letter that she acknowledged. And it is true as it is written in there, and that is what she confesses, and she defers to it.

To accusation 20, she said that it happened as she has said and declared in the sixth letter that was shown to her and that she acknowledged. And it is true as it is written there, and that is what she confesses, and she refers herself to it.

To accusation 21, she said that what this point says is very true; she said it and it happened this way; and she did not understand it then nor did she write it in the letters, even though once six months had passed and she had seen that Our Lord had given her many mercies, she accepted it as she has said in her confessions to which she defers.

To accusation 22, she said that she has already confessed in her general confession to what this accusation says and that it did not happen the way this accusation says but rather how she confessed it in the confessions to which she refers.

To accusation 23, she said that it did not happen the way the accusation claims. How it happened was that after the defendant had had the struggle with the demons each time for each different vice, the things happened that she has already said and confessed, and she refers to her confessions.

To accusation 24, she said it did not happen the way the accusation says and that what happened is that when the defendant had that struggle with the demons over the vices, as she has said, after it was all over she understood clearly the way the demons could make people offend God with those vices. And in satisfaction for those vices she understood the way that virtues could counter the same vices, as she has written in the vows that she has written in her own hand, which were contained in the box and recopied by Miguel Ruíz on some papers like a small book. And that that is what happened in what this accusation says.

To accusation 25, she said that she did not say such a thing nor did such a thing happen to her any more than what she has already said in her confessions to which she refers.

To accusation 26, she said that there is nothing more in what the accusation says than the obligations that she has already said she made.

To accusation 27, she said that what happened here was that when the defendant and her sister Isabel Bautista and others who had joined them talked about getting a house to start the convent, three of them were together: Magdalena de San Francisco, Catalina de San Francisco, and María de San Jerónimo. And they were talking about how they would leave their mothers' houses to join this congregation that they wanted to form but their mothers would not let them. And while they were talking about this and other things, the defendant went to them. And Magdalena de San Francisco said, "Surely if I enter this community I will be Judas." And then the defendant said, "You will not be Magdalena, but you will be John the Evangelist because you are loving. And Catalina de San Francisco, who embraces the cross and trials, will be Saint Andrew, because she will follow Saint Andrew. And María de San Jerónimo who is persecuted because of her lineage will follow Saint Paul." And her sister Isabel Bautista, because she was resourceful and a woman ready for anything, would follow Saint Peter, and this she said not in order to show that they were elect, because only God can do this, but to describe their conditions and characters in conversation. And this is what happened in this accusation. And most of the time these women were vexed by the devil.

To accusation 28, she said that she has already said and declared in her confessions what this accusation says, so she defers to that.

To accusation 29, she said that she has already confessed what happened in this accusation in her confessions, to which she refers.

To accusation 30, She said that she has already said and declared in her confessions what is contained in this accusation, and she refers to that, and it happened as she has confessed and not as the accusation states.

To accusation 31, she said that, regarding this accusation, she has already said and declared what has happened in her confessions, to which she refers.

To accusation 32, she says that she never said that, it is not true, and it did not happen to her.

To accusation 33, she said that she never said that nor did it happen to her.

To accusation 34, she said that she does not remember having said that nor would she say such a thing.

To accusation 35, she said that she has not said that nor has anyone said that to her.

To accusation 36, she said that she has not seen her sister in ecstasy, that she did not say such a thing as the accusation states, and that it did not happen.

To accusation 37, she said this is a great lie, because she has never said that nor is such a thing true.

To accusation 38, She said that it is not that way and that what happened to her regarding the betrothal mentioned in the accusation is that after the victory of the devils, one day after receiving communion, the defendant gave thanks to Our Lord because He had given her that victory, asking Him that He give her those virtues to which she had committed herself against those vices. She felt a very great fervor in her heart and a great communication of the love of Our Lord, and she esteemed Our Lord greatly for what had happened with the devils. And in payment for that, the defendant felt within herself a desire that Our Lord be wed to her soul, and she felt a great movement in her heart out of that love that Our Lord communicated to her. And from that feeling, a great strength remained in her to resist all the vices and to exercise with ease the virtues that she had vowed to uphold. And that is what happened and what she has to say about this accusation.

FEBRUARY 7, 1576

To accusation 39 that was read to her, she said it is a lie and false because she has not said that nor did that pass through her mind, although the defendant has talked a few times about how her sister Isabel Bautista had gone to Rome to try to found the convents.

To accusation 40 that was read to her, she said she has never said that and that it is false and she had never experienced those things and that if this refers to Juan de Dios, three days after she saw him she understood him to be a prophet, but that she did not say what the accusation states. And about having understood him to be a prophet, she has already talked about that in her confessions, to which she refers

To accusation 41 that was read to her, she said that she has already described in her confessions what happened in this accusation and she refers to it. And she has already said that her sister wrote a letter, and she does not remember now what it said, and that she showed it to a friend and she [i.e., the friend] must have said those things.

To accusation 42 that was read to her, she said that she has never said that nor did it pass through her mind. She said that what she said to a friend (she does not remember which) on Christmas Eve about two months after her sister left is that she had recollected herself that night in prayer in consideration of the birth of Our Lord, recently born [i.e., as a tender newborn baby], and there in the interior of her soul was communicated the tenderness that Our Lord had for people and how he was made human. And as she considered this, she felt a great pain, because she had no news of her sister Isabel Bautista, whether she had arrived in Rome or whether she had been shipwrecked. And in that prayer she was consoled that her sister was fine, and it was a consolation that Our Lord gives in the interior. And the next morning she told her friends that now she was not so worried about her sister because the previous night she had been consoled in thinking that she was fine. And this is what happened and nothing else, and this is what she told the friend.

To accusation 43 that was read to her, she said that she had not said that, but that she has believed that her sister is a good woman and that the letters she wrote from Rome were full of sadness and nothing in them had to do with what the accusation says.

To accusation 44 that was read to her, she said that this is about the judgment and it did not happen that way but the way she said in her confession, to which she refers.

To accusation 45 that was read to her, she said that she has not said that, but what she has said and declared in her confession, to which she refers.

To accusation 46 that was read to her, she said that she has already confessed in her confessions, and it happened the way she confessed it and not the way the accusation states.

To accusation 47 that was read to her, she said that it did not happen that way nor had she said such a thing.

To accusation 48 that was read to her, she said that she has already said what has happened in this matter and she defers to that, and it happened the way she has said and not in any other way.

To accusation 49 that was read to her, she said she had not said such a thing.

To accusation 50 that was read to her, she said that it was false, that that had not happened to her nor had she said such a thing.

To accusation 51 that was read to her, she said that she had not said that, did not know that, and had not seen such revelations.

To accusation 52 that was read to her, she said that she will respond to that, that that was a servant of Leonor de Mendoza who was very sad because she said that she could not perform the penances that the others did. And the defendant told her that she was a sweet servant and that she could devote herself to prayer and abstinence, thanking Our Lord for the mystery of the Incarnation and the most holy sacrament and the passion and solitude of Our Lady. And in what it says that the defendant said, that disciplines were penance of commoners, it is true that she said that, but not to disparage the penance of the discipline, because it is good, but to make her understand that the discipline is for young women who are strong and that nearly all the women who were there in her house were older and they could not discipline themselves much. And once, when they tried it, they later became sick. And she was not going to push them too hard and left it that each one would do what she could, and that is what happened.

To accusation 53 that was read to her, she said that she never said such a thing or even thought it, although it is true that she said to those who were there in the community that all the prayers they offered were for the exaltation of the Catholic faith and the state of the church, which they said was in great need, especially when they made petitions, and that in the sermons they were asked to pray for the needs of the church and this was her intent; and Fray Juan Bautista encouraged them in this every time he came to their house.

To point 54 that was read to her, she said that it did not happen the way it states there, but what happened is that when Fray Juan Bautista saw that they were trying to gather together in that convent and be virtuous, he said to the defendant that since she had been in a convent before and knew about religious things, she should teach them the way of the order. And thus as she was reading the rule, they themselves asked the defendant to teach them, and so the defendant did that twice, as a teacher and not as an abbess, and thus the defendant first said her faults to teach them. And this bit about the stones was when Porras and the curate from Navahermosa tried to go to Rome about this business and they were all happy about it. And the defendant said to them that they should be grateful for the good fortune that God had given them two people who take this to heart and that they would not have to suffer the trials that the defendant and her sister had suffered and that it seemed that they were good because God had treated the defendant and her sisters like great rocks and this is what happened.

To accusation 55 that was read to her, she said that that was not her intent, but that one of the women who was there, who is a very good woman named María de Jesús, wanted them to observe the rule of Saint Jerome, and she said to the defendant that it would be a good idea. And as they were reading the rule they kept it, and another who was there named María de San Jerónimo said that the defendant should be the caretaker, and the defendant said to her that this was opportune, and it was out of their respect for her that this was done, not because it was the defendant's idea.

To accusation 56, she said that it was certainly very false and that what happened was that Fray Juan Bautista brought into the defendant's company a young woman named Luisa de los Angeles who was very unwilling to sew and be enclosed because she said she was not accustomed to that without being in church and that she had always had someone to feed her and attend to her needs. And one time when the defendant felt pressured to see what she could do to make her sew and not leave the enclosure of the house, the defendant said to her, "Señora Angeles, you know I have thought that perhaps you are not meant to be in this congregation, for the person who is not dead to the world is not meant for this crucible. We must be like people entombed, we cannot leave the house, and we must live by our work." And she grew angry, saying that this was said in order to throw her out of the house and that others should leave and she would stay. And it could be that the defendant said this more than once, and this is what happened about this and nothing else.

AFTERNOON SESSION OF FEBRUARY 7, 1576

To accusation 57 that was read to her, she said that this did not happen to her and that one time she showed the women in her house the place in the book of the chronicles of Saint Francis where Saint Clare and Saint Ines suffered so many trials from their families for following the path of virtue and that God was calling them. And she said, "This seems like what is now happening to María de Jesús," who was there because she had entered there against the will of her mother and relatives. And they said that they would drag her out of there if she would not leave on her own, and she was determined not to leave there. And for that reason Francisca showed them this, and not because of a revelation or any other reason.

To accusation 58 that was read to her, she said that she never said that, it is not true, it did not happen, and she never put anything on the altars.

To accusation 59 that was read to her, she said that she had not said that nor had she been given to understand that the rule had to be confirmed.

To accusation 60 that was read to her, she said that she had not said that nor had it happened.

To accusation 61 that was read to her, she said that regarding what is contained in the accusation the defendant has already said what happened in her confessions, to which she refers.

To accusation 62 that was read to her, she said that that is nonsense, that she never said such a thing nor did it happen.

To accusation 63 that was read to her, she said that about this she has already said in her confession what happened, and she defers to that, and that she never burned anything nor did anything happen more than what she has confessed.

To accusation 64 that was read to her, she said that she had not heard this of the girl and that the defendant praised her greatly for her simplicity in the ways of God and in other things, because she was so simple.

To accusation 65 that was read to her, she said that she has already said what happened and nothing more happened than what she has already said.

To accusation 66 that was read to her, she said that she had not done that and that they themselves said to her as they were reading the rule of Saint Jerome that it said that no one had their own property, so they wanted to renounce what they had, which was all their clothing, because they had nothing more. And that was to be collected so that anyone who needed something could have it. And she said that it should be this way, so her sister Isabel Bautista and two others took charge of it.

To accusation 67 that was read to her, she said that nothing more happened than what was said in the accusation before this and that she did not take anything that the women themselves put into the community chest and that it remained there without the defendant having asked for it or taken it.

To accusation 68 that was read to her, she said that that never happened to her nor did she say such a thing, that the women themselves felt a great impulse to do that and that they did not keep anything [i.e., any property] for themselves.

To accusation 69 that was read to her, she said that it did not happen that way but the way she has already said and declared in her confessions, to which she refers.

To accusation 70 that was read to her, she said that that has never happened to her nor has she said such a thing. And that because María de Jesús had such a strong desire to keep the rule of Saint Jerome, the defendant said to the others that they should tell her to keep the rule, and that is what happened. And this happened because of what María de Jesús said and not for any other reason.

To accusation 71 that was read to her, she said that she has already said what happened about the aforementioned in her confessions, and she referred to it.

To accusation 72 that was read to her, she said, "That is Juan de Dios who went to Rome and said that about the destruction"; and that she had not said anything of what was in this accusation; and that Juan de Dios said he would go to Rome to free the archbishop; and that she and the others laughed at that.

To accusation 73 that was read to her, she said that that had never occurred to her nor had it happened to her. What did happen was that in the convent of San Antonio there was a great controversy over who would be abbess, and a nun in the convent, who was a good friend of hers, told her that she should pray to God about it. And the defendant did. Afterward she returned to the convent and told that friend of hers that they were having this controversy because she had understood that Magdalena Evangelista should be the abbess—although the defendant did not know her nor had she spoken with her. And afterward the woman emerged as abbess, and those nuns who were against this said many things against the defendant and those who supported her said that the defendant was a saint. And this is what happened in this matter because she did not say all that about John the Evangelist.

She was asked how she came to predict that or how she was told that that woman should be abbess or how that happened—that she should say and declare how this came to pass.

She said that after the first time she spoke to her friend, she was made to understand in her interior that that woman should be the abbess because she had a talent to be abbess.

She was told that this seems to contradict what she first said because before she said that she had never seen the nun but that in her interior she understood that she should be abbess, and thus she told her friend the nun who asked her to pray about that. And now she says that later the voice in her interior seemed to say that she should be abbess.

She said that that friend told her the names of those who were qualified to be elected abbess and asked her which one out of those should be abbess; and the defendant prayed to God about it and was given in her interior the name of one nun more than the other, and for this reason she said what she said.

She was told that this was where the contradiction was, because now she says this, and she just finished saying that later, when she saw Magdalena Evangelista, she was told in her interior that she should be abbess because she had skill and talent for it.

She said that she believes what she said has not been understood or she hasn't explained herself well. What she means to say is that her friend told her the names of those who were qualified to be chosen and that when she held the matter up to Our Lord, as she has said, it seemed that the spirit settled on the name of one more than the other. And when she went to the convent she said this to her friend, and while the two of them were together, Magdalena Evangelista arrived there and made a sign to her friend, who said this is one of them and told the defendant her name, and when the defendant saw her, all that had happened in her interior was confirmed for her because she saw that from her manner she was a strong enough woman to take on the task, and this is what happened.

To accusation 74 that was read to her, she said that she had never seen that nor had she said it.

To accusation 75 that was read to her, she said that she neither saw that nor did she say it.

To accusation 76 that was read to her, she said that she has never said that nor is it the truth.

To accusation 77 that was read to her, she said that that had never happened nor had she said it.

To accusation 78 that was read to her, she said that this is as false as the devil because she has never said it nor has such a thing happened.

To accusation 79 that was read to her, she said that that had never happened to her nor had she said it.

To accusation 80 that was read to her, she said that that had never been revealed to her nor is it the truth.

To accusation 81 that was read to her, she said that this is not true nor has she said it.

To accusation 82 that was read to her, she said that she did not do that in that way nor had she said that, but that in speaking with some of them who were speaking about virtues the defendant said to them that she tried to follow questions of virtue according to the call that Our Lord made in her interior, and this is what happened and not anything else.

To accusation 83 that was read to her, she said those are the vows that I made and they are contained in my confessions to which I refer.

To accusation 84, she said that she has not seen anything about the nuns other than what she has said in her confessions to which she refers.

FEBRUARY 8, 1576

To accusation 85 that was read to her, she said that she had responded to that in her confessions about the way it happened and she refers to it.

To accusation 86 that was read to her, she said that regarding the vows it is true that the defendant read them once to women, telling them to dedicate their works to that end. And with respect to what it says about not saying what happened to outsiders, she did not say that. What she said was that when Porras wanted to go to Rome she had taken a notary there before whom they had given him power to go to Rome and make the necessary arrangements for the convent. Then Porras told her and her sister to advise the women that they not say anything about it outside their community, and the defendant advised them of this, and nothing other than this happened.

To accusation 87 that was read to her, she said that on the eve of Saint Michael's, two days before they brought her here more or less, she was reading a vow that she had made to Our Lord that was written on a piece of paper, and a great lump arose in her throat that would not move up or down; and she began to experience some blockage in the throat and could not talk at all. When this had passed, the defendant said, "It's true this is a temptation of the devil, and I must finish reading this," and thus she finished.

To accusation 88 that was read to her, she said that it did not happen that way but in the way that she has said.

To accusation 89 that was read to her, she said that she never said such a thing nor had such a thing happened to her.

To accusation 90 that was read to her, she said that she has never said that he had to leave by a miracle or in that way. What she had said many times is that she believed that the religious houses would never be established, particularly the one for priests, if God did not work some kind of miracle—like granting a revelation to some pope, as has happened in the foundation of other religious orders, or if God were to take the archbishop out of prison and were to move or guide him [i.e., to support the sisters' religious house]—because the defendant understood that no one would believe it. And she has not said anything else.

To accusation 91 that was read to her, she said it was not true and that one night she dreamed that she saw a place where there were many flames and she saw a soul burning in them and it was screaming, saying, "Get me out of here and have a mass said for me!" And the defendant woke up sweating and screaming and when she was asked what was going on, she said that she had dreamed something. But she did not pay attention to it nor did she have the mass said.

To accusation 92 that was read to her, she said that she does not remember having said that in that way and that not eating meat on the eve of the Incarnation is a custom that she has observed for many years. And the defendant said to women who were there that whoever wanted to could observe it [i.e., her custom].

To accusation 93 that was read to her, she said that she did not say that in that way and that they were the vows that she has described.

To accusation 94 that was read to her, she said, "That is the letter about what happened at the Sagrario."

To accusation 95 that was read to her, she said this is the same as what happened at the Sagrario and that it is true and it happened to her in that way.

To accusation 96 that was read to her, she said that this happened that way and that it is true and it is in her letter.

To accusation 97 that was read to her, she said it is true and it happened to her that way.

To accusation 98 that was read to her, she said that it was true and it happened to her that way.

To accusation 99 that was read to her, she said that it was that way and that it is true.

She was asked to say more about how this happened and what these new tribulations were.

She said that she felt great battles within her and with them many torments in her body and they took her out of her senses, so she went to the hospital to speak with Miguel Ruíz. And because her mind was troubled, she could not manage to talk with him about how she felt; and then they stopped depriving her of her senses, and all those demons who were inside her spoke through her and declared to Miguel Ruíz that they were the demons of pride. Then, when the defendant returned to herself [i.e., returned to her senses], Miguel Ruíz told her to have patience and explained to her all that the demons had said. And all the other demons that were inside her acted in this way until Our Lord gave her victory over them all because they experienced in her all the vices that they had made people engage in. And after the devils experienced the vices in the defendant, Our Lord gave the defendant victory so that she would never fall back into those vices. And thus five or six or maybe eight or ten days before All Saints Day of 1574, all the demons came back to give themselves over as defeated, saying that Our Lord had ordered them to give up and to come tell Miguel Ruíz what they had done. And it was in this way: after the defendant had received communion, Our Lord gave her to understand how He had been offended with each type of vice in which they [i.e., the demons] had made people live. And thus the defendant felt in her interior how she had to make a vow against each vice in conformity with the way Our Lord wanted to be satisfied. And in this way, since the defendant felt this after having received communion, she wrote it down, and when she finished writing it down, it was about seven in the morning. Then those demons that had possessed her of that vice took the defendant's senses away from her and said to Miguel Ruíz themselves through her mouth, "Write, Miguel, by the command of God who commanded me to submit to surrendering this vice." And Miguel

Ruíz wrote down what the demons said, and in all this the defendant suffered a great deal, because each thing they said caused her to feel torn apart in her body. At the end they concluded by saying that they had vexed her[30] with this vice and that they subjected themselves to Miguel Ruíz. And the defendant does not know whether some of them said that they subjected themselves to the defendant, giving themselves over to her because they were defeated by her. And this process occurred with each type of demon, and she thinks there were seven types of demons, and some, she believes about five types, stopped around All Saints. Others came around the feast of the Incarnation and that was about three months ago, and others came around the feast of Saint Bernard and this was the process with all of them. And this must be written down in Miguel Ruíz's hand because he wrote it down and then he showed it to her after she returned to her senses, and he said, "This is what the demons have said," and this is what happened. And once everything was written down, the defendant felt freed and tranquil and was left with a gentle feeling. And in all this time these were the greatest combats and torments of spirit that one could describe and all those vices inside her soul gave her great suffering, more than she could say. After they were over, she remained with the greatest peace and tranquility in the world, and since then, she has not experienced any vice nor has she felt combat from demons; and she has been very calm and without torment. And all the time that this happened with the devils nothing happened to her of what she has said about Our Lord.

FEBRUARY 9, 1576

She was told that in the past session, in responding to accusation 99, she said with regard to the new types of tribulations that she feels in her, that the demons had taken away her senses and talked with Miguel Ruíz; and they said that they were the demons of pride or those of another vice with which she was then tormented that day. And that she had said that after this Our Lord gave the defendant to understand that she had been victorious over that vice and that after that all the devils gave themselves up as overcome. They said that Our Lord ordered them to give themselves up and come to give an account to Miguel Ruíz of what they had done and that they themselves told

---

30. Or, more benignly, "troubled her." The word "vejar" could here have the more pointed meaning of actual vexation or possession by demons or the more general meaning of an annoyance, referring then to Francisca's suffering. Since Francisca reports no residual effect after the experience, but rather an internal peace and calm, the "vexation" appears to be a temporary state of distress, caused, as she understood it, by the immediate presence and activity of the demons, who then left her.

Miguel Ruíz through the very mouth of the defendant, "Miguel, write by the order of God who ordered me to subject myself to surrender this vice," and that Miguel Ruíz was writing what they told him they had done. And they concluded by saying that they would stop using this vice and they subjected themselves to Miguel Ruíz. And the defendant does not know whether some of them said to the defendant that they were vanquished by her. She should say and explain if she has had word of this victory that she had over the demons and their vices by any means other than what she has said.

She said nothing more than that she felt that after Miguel Ruíz had written all that down and she had made that vow that was against that vice they had tormented her with, she felt a great peace and tranquility without fatigue. And she saw that those torments that she had experienced were like those of someone who had left hell and entered into glory, which accorded with the peace that she had after having experienced this. And for this reason the defendant came to understand that she had had victory over those devils and not for any other reason.

She was asked what she calls victory over the devils.

She said that I call victory over the demons seeing oneself free from those enemies with whom one has had so much struggle and not to have any more trouble with them; and what she calls having victory over the enemies is to have seen herself not fall into any of these vices.

She was told to say more about the way in which these devils subjected themselves to Miguel Ruíz. What kind of subjection was that which they made?

She said she does not know more than that word she heard them say and that they had so tormented her senses when this was happening that she heard all that they spoke through her mouth as if she were a simpleton.[31]

She was asked to describe the vow that she made to Our Lord.

She said that she has already talked about that many times: when she received communion, before the demons came to her, Our Lord inspired her and it was communicated to her in her soul how the devils had made people offend God with that vice. And the communication made to the defendant was that she vow to live in righteousness and holiness with respect to that vice, just as with the vice of pride, when she vowed to make satisfaction for that pride by living in subjection and humility.

She was told to say more about that communication that she says was made in her soul about how the devils had made people offend God with that vice.

31. "como oirlo enbobeda."

She said she does not know how it began if not in this way, which she will now explain: after having had contact with all those demons twelve or fourteen days before All Saints, she felt herself one day free of that way of suffering. And that day, as she recollected herself to receive communion, she felt a great light enter her soul, and within that light she felt inside her interior a voice saying to her with great gentleness how all those struggles were over. And because this voice was inside her interior she felt that it was from Our Lord—and also because of the gentleness with which it spoke to her. And a communication occurred inside her by which she was made to understand that she should fast that next week because Our Lord wanted to make those demons subject themselves and explain all the ways they had made all creatures offend God. And the defendant, in making the fast that she has spoken about, felt again the experience inside herself of all those vices that she had experienced earlier in the same way with the vice of pride. And when she had received communion she was free of this torment, and this communion helped her to understand in her interior how offended Our Lord had been by that vice that she had experienced, and she was given a great understanding of it. And within that knowledge, Our Lord gave her to understand how He wanted to be satisfied for that vice and that was in the way the defendant wrote it down in her vows, and she does not know how to say any more because it is a knowledge that she was given inside her soul.

She was told that she has not said what she was asked about and that she has in fact added more doubts.

She said that she does not know another way to talk about this except as she has spoken.

She was told that in the response she has just given to the question asked her, she said she felt inside her interior that she was told with great gentleness that all the struggles had ended. And she felt that that voice inside her interior was from Our Lord because of the gentleness with which it spoke. She should say how she knows that this was from God and not from the demons, since, as she has said in this session and in others, during those same days she was tormented by demons and they spoke through her mouth and she was tormented in her interior by them in such a way that internally and externally they spoke with her. So it remains to be seen whether this tenderness that she speaks of is from God and not the devil.

She said, after it [i.e., what the inquisitor said] had been read and explained to her, that she understood it to be from God and not the devil because when she was tormented by the devil both in her interior and her exterior her soul was always plunged into great darkness, with all of her senses and her body tormented. But when this light she described entered her soul, she felt herself outside of all this darkness and its torments and felt a great tenderness and love of Our Lord inside her—so much so that her own body also participated in that joy. And she understands that this was from God too, because she was given a great knowledge of His Majesty, and this knowledge was placed inside her within her own understanding, and since she had never experienced this kind of thing when she was in combat with the demons, she knew that this was from Our Lord. Also, she felt inside her soul that that light she had in her soul was from God, although she does not know how to explain it in any other way than what she has said.

She was told not to trust that, because the devil has so many ways to deceive and trap souls that he will look for and find these inventions and other even greater ones because sometimes he combats the soul with bad thoughts and reveals himself in the figure of a man or woman, and other times, seeing that he cannot do harm that way, he gives these inspirations and poses as a holy person in order to place in her a work that seems good but that has entered with a bad one. And this must have been the same way, because for her to suggest that Our Lord would have such particular communications with a person who has not performed greater abstinences and deprived herself of more things than she has is deceit, especially because it is mixed up with these incidents with demons.

She said that she is not capable of responding to such true and sensitive things as this nor does she know how to respond any more than what she has already responded. And with respect to what was just said, she knows she herself does not deserve any favor Our Lord has given to her, but because His Majesty wants to grant it, thus He is served.

She was told to say more about the way or process the devils had in giving an account of sins and the ways that they had made people commit them and the manner of subjection they made to Miguel Ruíz and to her.

She said that this was written in Miguel Ruíz's hand and she refers to it. And she does not remember it any more than that the demons were saying and explaining through her mouth of the ways they had of making people commit this kind of sin in all kinds of states, married people and clerics. And some said that so many years had been given over to this vice and other years in another vice and that the people did not stop committing the vice or leave their state and the demons did not explain all of this to Miguel Ruíz. And the vows were also written in Miguel Ruíz's hand and the hand of the defendant.

She was told to describe what this victory that she had over the demons was like, to say and explain it so that it can be understood and to describe what this struggle was like and what the victory was like because she has not described it in detail.

She said that she had felt combat from each vice that those demons put in her soul, from pride to the vice of indecency and all the other vices. Our Lord gave the defendant the grace not to fall into any one of those vices. And this is what the defendant calls victory over the demons, because not a single legion of demons overcame her with their vice, even though they wearied her terribly. And afterward they gave an account to Miguel Ruíz, which he has written down as she has said, and the defendant does not know how that account went, except that Miguel Ruíz has it written down. And what Our Lord helped the defendant to understand when He showed her all that sin that she has described [i.e., in the judgment vision] was that it was for His great love of the world that He wanted those demons to give an account of the way they had made people offend the Majesty of God and after that to throw them [i.e., the demons] into hell after the defendant had first had victory over them. And because the defendant had victory over them, God then threw them into hell; this was her understanding of what Our Lord wanted, and thus it is written in what Miguel Ruíz wrote down. And the demons said that they were making people abandon God in the world, and thus at the time that they gave their account of sins through the defendant's mouth, they said great things about how they had to give an account of that evil that they had made happen, and they said, "God is the one who has such power to make us give an account of how we have trapped the world and now He throws us into hell."

FEBRUARY 11, 1576

She said she has nothing more to say than what she has said and asked why she would suffer the things she has suffered if it weren't in order to serve Our Lord? And these things could not be suffered if Our Lord did not want it because she is so frail that she could not have suffered them if it were not the will of Our Lord and if He had not favored her in it.

She was asked to describe the vows she had made and what purpose they had and if she could have made them without going through the trials and torments that the devils gave her as she has described.

She said that she has already said that before and after she received communion Our Lord gave her a great knowledge in her interior of the ways Our Lord was offended in that sin and that He wanted all creatures to make satisfaction to Him for that sin. And with that great knowledge she felt in her interior a great clarity about how Our Lord wanted to be satisfied, and with that clarity she made that vow to serve God as she has said with righteousness and humility and thus in that way to counter all the vices. And the reason she made that vow was as she has already said, and she said that she could have served God fine without having had these trials and torments, but that it all comes down to the law of God and His precepts and gospel, which all creatures are obliged to keep willingly.

She was told that if this is so, what were those trials she was given by those demons? Because that seems to be a superfluous thing.

She said that she has not understood it to be anything more than that Our Lord wanted the demons to give that account and then to throw them into hell.

She was asked why the account that the demons had to give was only of the past seventy years and not one hundred or two hundred.

She said that she does not know except that the demons said so.

She was told that in the past session and in others she has overesteemed the victory she had over those demons. In the first session with her on October 5 of this past year she said that Our Lord asked her if she would allow the demons that she had seen in that rapture to enter into her so that they could give an account of what they had done in the world to make creatures offend God. And the defendant waited for six months, and in this time Our Lord showed her many things before she accepted what was being asked of her. And afterward she grew bold enough to accept what Our Lord asked her because she had read in a chapter of Catherine of Siena [i.e., Raymond of Capua's *Life of Catherine of Siena*] about something similar in which Catherine asked demons to come over her. And thus she said to Our Lord that if it would serve His honor and that of the church, she would accept it in good will, if He would give her grace not to offend Him.

And she suggests that after that the demons came inside her and tormented her in the way she has said. And this was because Our Lord wanted to renew the earth and send His spirit. And thus the defendant heard Our Lord say these words, "Send out your spirit and renew the face of the earth." She should say and declare how this is, because it is a new way in the world for people to negotiate with God and God with humanity. The temptations that come into people in whatever form of sin are very ordinary desires, and the devil does this without asking for the consent of the man or woman tempted by these in accordance with the strength that God gives them. And with the efforts the tempted person makes, he or she emerges victorious. And this is something that happens every day to millions of people in the world, who emerge victorious with the favor of God, and Our Lord does not use as many preambles nor does He ask their consent and there are not as many ostentatious visions and raptures of spirit.

So she must say and explain more of this, so that it can be understood and believed, because things said without foundation and reason must be likely to be true in order to be believed and this and the other things she has said are far from credible. Having read all this word for word and the Lord Inquisitor having explained it to her and after she said that she had heard and understood it, she said, "Certainly, Sir, I do not know what to say to that, because I did not understand that 'Send your spirit' was connected to the other, except that I saw that Majesty and before it that cloud, and they signified the sins." And she offered herself in order to make satisfaction to Our Lord with the great desire that His Majesty would have mercy on the world. And then the defendant was shown the reason that the world had committed the sins and that it was those demons who had everything trapped in sin; and she was shown that His Majesty, for the great love He had for the world, wanted to get rid of the demons and wanted them to give an account and to throw them into hell; and she did not understand anything more than this or any other purpose nor does she maintain another purpose in this.

She was told that here they are trying to set her straight in case she is deceived in these things; and that since this deceit is in the understanding, it is necessary for the defendant to dispose herself to understanding the truth, and she is not doing this; and that it is humanly impossible for her to leave this deceit she appears to be in, if it is in fact deceit and not willful, because she still doubts that she is deceived. To get her to leave this deceit, they will give her reasons and clear demonstrations, and she must hear them and want to understand them because any other approach will not work. And having read this to her and the Lord Inquisitor having explained it to her with many reasons and having said that she has heard and understood it, she said that she has said what happened to her and that she has no other way to explain it. How is she to understand that things were not that way? What happened to her was that her judgment had been taken away and she suffered many trials and others, not herself, had to make an account through her own mouth.

She was told that in what she has just said can be seen the deceit in which she dwells because she has always confessed that those things were said by the demons through her mouth, and she already knows this. And it is true and is known that the devil is the father of all lies and deceits, and if he at times tells the truth or appears to lead people on the right path, it is to persuade people into greater lies and deceits; and thus she should believe that everything the devil said through her mouth is a lie and false and without foundation.

She said that she does not enter into whether it is true or not true but that she has said what happened.

She was told that this is not a good reason to give because in the first audience they had with her and in today's and in all of them that they have had, she has recounted these things as true and certain, and now she says that she does not enter into whether or not it is true. But she must now try to understand the deceit in which she has remained and how all that is a lie and false. And having read it to her and the Lord Inquisitor having explained it to her, she said, "What I say is that those devils said that and I could not resist them. Whether or not what they said is true, I cannot say. But in everything else I have said, it all happened. Why else would I have said it? Wretched am I if it did not happen!"

She was told that this in order for them to continue talking with her, she must say which things she does not know to be true and which things are certain.

She said, "Your grace has not understood my 'wretched am I.' What I say that I do not know if it is true or if it is a lie, is what the demons said and what was written about what happened. Even if they asked me for ten years, I have no more to say, so may God save my soul or you condemn me; remembering this is destroying me."

She was asked to say what, out of what was written down that the demons said, is a lie and what is true.

She said that what the demons said through her mouth about how they had made people sin in this vice or in that vice is what she does not know whether it is a lie or the truth because only God can know that. And that the rest of what she has said happened the way she has said.

She was told that from here on out that she should presume that she will not be asked any more about what the demons said about how they had made people sin, because it is very clear that the defendant cannot know about its certainty, but that they are asking now about that which she says happened to her and what she saw and not about any other thing. And returning to what was said to her, she was told that those two things that she has esteemed so much and has written about, which are the victory over the demons and the vow that she made to God, in which she thought she performed a work of great perfection and spent so many months considering before consenting to, seem false and without any semblance of truth for the reason that has been told her. And it is even more dubious because it has never been known before that Our Lord asked for the consent of anyone to be tempted; and she says that God asked this of her and she spent time thinking about accepting it. And having read this to her and the Lord Inquisitor having explained it to her, she said, "Lord, I do not have a way to respond to that. It is one thing to be tempted and another to receive a hundred thousand armies of demons." And insofar as Our Lord asked for her will she does not know how or why, and the fact that she spent some time without accepting this task was because

Our Lord permitted it, in order to make her stronger. And during those months Our Lord did many things for her, and He gave her that great love that she has described in her confessions. And this gave her greater strength than what she read about Saint Catherine. And may God make His Lordship understand and may he ask God why she would say this.

She was told that not for receiving demons nor for any other thing has God been known to ask for any person's consent. And besides that, all these legions of demons had been trying to tempt her to commit a vice, and the person avails himself and God comes to his aid and grants the favor to resist. And it is not necessary [for God] to ask for consent, but what is necessary here is strength. Thus many saints were tempted and they emerged in a manly way from these temptations, without God having asked them for their consent. And many other people are tempted each day and they [i.e., the demons] leave them. All this was read to her, and the Lord Inquisitor explained it in detail and how it is contained in her confessions, which she heard and understood.

She said, "Lord, I did not understand that God asked for my consent in those things, because each day I have had my temptations. But rather God wanted to take them away from the world; and so that we might understand that God had taken them away, they [i.e., the demons] gave that account." And these are secrets of God that she does not grasp, and she did not do anything more than experience this and move onward.

She was told that she is blinding her understanding to the truth and that even if she falls short of understanding the truth, she is not confessing it, but rather, with what she says and has said, she is showing the falseness of her case. For it is clear that when the Majesty of God Our Lord decides to make such great revelations, it will be in a person who is well-versed and well experienced in prayer, disciplines, fasting, and other acts of virtue, something that is not true of the defendant, even though the defendant appears to be a virtuous woman.

In the second place, she said in the first session that one Monday her spirit was enraptured and she felt her spirit enraptured after receiving communion and that when she arrived at the Sagrario she saw that in that rapture Our Lady interceded with her Son on behalf of the state of the church and asked for Him to give them the Archbishop Bartolomé who is imprisoned in Rome. And in this she saw how Our Lord was very moved by the prayers of His mother and He was overcome by His mother's entreaties. And in this the defendant's vanities are seen because, besides the fact that this proposition is not true, Our Lord would then have to free the archbishop by force and this has not yet occurred two years after this revelation.

The other point is that later, the following Tuesday in the same place, she was enraptured again, and she saw the abovementioned and all that happened about being asked for her consent regarding the demons entering into her to torment her and many other things that are contained in the course of her trial; and the prosecutor asked her about them as they were read.

And because it was time to suspend the session she will respond to this another day.

FEBRUARY 14, 1576

She said that she has been sick to her stomach and has had a fever, and so she has not been able to think about what they said to her and she cannot say anything more about what happened. May God condemn her to hell if she has not said what happened and what she saw. And if she has been deceived, even though she has not felt that she has been, the Lord Inquisitor is here for that reason, to take away her deceit. And she was grateful for that, because her desire really is to serve God in spirit and in truth.

She was told that here they are trying to take her out of this deceit as a service to God Our Lord, but this cannot happen if she does not accommodate her will and understanding for that and become determined to believe the proofs they offer, which would be enough to see her deceit. So they will read over again what was said to her at the end of the past session so that she can respond to it. And then all the above was read to her word for word, and the Lord Inquisitor explained it to her with many reasons, and having read and explained it to her and after she said that she had heard and understood it, she said that she does not know what more to say. She sees that everything actually happened the way she has said it and the way it is written in that letter and that all of it is a mystery of God. And she was not told there when it would happen nor was it [i.e., the vision] more than as if a person stopped at a window to watch a procession, and she does not see the reason for her experience any more clearly than if she had never seen it.

She was told that in this she will see that these are not affairs of God, because if they were, they would have had some effect, which they have not had nor are they expected to have one; at least there is no trace of one. With respect to founding the religious houses of men and women, she sees how far that is from happening, and with respect to the release of the archbishop that God had promised Our Lady, which she said she saw, two years have passed, and there is no sign that what Our Lord promised Our Lady has occurred. And besides all this, all these things that appeared to her at that time and at other times were without purpose and foundation, which is not fitting for

Our Lord nor does it even make sense on a human level. And in addition to this is seen the lack of foundation that this revelation has, because there are many men and women who find themselves very oppressed by temptations from the devil, but they do not make so much of it, because if they did we would not have the occasion to be virtuous. And thus asking the defendant for her consent to go through these temptations of the demons was without fruit and without meaning and so were the vows she made for the victory God gave her against the demons. She should not think these things were so extraordinary that any good Christian does not perform them each day in order to be a Christian. She must say and explain why these works of hers are so great and why God gave her such great mercies and why before giving them to her she was sent those revelations.

And to say that Our Lord asked for her consent so that the devils would enter her and give an account through her mouth of the ways they had made people offend God and then to throw them in hell is far-fetched and is not something a person of good judgment would say; and besides this, there was no purpose in coming to give this account. After this was read and explained to her by the Lord Inquisitor and she had heard and understood it, she asked them to say each thing one by one so that she could respond to each point. The Lord Inquisitor explained each thing of the abovementioned in particular and after she had heard and understood it, she said that the things about the religious houses and the archbishop and the demons are secrets of God and that she cannot account for them because she does not understand them nor can she say anything more than what happened to her. And she has already responded to the point about the vows. And in what he says about being far-fetched to have said that Our Lord asked for her consent so that the devils would come and give an account through her voice to show her weakness and in the rest, about giving an account, what does she know about what God wanted to accomplish in that? She cannot say anything more than how it happened to her.

She was told that this is not a good response because what is at issue here is not that this did not happen, but rather to show her that it was all an illusion and deceit of the devil. And for this reason they have given her all these reasons that she has seen and heard. And to say only that these are judgments of God is to choose to close the ears of her understanding to all the reasons that they could give her because the judgments of God are never without some great foundation and this is true even more so in something like what she has described.

She asked what more she could respond except to say what she saw? And regarding what they suggest, that it is a deceit of the devil, the defendant did not understand that it could be from God or could be from the devil, but what she did was leave what she saw and not take notice of it except to leave it to the will of God and perform works that conform to what God has commanded, which is to observe His law, and if she did some things understanding that they were the works of the devil, then they were, but that she did not do more than see what they proposed and perform works according to the law of God.

She was told to persuade herself to believe the truth and thus to believe that everything was from the devil and that God did not take part in it, but that the devil did it in order to deceive the defendant and her sister and the other women with these illusions. And the defendant and her sister Bautista were going about so involved with demons that spoke through her mouth that it is more likely to be believed that this was their [i.e., the demons'] work and not God's.

She said, "Lord, when this happened to me the demons had not even come into me yet, and they did not come during those five [*sic*] months."

She was told that before and after this happened [i.e., she was troubled by demons], and now they are trying to take her out of her deceit and she says she wants to be undeceived; but after convincing her with reasons she does not now want to confess. She should be careful because seeing her so pertinacious in this gives occasion to believe about her that nothing of what she says is true and that all she has said are inventions she has made up. And having read this to her and the Lord Inquisitor having explained it and having said that she heard and understood it, she said, "Certainly I do not know what to say to that. I have said that it could be from God and I have described it and how the works that I felt when they happened were from God as well as those that He did afterward." And she cannot say more. She did not do anything to ask for that nor does she understand it or know more than what she says; she spoke with Miguel Ruíz about everything that happened to her, and he told her that those things ought to be left to the ordination of God and that they should not be believed or disbelieved but that nothing went against the law of God. And he looked at the gospel saying that this was what they had to do and that if an angel told them the contrary they would have to believe it; and the defendant did this without laying great stress upon what happened to her, and she could not resist what happened to her, and she has nothing more to say than this.

She was told that it remains for her to say what opinion she has about those things and revelations, whether she believes that they were from God or from the devil.

She said that she will not make a determination about whether they were from God or from the devil any more than to say that whatever the Lord Inquisitor says and instructs her, that is what she will believe.

She was told that for the reasons she has heard and many others they have not gone into throughout the course of her trial, especially about the demons giving an account, it is a very certain and confirmed thing that none of those revelations was from God, and to believe anything else would be a very great deceit.

She said that she has said what really happened to her and what truly came from her mouth but that if the Lord Inquisitor says to her that this is deceit, she will believe that it is deceit, and thus she believes, but she does not stop believing what she saw.

She was asked what she believes of what she saw.

She said that she cannot stop believing what she saw and that she suffered those torments and that those things that were said through her mouth were true but that she never believed what they said.

She was told that here she is not being told not to believe that she did not suffer those torments that she says she experienced nor all that about the devil speaking through her mouth or other such things, but that what she is being told she should not believe is that that vision or revelation of Our Lady speaking with Our Lord about the archbishop and the other one about the cloud and the other one about the Majesty of God and the decree and all the other revelations that she has talked about, she must not believe are from God or Our Lady or any of the saints or from any angel, but rather an illusion of the devil or a weakness in her mind. And that to believe otherwise is a great error and an offense to God, and to speak about it is a thing worthy of great punishment, especially now that she is undeceived about it, because besides what the revelations say, in these same revelations there are things that offend Our Lord greatly.

She said that she believes all that the Lord Inquisitor tells her because he is a person with more light from God to understand those things than she is. And she says that she has not said or presumed to do anything that is an offense to Our Lord, and if she were to understand that it was, she would not do it for heaven or earth.

[At this point Valdés returned to the specific accusations in order to continue the investigation.]

To accusation 100 that was read to her, she said that she says what she has already said and refers to it.

To accusation 101 that was read to her, she said that she says what she has already said and refers to it.

To accusation 102 that was read to her, she said that she has already responded to this and she refers to it.

To accusation 103 that was read to her, she said that she says what she has already said and refers to it.

To accusation 104 that was read to her, she said that she has already responded to this and she refers to it.

To accusation 105 that was read to her, she said that she says what she has already said and refers to it.

FEBRUARY 15, 1576

She was told that in the previous session she said she believed everything the Lord Inquisitor told her, as a person who has more light from God to understand these things than she does; she should say and declare what she really believes because she has not declared it; she should say what specifically she believes.

She said that she believes what she has been told.

She was told that it was not enough to say that in such a general way but that she should say and explain in detail.

She said that all the things together that have happened to her and that she has confessed—in all of that she believes as the Lord Inquisitor has told her, and she believes that they are illusions of the devil or vanities in her mind. But besides having discussed these things with Miguel Ruíz, she also talked about them with three other friars, the prior of the Sisla and that of the Trinity and with the discalced friar Juan Bautista. And one of those, even all of them, did not approve or receive it. The current prior of the Sisla told the defendant that there was nothing wrong and that she did not have anything to fear, but that she should not think about these things, and that in praying as the defendant has confessed, what she felt could be from a powerful imagination that was enough to cause in her those things and to make her think that they were true, and so she committed herself to all that was good and not the rest.

She was told that this is a matter of saving her soul and clearing her conscience, so she must say and explain if this was something that any person put her up to or if they were things that proceeded from herself.

She said that under her oath they proceeded from herself without her having spoken to anyone else.

To accusation 106 that was read to her, she said that she says what she has already confessed in this session and in the previous one to which she refers, although it is true that in her naiveté she had told it as the truth, with the desire that all people make satisfaction for the passion of Christ.

[At this point in the trial, Francisca withdrew from the interrogation and used the formulaic answer, "She said she says what she has already said in this investigation and refers to it." She uses this answer to each accusation, 107 through 144. Thus the transcript reads from here on out:

To accusation 107 that was read to her, she said that she says what she has already said in the accusation before this one.

To accusation 108 that was read to her, she said that she says what she has said in this session to which she refers.

Etc.

To accusation 144 that was read to her, she said that she says what she has said in this session to which she refers and that she does not know about others any more that what she has said.]

At the end and conclusion of the accusation that was read to her, she said that she has nothing more to say than what she has already said about herself or about any other person and what she has said is the truth under the oath she has made.

[On February 21, Francisca said she had nothing to add in her defense. Her entire testimony from each session was read, and she ratified it with the following oath:]

She said that what she has said and confessed to the accusation by the prosecutor is true and it was written as she said it; and she has nothing to change or take away because it is true and she ratifies it; and if it were necessary she would say it all over again; and it is true under the oath she has made.

FRANCISCA'S APPEAL TO RECEIVE THE SACRAMENTS[32]

[On January 9, 1577, Francisca was brought into chambers because she had asked for a hearing.]

She said that it is true that she has asked for this session and that she wants it because she wants to say how difficult it is for her to be deprived of the rituals and sacraments of the church and that it seems to her she cannot suffer this and the trials of prison and therefore much less will she be able to suffer those of hell. Therefore she begs their lordships not to separate her from the church but instead to incorporate her into it. And if, because of pride or vanity or her lack of understanding, she was deceived by the devil, as she has been made to understand by the holy admonitions they have made to her in this Holy Office, she asks that if she ever falls into a similar offense to Our

32. Fol. 242r.

Lord in the future that they give her the most rigorous punishment that in this Holy Office they can; but that out of reverence for Our Lord and His holy blood she begs their lordships that she be treated mercifully because she has confessed everything carefully; and that it was not malice but pure ignorance and that she did not understand or capture the subtleties of the deceits of the devil. And she asked to be received in the mercy of Our Lord, taking into account the trials she has borne in these prisons, all of which she begged with tears and anguish. She was told to return to her cell.

ADDITIONAL ACCUSATIONS AGAINST FRANCISCA, PRESENTED ON MARCH 6, 1577[33]

[On February 28, 1577, the cleric Don Vicencio testified that Francisca de los Apóstoles had conversed with another prisoner, el Licenciado Hernando Velasco, and they had made plans to marry and that Francisca, when leaving her cell for her meals, revealed her body to him. This testimony to licentiousness was used to further the case against Francisca by attempting to discredit her sexual virtue. And so, on March 6, 1577, Francisca was brought out to hear new charges brought against her by the prosecutor.]

1. First, the woman, pretending to be and giving the impression that she was holy and saying publicly that she had revelations of Our Lord; and that God had betrothed Himself to her; and that God had asked her father for permission to do that; and that God had said that He had found a just and holy soul who would make satisfaction for the world and for sinners; and that He had asked for the signs of betrothal; and that He had given her virtue enough to be holy or resist temptations; after saying and doing all these and other things in public, in these prisons she has secretly talked with and planned to marry a certain person, and she calls him her husband and he calls her his wife, and she tries to see and speak with him, and she has in fact done so.

2. In addition, Francisca de los Apóstoles used many words of love and sensuality to the man talking about their members [i.e., sexual organs] by name.

3. In addition, the aforementioned said and wrote to the man that she was tired of fasting for twenty years and that, in leaving the prison, she and he would be joined and have carnal relations one with the other, describing it with dirty words, and that they would do this wantonly.

33. Fols. 243r–244r.

4. In addition, that the defendant wrote to the said person that she had been with her flower [i.e., menstrual period] and that she was now clean and she had washed herself well and put on a clean shirt and, lying down in bed, she had said, "Come here, so-and-so," naming the person, and asking him to have relations with her . . .[34]

5. In addition, that the abovementioned sent the person some pieces of cloth about the size of a hand and that she sent him a paper that said that those cloths she sent she had kept in her private parts and that she also sent a piece of colored cloth about the size of a fingernail and that she wrote him to say that that colored cloth was the flower of the tree [i.e., menstrual blood].

6. She wrote him to say that she was pregnant from him and that her middle was already swelling, and she writes him every day.

7. In addition, that in addition to the aforementioned, it is to be presumed that Francisca de los Apóstoles has said and done and committed many other dirty and dishonest things as a shameless and sensuous woman, for which reason I ask your grace to punish her as I have asked and I swear before God that I do not make this accusation out of malice.

FRANCISCA'S RESPONSE TO THE ADDITIONAL ACCUSATIONS AND LETTER[35]

After the above accusation was read aloud, Francisca responded:

To the first point of the accusation, she said what she has already said and explained.

To the second point of the accusation, she said it is true that she has written many love letters and childish things to Hernando Velasco, but they were not with dishonest words as the accusation claims.

To the third point of the accusation, she said she does not remember having said that and that she is a maiden.

To the fourth point, she said that it is true that she wrote a note to Hernando Velasco in which she had said that she had been ill with the illness of women and that she told him similar things like those that are contained in this point and that she called him "Bernaldinico" because he had an uncle with this name.

---

34. The text contains some colorful language here, which I cannot render in any satisfactory English. It reads, "Hazme un bernardinico y tu bello que no lo quisiste hazer. Y hallo que se [h]avia hallado en bazio."

35. Fols. 244r–245v.

To the fifth point of the accusation, she said it was true that she sent him a colored cloth but she sent it as a sign to see if the man who was carrying her card was Velasco and not for the reason the accusation gives and that she sent cards wrapped up in some dirty cloths so that the cards would be more easily concealed and not for the reason that the accusation says.

To the sixth point, she said that it is true that she wrote that she had dreamed that she was pregnant from him.

To the seventh point, she said that she had not done more than what she had said and testified.

Asked if she ever saw Licenciado Velasco in some secret place, she said not except to have seen him by accident.

Asked what she used to write to Licenciado Velasco and who gave her paper and ink for that, she said that she ground up a little bit of coal and mixed it with water and vinegar and that she wrote with the feather of a chicken on the scraps of paper on which they gave her spices or other similar things.

Asked who taught her to make the ink from carbon, she said that, because her father was a painter, he ground up coal that way, and that they used it to draw many times.

Asked if herself or through another person she had written to any other prisoner after she had been imprisoned, she said that she had not, either alone or through another person, written to anyone in the prison or outside it.

Asked if she or any other person she knows has received any letters from a person who is imprisoned in this Holy Office or outside of it, she said that she does not know of anyone who has received a letter from anyone imprisoned in this Holy Office or outside of it and that this is the truth under the oath she has made.

FRANCISCA'S HANDWRITTEN RESPONSE TO NEW ACCUSATIONS[36]

To the first point I say that I have already responded that it is false and what proves it is that I have never considered myself a saint nor have I done works to be one, but rather I consider myself a great sinner and, as a woman, imprudent. And having little experience in the things of Our Lord, I spoke with those I took to be friends about the things I have described in these sessions. And these friends have recounted these things in a spirit contrary to the way I spoke with them, especially Magdalena de San Francisco, the *beata* who was

36. Fols. 246r–247r.

possessed by the devil, as I can prove because Alonso Hernández, chaplain of the Capilla de los Reyes, conjured her, along with other people who lived in the house, and this woman said to us (or the devil through her mouth) every day that we would be taken to the Inquisition. I laughed at this, and she turned to me and said that I should not underestimate what she said because it was not her but the devil. This happened many times in the presence of Catalina de San Francisco and María de San Jerónimo, *beatas*.

Thus I say that I have told truthfully all the things that have happened to me, and because I thought that I was proceeding along a certain path toward my own salvation, I did not understand, as an ignorant woman of little experience, the deceits of Satan, who perhaps wanted to deceive me as he has others. But now that I have seen, in the sessions that they [i.e., the inquisitors] have had with me, which have made it known to me that I was deceived on the road that I thought was secure in the service of God, I have decided to close my understanding with respect to all these things that have happened to me and only to believe what the Holy Office has instructed me. And if an angel were to tell me the opposite, I would not believe it, but would rather think it was the devil wanting to deceive me.

And seeing myself in the difficulties that this affair has caused me and understanding my liberty to be in great danger, I have decided to change my estate and marry because perhaps I will save myself better than in this other estate, because all that I have said in my confessions that was related to this was with the condition that if the convent were founded, I would live out my vows there and if not, I would not. And now, seeing that not only has this convent not been founded, but that it has been the occasion for the great trials in which I find myself—because only God knows the great combats of spirit and tribulations that I have experienced in this cell, especially these past eight months in which I have been alone—it has so happened that during this time a man named Licenciado Velasco came here, and in hearing him talk I recognized him, because one of his brothers was a neighbor of mine, a man named Herrera, who was studying to be a priest in this city. And from things I heard about Licenciado Velasco from his brother I understood that it was him, but not because I had ever seen him before in my life in this house nor in any other, but rather because of the knowledge I had of him. And I spoke with him from my cell and he from his, which have a cell in between them.

So, finally, for many reasons that we discussed, we gave each other our word that we would marry and all the people who are here understand our communication and its end, which was to be husband and wife. And then they moved him along with his roommate and two others who were housed underneath this cell from here to the dungeon from what I understood, but

I wasn't sure because they always closed the door when someone passed by our cells. And the guard is very careful about this and every other thing, so that we cannot be certain about anything except in our imaginations.

And one month after he was transferred, when I went past the secretary, I heard, "Take what is by the desk," and because it was said suddenly, I didn't understand it nor did I know who told me that because the jail keeper was there and he is new to the place. And thus I did not know more than what was said and even that I did not hear well. I looked around that place each time I passed by it. And underneath a board that was next to the desk I found a paper in which he confirmed his word that he had given me and many other things about his love and his will, and I responded, confirming my response to what he had written to me. And in all these things I treated him as a wife treats her husband, and I spoke of many childish things and spoke of my love, but not in the way that the points accuse me of. I have behaved in all of this like a person who is to be married to the man who wrote to me—although I cannot swear it for the truth—because it could have been another person trying to trick me, since I have not heard from him since they moved him from here and I do not know if he is gone or if he is home or why they moved him from near my cell about half a year ago. I have written him five times more or less since before Christmas, and I have had a response from each one. But after that Christmas I have not received a thing responding to what I have written, which I take to mean that one of the inmates has turned on us and now he has informed your graces. And I am afraid of an Italian priest who was here in his company who was always against this business [i.e., the relationship] and who may have done me this wrong.[37] I confess my guilt to your reverence, and for what I have done I ask for mercy from God, but I ask that you do not do with me what this crime merits but according to the mercy of God and what your graces often use against sinners and that you be attentive to the fact that I am a woman and that I am almost desperate from having experienced many trials and illnesses in my life. And if your graces understood this you would encourage the will I have demonstrated in wanting to marry. I ask for the love of Our Lord that I may be favored in all this by your graces, since you are in the place of God to help souls. And in all of this I reply to the accusation from the first point to the end that the prosecutor has made against me without having anything more to say to it.

Francisca de los Apóstoles

---

37. Francisca's suspicions were correct. On February 28, 1577, a cleric named Don Vicencio testified against her and informed the inquisitor of the correspondence between Francisca and Hernando de Velasco. See fol. 163r.

RATIFICATION OF HER CASE AND FINAL QUESTIONS, AUGUST 9, 1577[38]

And afterward she was read word for word all that she has said, and she responded to the publication, letters, and papers about which she has been examined from the audience on the morning of the last day of July until this audience. And having said that she has understood it, she said that it is the truth and that she affirms and ratifies it, and, if necessary that she would say it again and that she has said it just as it happened to her. And that it is true that she told all those people who testified all the things that she has confessed happened to her, as she has known these witnesses, as a woman ignorant of matters pertaining to Our Lord and a person of little insight, because she thought that all those things she saw, since they pertained to the justice against the world, seemed to her to be urgent, and for this reason she told them all. And she wanted to tell everyone, according to her lack of judgment in this matter, with the desire that all might do penance as she had seen that Our Lord was offended. And because she was ignorant about matters pertaining to Our Lord, she did not understand that they could be deceits of the devil to lead her into the state to which he has led her. And thus not recognizing it for what it was but understanding it all to be from our Lord, she spoke of it with everyone so freely. But now that in this Holy Office she has been made to understand the opposite, she renounces all that she has confessed and spoken of in her confessions and only believes and will believe what they have taught her in this Holy Office. And thus she places herself in the hands of Our Lord and the Lord Inquisitor, as the person who is appointed to give light in the church of God and take her from errors and ignorance. And because she does not understand herself to have fallen into error and if she has fallen she did not recognize it, she asks for the mercy of Our Lord that she be received into the bosom of the church and that what she has suffered during these past two years in prison be taken as penance for her ignorance, lunacy, and vanity. And with this she has nothing more to say.

She was told that what she has just said, which concludes her confessions, is well said, but that there remains a final satisfaction to conclude her

---

38. Folios 248r–267r are a copy of the Publication of Witness Statements, a listing of charges made against Francisca that the prosecutor had converted into the 144 formal accusations made against her. The Witness Statements were read aloud to her, and, on July 31, 1577, she began a response to each accusation point by point, referring at all times to her previous confession, but continuing to explain herself and her actions as a woman of good faith. This questioning continued through August 8, 1577. Then her letters and obligations were also reread, and she recognized them and made a few more explanatory comments in response to questions by the inquisitor. On August 9, her new testimony was read back to her for ratification.

case and to completely understand the truth of it, and that is that she declare if the things that have been testified and read to her and the things she has said and confessed and all the rest of what happened to her in this business are of her own invention or of some other person, because she has already been told that they are not works of God nor does any single thing appear to be so; and if it is only an invention of the devil it appears to have little cunning, and many things even contradict each other, and so it leaves the suspicion that they are women's matters (*cosas de mujeres*). She should say what is the case here and who was the inventor of this business and who continued it and by whose order it was taken forward because in knowing this about what she has said, they will have entire satisfaction that what she has just said is said with a good intention and is true so that she can unburden her conscience and tell the entire truth.

She swore by her salvation and the oath she has made that it has not been her own invention nor was she taught by anyone but it was exactly as she has confessed from the beginning to the end and that if she were to understand that it were anything else she would declare that because of the great desire she has for her salvation. For she understands that whatever she does not confess here will in no way be absolved and thus her soul would remain condemned forever; and she would not do that even with all the dishonors of the world that might come or all the punishments that this Holy Office might give her because she holds her salvation in greater esteem. And thus she has declared the entire truth as it happened without having to say or declare anything more about it.

She was told to think carefully about her case and unburden her conscience, and having reread everything she said in this audience back to her, adding to it the ratification of her confessions, and having said that she understood it, she said that it was well written and that she said it that way and that it is the truth and she affirms and ratifies it and, if necessary, she would say it again, and then she was ordered to return to her cell.

[The Inquisitors deliberated on the sentence on October 5, 1577.]

SENTENCE AGAINST FRANCISCO DE LOS APÓSTOLES

We have followed with attention the acts and merits of this case and the guilt of Francisca de Avila, alias de los Apóstoles, and if we were to act within the rigor with which we can rightfully proceed we could punish her most gravely, but we recognize her good confession and the signs of repentance she has given. And for other reasons that move us, using kindness and mercy with her, we order that she be punished for these vanities and errors to give others an example and that she walk in this present auto de fe in person with a wax candle in her hands, a rope around her neck, where her sentence will be read, and that she abjure her fault *de levi*. And after that we order that she be given one hundred lashes on the customary streets of this city and her crime be read publicly and she be exiled from this said city of Toledo and five leagues around it for the time of three years, and if that exile is broken, this time will be doubled. And we warn her that from now on she must refrain from committing the crimes or any other similar ones and that if she does the opposite she will be punished with all due rigor. And this our sentence is to be spread as we pronounce it and order it.

Signed: El Doctor Juan de Llano de Valdés, El Licenciado Antonio Matos de Noroña, El Licenciado Alonso de Reinoso, and El Doctor Juan de Obregón.

[The auto de fe was held in the main square of the city on April 13, 1578, and Francisca abjured her errors. The lashes were administered on April 14, 1578.]

APPENDIX A

THEOLOGICAL ASSESSMENT OF FRANCISCA DE LOS APÓSTOLES'S PROPOSITIONS

First witness, Magdalena de San Francisco

1. To say that Our Lady begged her Son not to destroy the world and that she would give him four people who would make satisfaction for the sins of the world who are Bartolomé the imprisoned archbishop, Miguel Ruíz, Isabel Baptista, and the said Francisca, her sister; this proposition is heretical in the part that says that four people could make satisfaction for the sins of the world, and the part that says that Our Lady said these words to her Son is shameful blasphemy and goes against the innocence and honor of Our Lady. And to say that what is contained in the proposition was made known to her by Our Lord and that she felt this in her heart and saw it clearly in her spirit is a heretical proposition of the *alumbrados*.

2. She says that while offering up prayers and fasts for the sins of pride in the world, she felt that many legions of devils came over her, which tempted her to commit this sin. And in suffering these temptations the devils confessed through her mouth to Miguel Ruíz that they would not weigh down humanity and in that way she was making satisfaction for other sins of the world. All this is rash and arrogant.

3. For Francisca to say that she was taught in spirit that God would make her holy and reform the apostolic life, insofar as she says that she was taught in spirit, this is the language of the *alumbrados* and the rest is heretical.

4. To say that she was taking the apostolic life out of the hands of the devils where it has been darkened by the state of humanity and that this was hard work is very rash and arrogant.

5. To say that Our Lord said, "Commit yourself to making satisfaction for the sins of humanity and if you do it, I will abandon my wrath," and that she said, "Yes, I commit myself with your divine favor" is a proposition that has the same judgment as the earlier ones that also talk about satisfaction, and insofar as it says that Our Lord said this to her, it is blasphemy against Our Lord.

6. Insofar as she says she felt fear within herself in doing this and that she thought Our Lady said, "Don't be afraid; I will be your advocate and will grant you favor so that you can do it" is injurious and blasphemy against Our Lady.

7. And for Francisca to speak as if in the voice of God and to give the names of the apostles to women with words that conveyed that they had to exercise the office

of Saint Peter and the other apostles whom she named is heretical, because she seeks to make a new church and give the office of Saint Peter and other apostles to women.

8. To believe with readiness what is given in one's interior, understanding it to be the teachings of Our Lord, and to believe in dreams is the heresy of the *alumbrados*.

Catalina de San Francisco

9. To say that Our Lady would miraculously release the archbishop of Toledo is injurious to Our Lady and the Holy Office.

10. This second witness says of this same woman the second proposition of the first witness [i.e., point 2 above], which is already assessed.

Until here Catalina de San Francisco

11. To say that Saint Inez and other saints who were martyrs had put their necks against the knife and that one day many women had died and suffered much but that she had suffered more than these saints for the love of God is a rash proposition and injurious to the holy martyrs.

12. To say that Our Lady dressed a woman in the habit of certain nuns of a convent that she was to found and that for this reason Our Lady came down from heaven or that person had risen to heaven in order to be robed is a rash, blasphemous, and arrogant proposition and is the language of the *alumbrados*.

13. She said that a crazy man who declared many heresies was a prophet of God and that she would believe anything he said as if it were the creed and the faith, and this is a heretical proposition.

14. For a person to say of herself that she is a saint is a rash and arrogant proposition.

15. To say that a woman is holier than Catherine of Siena is a rash proposition injurious to the saint.

16. To say that those who live in Toledo and are sick are possessed by spirits and that it is a waste of money to call in doctors is rash and dangerous.

17. To say that Our Lady of the Sagrario promised to give her a great gift that was the archbishop of Toledo is of the same tenor as proposition 3.

18. To say that a crazy man . . . This is the same as what was assessed in the testimony of the third witness, proposition 13.

19. To say that she had seen a woman rise to heaven and that her face shone and that she had seen God and He had told her things about a convent and the habit and the order they would represent is a proposition of the *alumbrados* and rash and injurious to Our Lord.

20. For a person to say that while taking the form of a cross, her spirit had arisen to heaven and that she had seen Our Lord is a proposition of the *alumbrados*.

21. For a person to say of herself that having risen to heaven and seeing Our Lord who wanted to destroy the world, she asked Him not to destroy it; and that Mary Magdalene told Him to destroy it because the poor were dying of hunger; and that she told Mary Magdalene that she used to gad about in the world and had been a sinner; and also that Saint Peter said to Our Lord that He should destroy the world because humans were liars and blasphemers; and that she said to Saint Peter, "Be quiet

old man; you also denied Our Lord"; and that Our Lady said to Our Lord that He should destroy it because people grow more evil each day are propositions of the *alumbrados* and injurious to the saints and particularly to Our Lady because it shows that this person disparages Our Lady's mercy for sinners.

22. For a person to say of herself that she had promised and told God that since He had died she too wanted to die and suffer travails so that He would not destroy the world sounds like earlier propositions that were already judged that address satisfaction [i.e., of sin].

23. For a woman to say of herself that, having risen to heaven in spirit, Our Lord said to her, "Do not go. My pleasure is to be with humans and even more with you because you please me greatly" is a proposition of the *alumbrados* and arrogant.

Until here Isabel de Rincón

24. To say that a prophet had come who announced that all laws would become one and other things that are heresies and lies and that no one should doubt it and that what the prophet foretold would happen and that she believed it as she believed she should die is a heretical proposition.

[Taken from the testimony of Catalina de Jesús.]
Signed: Dr. Barrionero, Fr. Marcus de Valladolid, Fr. Alfonso de Motulus, Fr. Antonio Manrrique

APPENDIX B
ANALYSIS OF ACCUSATIONS
AGAINST FRANCISCA

Type of Accusation	Accusation No.	Percentage of Accusations
Visions		
Francisca received visions or revelations from God	9, 10–12, 15, 17, 42, 47, 48, 50, 57–59, 63, 68, 70, 73, 75, 79, 82, 90, 116, 125	15
Francisca had a vision of the Last Judgment	15, 16, 18, 20–22, 28–30, 44–46, 61, 71, 77, 85, 96, 105–8, 119, 122	15
Francisca defended the authenticity of her visions	135, 137–144	6
Francisca's sister Isabel had visions that Francisca believed	1, 41, 74	2
Intercessory Role		
Francisca claimed an intercessory or redemptive role for herself and/or her reform movement	14, 16, 19, 21, 22, 25, 33, 38, 45, 53, 84, 91, 97, 98, 102, 109, 111–16, 119, 123	16
Monastic Reforms		
Francisca's reforms were supported or justified by her visions	5, 6, 24, 27, 31, 60, 80, 89, 93, 120	6
Accusations against Francisca's community, its way of life, or Francisca's conduct as abbess	26, 27, 37, 54, 56, 65–67, 70, 76, 83, 86, 88, 118, 121, 122	10
Francisca's Raptures	12, 17, 94–96, 105, 110, 126	5
Ecclesiastical Reform		
Francisca's support of Carranza	11, 13, 59, 72, 90, 95	4
Visions that condemned clerics for ecclesiastical abuses	61, 71, 108, 131	3

Continued

Type of Accusation	Accusation No.	Percentage of Accusations
Other		
Francisca's torments at the hands of demons	23, 62, 87, 99, 100, 101, 103, 124	5
Francisca's belief that her sister was holy or able to perform miracles	7, 8, 18, 32, 34, 35, 43, 49, 51, 78	6
Francisca's association with Juan de Dios	2–4, 40, 72	3
Miscellaneous		4

APPENDIX C
CAST OF CHARACTERS:
BIOGRAPHICAL NOTES

Aguilar, Francisca de: At the time she testified in October 1575, Francisca de Aguilar was thirty-eight. She had never been married, and she and her niece Inés lived in the *beaterio* for four months. The substance of her testimony concerned the judgment vision and Francisca and Isabel's relationship with Alonso de la Cuadra. Francisca de Aguilar also testified that the women often had masses said and made processions specifically for the release of Archbishop Bartolomé Carranza, which they understood would have to happen through some miracle of Mary. See fol. 87v.

Aguilar, Inés de: The sixteen-year-old niece of Francisca de Aguilar, Inés testified in October 1575. She described papers that the women hid during the vicar's visit, and she mentioned that the sisters read aloud from spiritual books, including the book of Angela of Foligno. See fol. 99v.

Aguilera, Luisa de: An older *beata,* Luisa was bedridden when she became associated with Francisca in 1574. She was forty-seven when she testified against Francisca on December 15, 1574, and she related her concerns about Francisca to her confessor, the Jesuit Sebastián Hernández, before she died in early 1575. Hernández then went to the Inquisition to express his concerns as well. Luisa was technically still married, the wife of Gabriel Sánchez, but he had abandoned her, and she lived on the property of Pedro de Silva. She was the mother of Isabel Rincón and María de Jesús.

Ana: Maidservant of Francisca and Isabel, she apparently was friends with the younger *beatas* María de Jesús and Inés de Aguilar. She had a vision of John the Baptist and Jesus in the Jordan River.

Angeles, Luisa de los: An unmarried woman originally from Pastrana, Luisa was brought to the *beaterio* by Fray Juan Bautista when she was twenty-five or twenty-six years old. She apparently had a difficult time in convent life, although she had many experiences of prayer and was at first highly regarded by the sisters. She testified before the Inquisitional tribunal on July 15, 1575.

Avila, Cebrián de: He was Francisca's brother and a painter. On Ash Wednesday of 1574 he experienced a form of conversion after which he made a general confession to Miguel Ruíz.

Bautista, Isabel: Francisca's sister, she was six years younger than Francisca and had the original plan to found a convent of women. She left for Rome in 1573 in the hope of securing official ecclesiastical approval of the rule she had written for the new foundation.

Bautista, Fray Juan: A discalced Franciscan friar from Italy, he first met the women when they went to visit him at the monastery of San Francisco outside the city walls. After getting to know them, he reassured Francisca about her desires to reform and intended to go to Rome with Marcos de Porras to secure official permission to found the convent. He was thirty-five when he testified against the women.

Busto de Villegas, Sancho: He served as governor of the Toledo archdiocese from 1569 to 1577. As the acting archdiocesan representative, he arranged and paid for a large distribution of alms on Christmas of 1573.

Carranza, Bartolomé de: Archbishop of Toledo, he was imprisoned first by the Spanish Inquisition, at Valladolid in 1558, then was transferred in 1559 to the jurisdiction of the Roman Inquisition. His Inquisitional trial ended with an ambiguous verdict in 1576, and he died soon after, never having returned to Toledo. He was seen by Francisca as a major figure of reform. See fol. 146r.

Cerezo, Andrés: Francisca's brother, he was a painter and was present during many conversations about the reforms.

Chacón, Pedro: A twenty-four-year-old cleric who testified on April 11, 1575, he was the son of Diego Chacón. He had known the sisters for four or five years and considered them women of good faith, although he disapproved of their attachment to Miguel Ruíz.

Concepción, Inés de la: Niece of Francisca de Santiago, she was a *beata* who entered the *beaterio* in April 1575.

Cruz, Mariana de la: Sister of Francisca, she was doorwoman of the house. See fol. 53r.

Dios, Juan de: An itinerant prophet who settled in Toledo, he was considered mentally unstable by many. His prophecies confirmed the sisters' desire to found the convent, and he spent time at their home, giving them advice. His association with the sisters proved to be somewhat damaging to their reputation.

Erasun, Juana de: The daughter of Francisco de Erasun and Leonor de Carabajal, she was a cousin of Francisca and Isabel. She testified before the Inquisitional tribunal on July 22, 1575, that the women had the reputation of being *endemoniadas*. See fol. 36r.

González de Mendoza, Pedro: A cathedral canon, Francisca said he was asking the magistrate about the sisters' wish to found a convent and that he would be able to be their "protector" or patron.

Hernández, Alonso: A cleric who specialized in exorcisms, he performed one on Isabel Bautista sometime around 1570. He was a cleric at the church of San Juan de los Reyes.

Hernández, Sebastián: A Jesuit preacher in Toledo, he was thirty-three years old when he heard the confession of Luisa de Aguilera on February 9, 1575, and, as a result, testified voluntarily before the Inquisition on February 11 of that same year. He believed that the sisters gave evidence of having a pact with the devil and felt their practices were "scandalous to the faithful." See fols. 18v–20v.

Jesús, Catalina de: A thirty-four-year-old *beata*, she had a vision that a march on Rome was being organized in Turkey and that the pope would die and Carranza would be taken back to Toledo. See fols. 2r–3r, 4r.

Jesús, María de: The older daughter of Luisa de Aguilera and sister of Isabel Rincón, she testified before the Inquisition on April 12, 1575, after her mother had died, as to the sisters' close association with Juan de Dios. See fols. 13v–15r.

López, María (María de San Agustín): She was a thirty-year-old woman associated with the convent of Santa María la Blanca. Francisca asked her to consider joining her new convent about two years before its actual foundation. María testified on October 5, 1575, about the judgment vision she had heard Francisca describe.

López, Mateo: A cleric who ministered to the women in the *beaterio* and a relative of Francisca's.

López de la Cuadra, Alonso: A major supporter of the women, he thought he had dreamed about them some twenty years before he met them (fols. 86v–87r, 96r). He gave them furniture and books, which he eventually asked them to return when he withdrew his support. He was concerned that they needed more clerical support, and he discussed going to Rome for permission to say mass at their house so that they would not have to leave the enclosure of the *beaterio*. He grew more suspicious of the women after learning about their association with Juan de Dios, whom he considered a fraud. La Cuadra believed that their "torments by the devil" were tests to purify them, and he compared Francisca and her sister to the popular saint María de Ajofrín (buried at La Sisla), and to Saints Catherine of Siena, Francis of Assisi, and Antony. His brother, Bezerra, a chaplain of the Capilla de los Reyes, felt that Francisca and Isabel were controlled by demons and grew concerned over Alonso's support of them. Alonso testified before the Inquisition on July 23, 1575.

Mendoza, Gaspar de: The brother of Leonor de Mendoza, he was a cathedral canon. He was skeptical about the women's holiness and did not approve of their revelations. Gaspar spoke with the son of Juan Gonzalez de Vernales, chaplain of Corpus Christi, about the women, complaining about their visions. Gaspar knew that Isabel had gone to Rome, but he did not support the new foundation. He was critical of his sister's involvement with the women. When Juan Bautista, the Italian friar, came to visit him asking about setting up a grille at Corpus Christi so that the women could receive communion there, Gaspar apparently gave him an earful about the women's revelations. He told Bautista, "If they were saints and not imposters, their inventions would cause them to be inclined toward disciplines and fasting and prayer." See fols. 31v–32r. He testified against the women on July 20, 1575.

Mendoza, Leonor de: The widow of Fernando Alvarez Ponce de León, she had founded the hospital of Corpus Christi in 1567. She was supportive of the women's reform efforts, considered endowing their foundation, and offered to pay the dowry for María de la Paz to enter the *beaterio*. She withdrew her support during the course of the inquisitorial investigation, shortly before the women were arrested.

Mesa, Isabel de: She accompanied Isabel Bautista to her exorcisms with Alonso Henares; she had left for the Americas by 1575. See fol. 171v.

Osorio, Isabel: She supposedly gave advice on the foundation of a convent, then later decided not to give financial support to the sisters; she may have been visited by Isabel Bautista around 1571–72. See fols. 54r, 47r.

Paz, María de la: A servant from the household of Leonor de Mendoza, she spent just seventeen days in the *beaterio*, beginning on July 8, 1575. She was thirty years old when she testified against the women on August 11, 1575. She describes how the women understood themselves to have an intercessory role for the church similar

to that of Catherine of Siena (fol. 28r), and she describes how Francisca owned a
book about Catherine and quoted from it. When María first entered the *beaterio*
and saw that the women were receiving communion daily, she questioned Miguel
Ruíz about this practice, saying that Fray Juan de la Vega had told her that daily
communion was not appropriate. Ruíz responded that there were various opinions
on the matter and that he would take the question on his own conscience. María
also told Ruíz that she had heard Dr. Hurtado say that the entire congregation was
full of *endemoniadas*, to which Ruíz replied that he would give his life for them and
that they were doing God's work. See fol. 29r.

Porras, Marcos de: Curate from Fonseca, he was a friend of Juan Bautista and talked with
López de la Cuadra and Bautista about taking a trip to Rome on behalf of the sisters. See fols. 180r, 219r, 223r.

Ribera, Blas de: Francisca's married brother, he lived in Madrid but returned to Toledo
in February 1574.

Rincón, Isabel del: The younger daughter of Luisa de Aguilera, she was 21 years old when
she testified on April 15, 1575; she speaks of Isabel's trip to Rome and Francisca's
references to Raymond of Capua's *Life of Catherine of Siena.*

Ruíz, Miguel: Cleric at the Hospital of La Misericordia, he was the priest most associated with the women and their reforms. He first met Isabel Bautista in 1572,
when he was asked to exorcize her. After she changed some of her clothing and
habits, he began to treat her with confession and communion, but when he testified before the Inquisition he claimed that she was still "not cured of the said
illness." See fol. 37r. He also said that two of Isabel's sisters were also *endemoniadas*
and that the devil spoke through Francisca's mouth, so that he never believed
what she said. He testified that of all the women in the community, only María
de la Paz seemed free of demonic influence. He said daily mass at the Hospital
de la Misericordia for the *beatas* and was arrested and imprisoned at the same time
they were. He testified on November 13, 1575. In his testimony, Ruíz describes
himself as a skeptic, but other witnesses testify to his passionate commitment to
the women.

Ruy, Luis: He was a cleric who testified in the vicar's investigation on May 27, 1575,
stating that they had taken a vow of obedience to Miguel Ruíz. See fols. 49v–50r.

San Francisco, Catalina de: A thirty-four-year-old *beata* who lived with the women,
Catalina was a reluctant witness when she testified on March 2, 1575. She was
from the parish of San Román and lived in the house of Arras Pardo. In her testimony she described Francisca's judgment vision. According to others, Catalina
had to be exorcised many times at the Hospital de la Misericordia.

San Francisco, Magdalena de: A *beata* who was apparently possessed by the devil and therefore took Miguel Ruíz as her confessor, she testified before the Inquisition on
February 28, 1575. See fols. 183r–v.

San Jerónimo, María de: The widow of Francisco Ruíz de Herrera, she lived with her
mother Catalina Nuñez. She stayed with Francisca in the *beaterio* from May through
August 1575. She had met Isabel Bautista in the chapel of the Hospital de la
Misericordia before Isabel left for Rome. At that time, Isabel told her that she was
meant to be a nun at the *beaterio*. María left the *beaterio* shortly before the women's
arrest with the permission of Miguel Ruíz, although Francisca was displeased over
her departure. See fols. 80v–83v.

Santiago, Francisca de: A *beata* who entered the *beaterio* in April 1575, she was the aunt of Inés de la Concepción.

Sarmiento, Francisca: She was a noblewoman of Novés and nun at Santa María la Blanca; Francisca grew up in her house. See fol. 170r.

Serrano: The archdiocesan vicar, he would not grant the women permission to found the convent.

Silva, Don Pedro de: A Toledo councilman in 1581, he was a reformer of almsgiving and health policies; Luisa de Aguilera lived on his property.

Sueldo, Dr. Esteban del: Parish priest of San Martín and confessor to Magdalena de San Francisco, he testified on May 27, 1575, saying that people in the city had murmured against the women because they had taken a vow of obedience to Miguel Ruíz.

Velázquez, Doctor Alonso: A canon of the cathedral to whom Luisa de Aguilera spoke about the *beatas*, he apparently disapproved of the women's visions, although he never testified against them. See fol. 46v.

Velasco, Licenciado Hernando: A former neighbor of Francisca's, he began to communicate with her while in the inquisitorial prison himself. They developed a plan to marry after they were freed. See fols. 163r, 243r—243v.

Ximénez, María de Jesús: She was the twelve-year-old niece of Juana Ximénez; they lived at the *beaterio* for four months. In her inquisitorial testimony on October 3, 1575, she described Francisca's writings, which were kept in a trunk. They consisted of the vision of the Last Judgment and other things—a great bundle of papers. See fol. 64v.

Ximénez, Juana (Juana Evangelista): The widow of Diego de Salazar, she lived on Calle de los Jurados. She was forty years old at the time she testified against Francisca in October 1575. Her testimony describes certain papers Francisca had written that were hidden at the time the vicar visited the *beaterio*. She also described how Juan de Dios was a frequent visitor of the *beaterio*. She complained once to Miguel Ruíz about whether or not Francisca and her sister were truly inspired and was told that she was the one deceived by the devil. See fol. 72r. She was the aunt of María de Jesús.

Zapata, Pedro: Francisca and Isabel rented his house and placed the sacrament there in preparation for the foundation of the convent.

APPENDIX D
CHRONOLOGY OF THE TRIAL OF
FRANCISCA DE LOS APÓSTOLES

1570
Francisca's sister, Isabel Bautista, now with a public reputation for wandering about the city late at night, begins to be exorcized by Alonso Hernández.

Fall 1571
Isabel Bautista is first exorcized by Miguel Ruíz. Within eight days of this treatment, she is cured of her illness and gives herself over to fasting and penance.

Fall 1573
Isabel Bautista goes to Madrid to consult with a noblewoman about founding a convent.

Fall 1573
Isabel Bautista composes a rule for a convent for women and reads it to Magdalena de San Francisco, Catalina de San Francisco, a *beata* from San Román, and María de San Jerónimo.

November 1, 1573
Isabel Bautista leaves for Rome.

January 1574
Francisca has her vision of the Last Judgment.

April 23, 1574
Francisca writes a letter to Isabel in Rome.

June 1574
Francisca accepts torments by devils.

June 29, 1574
Isabel writes to Francisca; the letter is received August 17, 1574.

July 18, 1574
Francisca writes a letter to Isabel.

Late July 1574
Francisca begins three months of fasting, prayers, and penance on behalf of the sins of the world.

August 24, 1574
Francisca writes to Pedro Chacón. This letter sounds very positive about the progress of the reform movement during August.

August 25, 1574
Francisca writes Isabel, saying, "They have confirmed our convent."

October 20, 1574
Francisca's torments by devils come to an end.

October 24, 1574
Francisca writes out her vows to overcome vices.

October 25, 1574
Francisca has a vision of victory over devils.

September–November 1574
Isabel Osorio withdraws financial support but writes a letter to the king's confessor in support of the convent.

November 1, 1574
Francisca has the vision of the Justice of God. She is ill for several days afterward.

November 11 or 13, 1574
Francisca has a vision of her own lowliness. She is reassured by God that His love will make satisfaction for sins and that she can be a model for how others can atone.

November 19, 1574
Inquisitional testimony of Catalina de Jesus (first accusation).

November–December 1574
The cleric Porras warns Francisca that she should go to the Inquisitional tribunal if she has anything to confess. She consults with the prior at the Hieronymite Monastery of La Sisla.

December 5, 1574
Francisca has a vision in which her body takes the form of a cross and hosts fall on her bed.

After December 10, 1574
Isabel returns from Rome, and the women begin to congregate. The rule has not been approved, but money has been promised to endow the foundation. The women approach Pedro Gonzalez de Mendoza about gathering together. They begin wearing habits.

December 15 1574
Inquisitional testimony of Luisa de Aguilera, who dies sometime between March 9 and April 12, 1575.

December 1574—January 1575
Isabel goes to Madrid to visit Isabel Osorio; Juan de Dios arrives in Toledo.

February 11, 1575
Inquisitional testimony of Sebastián Hernández, S.J., confessor of Luisa de Aguilera.

February 28, 1575
Inquisitional testimony of Magdalena de San Francisco.

April 1575
The women take up residence in a new house.

April 11, 1575
Inquisitional testimony of Pedro Chacón.

May 1575
Luisa de los Angeles enters the *beaterio*.

May 27, 1575
The vicar Serrano visits the *beaterio* and interviews Isabel and Francisca. He gathers materials from the *beaterio*, including papers written by Francisca. At this time, Serrano asks Francisca to name the *beatas* living in the house. She names seven sisters in order of their age in the community: Francisca, Isabel, Mariana, Magdalena de la Cruz, Juana Evangelista (aka Juana Ximénez), María de San Jerónimo, and María de Jesús (Herrera?). She also mentions three minors: María de Jesus Ximénez, Ana, and another Isabel, age 8. Francisca does not name Luisa de Agilera or Luisa de los Angeles.

June 28, 1575
Alonso López de la Cuadra returns to Francisca and says that Juan de Dios should not go to Rome on behalf of the women. Francisca agrees with him.

July 8, 1575
María de la Paz enters the *beaterio*.

July 10, 1575
Alonso de la Cuadra encourages his friend Juana Ximénez to leave the *beaterio*.

July 16, 1575
Juana de Erasun talks to Gaspar de Mendoza about the *beaterio*.

July 1575
Within the community, Francisca cites Capua's *Life of Catherine of Siena* as a model for her religious experiences.

July 17, 1575
Inquisitional testimony of Luisa de los Angeles; she is still living in the *beaterio* with the other women, and she calls the house a "convent."

July 19, 1575
Conversation between Alonso de la Cuadra and Fray Juan Bautista regarding their trip to Rome. They agree that Juan de Dios is under the control of the devil but that the *beatas* are all right. Juan Bautista and Porras still plan on going to Rome together on their behalf.

July 20, 1575
Inquisitional testimony of Don Gaspar de Mendoza.

July 22, 1575
Juana Ximénez leaves the *beaterio*, under the influence of Alonso de la Cuadra. The women are worried about the legal action that De la Cuadra is planning on her behalf.

July 22, 1575
Inquisitional testimony of Juana de Erasun.

July 23, 1575
Inquisitional testimony of Alonso López de la Cuadra.

July 24, 1575
Inquisitional testimony of Doña Leonor de Mendoza

July 25, 1575
María de la Paz leaves the *beaterio*.

Early August 1575
Francisca and Isabel visit Serrano, asking him what to do and whether or not the nine remaining women should stay with them.

August 11, 1575
Inquisitional testimony of María de la Paz.

September 28, 1575
Inquisitors in Toledo send a letter to Madrid informing them of the progress of the investigation of the *beaterio*.

October 1, 1575
An Inquisitional warrant orders Francisca's arrest and imprisonment.

October 3, 1575
Inquisitional testimony of María de Jesús Ximénez and Juana Ximénez.

October 5, 1575
Inquisitional testimony of María de San Agustín (aka María López); initial examination of Francisca.

October 8, 1575
Inquisitional testimony of María de San Jerónimo and María de Jesús Herrera; María de Jesús refers to Carranza's bleak situation during her testimony.

October 10, 1575
Inquisitional testimony of Francisca de Aguilar. She describes a conversation about the habit the women were to wear when the following were present: María de Jesús Herrera, Luisa de los Angeles, Mariana de la Cruz, Juana Ximénez, María de Jesús Ximénez, María de San Jerónimo, Ana, Isabel Bautista, Francisca de los Apóstoles, Mariana, Francisca de Aguilar, and Inés de Aguilar. Inquisitional testimony of Inés de Aguilar.

October 13, 1575
Inquisitional testimony of Catalina López.

October 19, 1575
Inquisitional testimony of Fray Juan Bautista.

October 20, 1575
Inquisitional testimony of Juana Bautista.

November 8, 1575
Inquisitional testimony of Isabel Bautista.

November, 23 1575
Isabel Bautista is cracking under the stress of her own trial.

November 28, 1575
Francisca complains of liver and heart trouble and torments by demons. She asks for company to calm these pains.

December 1, 1575
Francisca gives more testimony about her visions.

December 2, 1575
Francisca's testimony on visions continues.

December 5, 1575
Francisca's testimony on visions continues.

December 23, 1575
Inquisitional testimony of Francisco Sánchez de Ravanal and Inés de la Concepción.

January 1576
The Inquisitional prosecutor presents the official accusation against Francisca de los Apóstoles, consisting of 144 points.

January 27–February 21, 1576
Francisca responds to the official accusations over six sessions of testimony.

January 9, 1577
Francisca asks for an audience with the Inquisitor to request access to the sacraments.

March 6, 1577
The Inquisitional prosecutor presents new accusations concerning Francisca's conduct with another prisoner.

April 13, 1578
Auto de fe held in the main square of Toledo, where Francisca's sentence was read publicly and she abjured her errors.

April 14, 1578
Francisca receives one hundred lashes and is banished from Toledo for a period of three years.

SERIES EDITORS'
BIBLIOGRAPHY

PRIMARY SOURCES

Alberti, Leon Battista. *The Family in Renaissance Florence.* Trans. Renée Neu Watkins. Columbia, SC: University of South Carolina Press, 1969.

Arenal, Electa, and Stacey Schlau, eds. *Untold Sisters: Hispanic Nuns in Their Own Works.* Trans. Amanda Powell. Albuquerque, NM: University of New Mexico Press, 1989.

Astell, Mary. *The First English Feminist: Reflections on Marriage and Other Writings.* Ed. and intro. Bridget Hill. New York: St. Martin's Press, 1986.

Atherton, Margaret, ed. *Women Philosophers of the Early Modern Period.* Indianapolis, IN: Hackett Publishing Co., 1994.

Aughterson, Kate, ed. *Renaissance Woman: Constructions of Femininity in England: A Source Book.* London and New York: Routledge, 1995.

Barbaro, Francesco. *On Wifely Duties.* Trans. Benjamin Kohl. In *The Earthly Republic,* ed. Benjamin Kohl and R.G. Witt.. Philadelphia: University of Pennsylvania Press, 1978, 179–228. Translation of the preface and book 2.

Behn, Aphra. *The Works of Aphra Behn.* 7 vols. Ed. Janet Todd. Columbus, OH: Ohio State University Press, 1992–96.

Boccaccio, Giovanni. *Famous Women.* Ed. and trans. Virginia Brown. I Tatti Renaissance Library. Cambridge, MA: Harvard University Press, 2001.

———. *Corbaccio or the Labyrinth of Love.* Trans. Anthony K. Cassell. Second revised edition. Binghamton, NY: Medieval and Renaissance Texts and Studies, 1993.

Brown, Sylvia. *Women's Writing in Stuart England: The Mother's Legacies of Dorothy Leigh, Elizabeth Joscelin and Elizabeth Richardson.* Thrupp, Stroud, Gloceter: Sutton, 1999.

Bruni, Leonardo. "On the Study of Literature (1405) to Lady Battista Malatesta of Moltefeltro." In *The Humanism of Leonardo Bruni: Selected Texts,* trans. and intro. Gordon Griffiths, James Hankins, and David Thompson. Binghamton, NY: Medieval and Renaissance Texts and Studies, 1987, 240–51.

Castiglione, Baldassare. *The Book of the Courtier.* Trans. George Bull. New York: Penguin, 1967.

Christine de Pizan. *The Book of the City of Ladies.* Trans. Earl Jeffrey Richards. Foreward Marina Warner. New York: Persea Books, 1982.

———. *The Treasure of the City of Ladies.* Trans. Sarah Lawson. New York: Viking Penguin, 1985.

Clarke, Danielle, ed. *Isabella Whitney, Mary Sidney and Aemilia Lanyer: Renaissance Women Poets.* New York: Penguin Books, 2000.

Crawford, Patricia, and Laura Gowing, eds. *Women's Worlds in Seventeenth-Century England: A Source Book.* London and New York: Routledge, 2000.

Daybell, James, ed. *Early Modern Women's Letter Writing, 1450–1700.* Houndmills, England and New York: Palgrave, 2001.

Elizabeth I: Collected Works. Ed. Leah S. Marcus, Janel Mueller, and Mary Beth Rose. Chicago: University of Chicago Press, 2000.

Elyot, Thomas. *Defence of Good Women: The Feminist Controversy of the Renaissance.* Facsimile Reproductions. Ed. Diane Bornstein. New York: Delmar, 1980.

Erasmus, Desiderius. *Erasmus on Women.* Ed. Erika Rummel. Toronto: University of Toronto Press, 1996.

Female and Male Voices in Early Modern England: An Anthology of Renaissance Writing. Ed. Betty S. Travitsky and Anne Lake Prescott. New York: Columbia University Press, 2000.

Ferguson, Moira, ed. *First Feminists: British Women Writers, 1578–1799.* Bloomington, IN: Indiana University Press, 1985.

Galilei, Maria Celeste. *Sister Maria Celeste's Letters to her father, Galileo.* Ed. and trans. Rinaldina Russell. Lincoln, NE, and New York: Writers Club Press of Universe.com, 2000.

Gethner, Perry, ed. *The Lunatic Lover and Other Plays by French Women of the 17th and 18th Centuries.* Portsmouth, NH: Heinemann, 1994.

Glückel of Hameln. *The Memoirs of Glückel of Hameln.* Trans. Marvin Lowenthal. New introduction by Robert Rosen. New York: Schocken Books, 1977.

Henderson, Katherine Usher, and Barbara F. McManus, eds. *Half Humankind: Contexts and Texts of the Controversy about Women in England, 1540–1640.* Urbana, IL: Indiana University Press, 1985.

Hoby, Margaret. *The Private Life of an Elizabethan Lady: The Diary of Lady Margaret Hoby 1599–1605.* Phoenix Mill, UK: Sutton Publishing, 1998.

Humanist Educational Treatises. Ed. and trans. Craig W. Kallendorf. I Tatti Renaissance Library. Cambridge, MA: Harvard University Press, 2002.

Joscelin, Elizabeth. *The Mothers Legacy to her Unborn Childe.* Ed. Jean leDrew Metcalfe. Toronto: University of Toronto Press, 2000.

Kaminsky, Amy Katz, ed. *Water Lilies, Flores del agua: An Anthology of Spanish Women Writers from the Fifteenth Through the Nineteenth Century.* Minneapolis: University of Minnesota Press, 1996.

Kempe, Margery. *The Book of Margery Kempe.* Trans. and ed. Lynn Staley. Norton Critical Edition. New York: W.W. Norton, 2001.

King, Margaret L., and Albert Rabil, Jr., eds. *Her Immaculate Hand: Selected Works by and about the Women Humanists of Quattrocento Italy.* Binghamton, NY: Medieval and Renaissance Texts and Studies, 1983.Second revised paperback edition, 1991.

Klein, Joan Larsen, ed. *Daughters, Wives, and Widows: Writings by Men about Women and Marriage in England, 1500–1640.* Urbana, IL: University of Illinois Press, 1992.

Knox, John. *The Political Writings of John Knox: The First Blast of the Trumpet against the Monstrous Regiment of Women and Other Selected Works.* Ed. Marvin A. Breslow. Washington, DC: Folger Shakespeare Library, 1985.

Kors, Alan C., and Edward Peters, eds. *Witchcraft in Europe, 400–1700: A Documentary History.* Philadelphia: University of Pennsylvania Press, 2000.

Krämer, Heinrich, and Jacob Sprenger. *Malleus Maleficarum* (ca. 1487). Trans. Montague Summers. London: Pushkin Press, 1928. Reprint, New York: Dover, 1971.

Larsen, Anne R., and Colette H. Winn, eds. *Writings by Pre-Revolutionary French Women: From Marie de France to Elizabeth Vigée-Le Brun.* New York and London: Garland Publishing Co., 2000.

de Lorris, William, and Jean de Meun. *The Romance of the Rose.* Trans. Charles Dahlbert. Princeton: Princeton University Press, 1971. Reprint, University Press of New England, 1983.

Marguerite d'Angoulême, queen of Navarre. *The Heptameron.* Trans. P. A. Chilton. New York: Viking Penguin, 1984.

Mary of Agreda. *The Divine Life of the Most Holy Virgin.* Abridgment of *The Mystical City of God.* Abr. Fr. Bonaventure Amedeo de Caesarea, M.C. Trans. from French by Abbé Joseph A. Boullan. Rockford, IL: Tan Books, 1997.

Myers, Kathleen A., and Amanda Powell, eds. *A Wild Country out in the Garden: The Spiritual Journals of a Colonial Mexican Nun.* Bloomington, IN: Indiana University Press, 1999.

Russell, Rinaldina, ed. *Sister Maria Celeste's Letters to Her Father, Galileo.* San Jose and New York: Writers Club Press, 2000.

Teresa of Avila, Saint. *The Life of Saint Teresa of Avila by Herself.* Trans. J. M. Cohen. New York: Viking Penguin, 1957.

Weyer, Johann. *Witches, Devils, and Doctors in the Renaissance: Johann Weyer, De praestigiis daemonum.* Ed. George Mora with Benjamin G. Kohl, Erik Midelfort, and Helen Bacon. Trans. John Shea. Binghamton, NY: Medieval and Renaissance Texts and Studies, 1991.

Wilson, Katharina M., ed. *Medieval Women Writers.* Athens, GA: University of Georgia Press, 1984.

———, ed. *Women Writers of the Renaissance and Reformation.* Athens, GA: University of Georgia Press, 1987.

Wilson, Katharina M., and Frank J. Warnke, eds. *Women Writers of the Seventeenth Century.* Athens, GA: University of Georgia Press, 1989.

Wollstonecraft, Mary. *A Vindication of the Rights of Men and a Vindication of the Rights of Women.* Ed. Sylvana Tomaselli. Cambridge: Cambridge University Press, 1995. Also *The Vindications of the Rights of Men, The Rights of Women.* Ed. D. L. Macdonald and Kathleen Scherf. Peterborough, Ontario: Broadview Press, 1997.

Women Critics, 1660–1820: An Anthology. Ed. the Folger Collective on Early Women Critics. Bloomington, IN: Indiana University Press, 1995.

Women Writers in English 1350–1850: 15 published through 1999 (projected 30-volume series suspended). Oxford University Press.

Wroth, Lady Mary. *The Countess of Montgomery's Urania.* 2 parts. Ed. Josephine A. Roberts. Tempe, AZ: Medieval and Renaissance Texts and Studies, 1995, 1999.

———. *Lady Mary Wroth's "Love's Victory": The Penshurst Manuscript.* Ed. Michael G. Brennan. London: Roxburghe Club, 1988.

———. *The Poems of Lady Mary Wroth.* Ed. Josephine A. Roberts. Baton Rouge, LA: Louisiana State University Press, 1983.

de Zayas Maria. *The Disenchantments of Love.* Trans. H. Patsy Boyer. Albany, NY: State University of New York Press, 1997.

————. *The Enchantments of Love: Amorous and Exemplary Novels.* Trans. H. Patsy Boyer. Berkeley, CA: University of California Press, 1990.

SECONDARY SOURCES

Ahlgren, Gillian. *Teresa of Avila and the Politics of Sanctity.* Ithaca, NY: Cornell University Press, 1996.

Akkerman, Tjitske, and Siep Sturman, eds. *Feminist Thought in European History, 1400–2000.* London and New York: Routledge, 1997.

Allen, Sister Prudence, R.S.M. *The Concept of Woman: The Aristotelian Revolution, 750 B.C—A.D. 1250.* Grand Rapids, MI: William B. Eerdmans Publishing Company, 1997.

————. *The Concept of Woman: Volume II: The Early Humanist Reformation, 1250–1500.* Grand Rapids, MI: William B. Eerdmans Publishing Company, 2002.

Andreadis, Harriette. *Sappho in Early Modern England: Female Same-Sex Literary Erotics, 1550–1714.* Chicago: University of Chicago Press, 2001.

Armon, Shifra. *Picking Wedlock: Women and the Courtship Novel in Spain.* New York: Rowman and Littlefield Publishers, Inc., 2002.

Backer, Anne Liot Backer. *Precious Women.* New York: Basic Books, 1974.

Ballaster, Ros. *Seductive Forms.* New York: Oxford University Press, 1992.

Barash, Carol. *English Women's Poetry, 1649–1714: Politics, Community, and Linguistic Authority.* New York and Oxford: Oxford University Press, 1996.

Battigelli, Anna. *Margaret Cavendish and the Exiles of the Mind.* Lexington, KY: University of Kentucky Press, 1998.

Beasley, Faith. *Revising Memory: Women's Fiction and Memoirs in Seventeenth-Century France.* New Brunswick: Rutgers University Press, 1990.

Beilin, Elaine V. *Redeeming Eve: Women Writers of the English Renaissance.* Princeton: Princeton University Press, 1987.

Benson, Pamela Joseph. *The Invention of Renaissance Woman: The Challenge of Female Independence in the Literature and Thought of Italy and England.* University Park, PA: Pennsylvania State University Press, 1992.

Benson, Pamela Joseph, and Victoria Kirkham, eds. *Strong Voices, Weak History? Medieval and Renaissance Women in their Literary Canons: England, France, Italy.* Ann Arbor: University of Michigan Press, 2003.

Bilinkoff, Jodi. *The Avila of Saint Teresa: Religious Reform in a Sixteenth-Century City.* Ithaca, NY: Cornell University Press, 1989.

Bissell, R. Ward. *Artemisia Gentileschi and the Authority of Art.* University Park, PA: Pennsylvania State University Press, 2000.

Blain, Virginia, Isobel Grundy, and Patricia Clements, eds. *The Feminist Companion to Literature in English: Women Writers from the Middle Ages to the Present.* New Haven, CT: Yale University Press, 1990.

Bloch, R. Howard. *Medieval Misogyny and the Invention of Western Romantic Love.* Chicago: University of Chicago Press, 1991.

Bornstein, Daniel, and Roberto Rusconi, eds. *Women and Religion in Medieval and Renaissance Italy.* Trans. Margery J. Schneider. Chicago: University of Chicago Press, 1996.

Brant, Clare, and Diane Purkiss, eds. *Women, Texts and Histories, 1575–1760.* London and New York: Routledge, 1992.

Briggs, Robin. *Witches and Neighbours: The Social and Cultural Context of European Witchcraft.* New York: HarperCollins, 1995; Viking Penguin, 1996.

Brink, Jean R., ed. *Female Scholars: A Tradition of Learned Women before 1800.* Montréal: Eden Press Women's Publications, 1980.

Brown, Judith C. *Immodest Acts: The Life of a Lesbian Nun in Renaissance Italy.* New York: Oxford University Press, 1986.

Brown, Judith C., and Robert C. Davis, eds. *Gender and Society in Renaisance Italy.* London: Addison Wesley Longman, 1998.

Bynum, Carolyn Walker. *Fragmentation and Redemption: Essays on Gender and the Human Body in Medieval Religion.* New York: Zone Books, 1992.

———. *Holy Feast and Holy Fast: The Religious Significance of Food to Medieval Women.* Berkeley: University of California Press, 1987.

Cambridge Guide to Women's Writing in English. Ed. Lorna Sage. Cambridge: Cambridge University Press, 1999.

Cavanagh, Sheila T. *Cherished Torment: The Emotional Geography of Lady Mary Wroth's "Urania."* Pittsburgh: Duquesne University Press, 2001.

Cerasano, S. P., and Marion Wynne-Davies, eds. *Readings in Renaissance Women's Drama: Criticism, History, and Performance, 1594–1998.* London and New York: Routledge, 1998.

Cervigni, Dino S., ed. *Women Mystic Writers. Annali d'Italianistica* 13 (1995) (entire issue).

Cervigni, Dino S., and Rebecca West, eds. *Women's Voices in Italian Literature. Annali d'Italianistica* 7 (1989) (entire issue).

Charlton, Kenneth. *Women, Religion and Education in Early Modern England.* London and New York: Routledge, 1999.

Chojnacka, Monica. *Working Women in Early Modern Venice.* Baltimore: Johns Hopkins University Press, 2001.

Chojnacki, Stanley. *Women and Men in Renaissance Venice: Twelve Essays on Patrician Society.* Baltimore: Johns Hopkins University Press, 2000.

Cholakian, Patricia Francis. *Rape and Writing in the Heptameron of Marguerite de Navarre.* Carbondale and Edwardsville, IL: Southern Illinois University Press, 1991.

———. *Women and the Politics of Self-Representation in Seventeenth-Century France.* Newark: University of Delaware Press, 2000.

Christine de Pizan: A Casebook. Edited by Barbara K. Altmann and Deborah L. McGrady. New York: Routledge, 2003.

Clogan, Paul Maruice, ed. *Medievali et Humanistica: Literacy and the Lay Reader.* Lanham, MD: Rowman and Littlefield, 2000.

Clubb, Louise George. *Italian Drama in Shakespeare's Time.* New Haven, CT: Yale University Press, 1989.

Conley, John J., S.J. *The Suspicion of Virtue: Women Philosophers in Neoclassical France.* Ithaca, NY: Cornell University Press, 2002.

Crabb, Ann. *The Strozzi of Florence: Widowhood and Family Solidarity in the Renaissance.* Ann Arbor: University of Michigan Press, 2000.

Cruz, Anne J., and Mary Elizabeth Perry, eds. *Culture and Control in Counter-Reformation Spain.* Minneapolis: University of Minnesota Press, 1992.

Davis, Natalie Zemon. *Society and Culture in Early Modern France.* Stanford: Stanford University Press, 1975. Especially chapters 3 and 5.

———. *Women on the Margins: Three Seventeenth-Century Lives.* Cambridge, MA: Harvard University Press, 1995.

DeJean, Joan. *Ancients against Moderns: Culture Wars and the Making of a Fin de Siècle.* Chicago: University of Chicago Press, 1997.

———. *Fictions of Sappho, 1546–1937.* Chicago: University of Chicago Press, 1989.

———. *The Reinvention of Obscenity: Sex, Lies, and Tabloids in Early Modern France.* Chicago: University of Chicago Press, 2002.

———. *Tender Geographies: Women and the Origins of the Novel in France.* New York: Columbia University Press, 1991.

———. *The Reinvention of Obscenity: Sex, Lies, and Tabloids in Early Modern France.* Chicago: University of Chicago Press, 2002.

Dictionary of Russian Women Writers. Edited by Marina Ledkovsky, Charlotte Rosenthal, and Mary Zirin. Westport, CT: Greenwood Press, 1994.

Dixon, Laurinda S. *Perilous Chastity: Women and Illness in Pre-Enlightenment Art and Medicine.* Ithaca, NY: Cornell Universitiy Press, 1995.

Dolan, Frances, E. *Whores of Babylon: Catholicism, Gender and Seventeenth-Century Print Culture.* Ithaca, NY: Cornell University Press, 1999.

Donovan, Josephine. *Women and the Rise of the Novel, 1405–1726.* New York: St. Martin's Press, 1999.

Encyclopedia of Continental Women Writers. 2 vols. Ed. Katharina Wilson. New York: Garland, 1991.

De Erauso, Catalina. *Lieutenant Nun: Memoir of a Basque Transvestite in the New World.* Trans. Michele Ttepto and Gabriel Stepto; foreword by Marjorie Garber. Boston: Beacon Press, 1995.

Erdmann, Axel. *My Gracious Silence: Women in the Mirror of Sixteenth-Century Printing in Western Europe.* Luzern: Gilhofer and Rauschberg, 1999.

Erickson, Amy Louise. *Women and Property in Early Modern England.* London and New York: Routledge, 1993.

Ezell, Margaret J. M. *The Patriarch's Wife: Literary Evidence and the History of the Family.* Chapel Hill, NC: University of North Carolina Press, 1987.

———. *Social Authorship and the Advent of Print.* Baltimore: Johns Hopkins University Press, 1999.

———. *Writing Women's Literary History.* Baltimore: Johns Hopkins University Press, 1993.

Farrell, Michèle Longino. *Performing Motherhood: The Sévigné Correspondence.* Hanover, NH, and London: University Press of New England, 1991.

The Feminist Companion to Literature in English: Women Writers from the Middle Ages to the Present. Ed. Virginia Blain, Isobel Grundy, and Patricia Clements. New Haven, CT: Yale University Press, 1990.

The Feminist Encyclopedia of German Literature. Ed. Friederike Eigler and Susanne Kord. Westport, CT: Greenwood Press, 1997.

Feminist Encyclopedia of Italian Literature. Ed. Rinaldina Russell. Westport, CT: Greenwood Press, 1997.

Ferguson, Margaret W. *Dido's Daughters: Literacy, Gender, and Empire in Early Modern England and France.* Chicago: University of Chicago Press, 2003.

————, Maureen Quilligan, and Nancy J. Vickers, eds. *Rewriting the Renaissance: The Discourses of Sexual Difference in Early Modern Europe.* Chicago: University of Chicago Press, 1987.

Ferraro, Joanne M. *Marriage Wars in Late Renaissance Venice.* Oxford: Oxford University Press, 2001.

Fletcher, Anthony. *Gender, Sex and Subordination in England, 1500–1800.* New Haven, CT: Yale University Press, 1995.

French Women Writers: A Bio-Bibliographical Source Book. Ed. Eva Martin Sartori and Dorothy Wynne Zimmerman. Westport, CT: Greenwood Press, 1991.

Frye, Susan, and Karen Robertson, eds. *Maids and Mistresses, Cousins and Queens: Women's Alliances in Early Modern England.* Oxford: Oxford University Press, 1999.

Gallagher, Catherine. *Nobody's Story: The Vanishing Acts of Women Writers in the Marketplace, 1670–1820.* Berkeley: University of California Press, 1994.

Garrard, Mary D. *Artemisia Gentileschi: The Image of the Female Hero in Italian Baroque Art.* Princeton: Princeton University Press, 1989.

Gelbart, Nina Rattner. *The King's Midwife: A History and Mystery of Madame du Coudray.* Berkeley: University of California Press, 1998.

Glenn, Cheryl. *Rhetoric Retold: Regendering the Tradition from Antiquity through the Renaissance.* Carbondale and Edwardsville, IL: Southern Illinois University Press, 1997.

Goffen, Rona. *Titian's Women.* New Haven, CT: Yale University Press, 1997.

Goldberg, Jonathan. *Desiring Women Writing: English Renaissance Examples.* Stanford: Stanford University Press, 1997.

Goldsmith, Elizabeth C. *Exclusive Conversations: The Art of Interaction in Seventeenth-Century France.* Philadelphia: University of Pennsylvania Press, 1988.

————, ed. *Writing the Female Voice.* Boston: Northeastern University Press, 1989.

Goldsmith, Elizabeth C., and Dena Goodman, eds. *Going Public: Women and Publishing in Early Modern France.* Ithaca, NY: Cornell University Press, 1995.

Grafton, Anthony, and Lisa Jardine. *From Humanism to the Humanities: Education and the Liberal Arts in Fifteenth-and Sixteenth-Century Europe.* London: Duckworth, 1986.

Greer, Margaret Rich. *Maria de Zayas Tells Baroque Tales of Love and the Cruelty of Men.* University Park, PA: Pennsylvania State University Press, 2000.

Hackett, Helen. *Women and Romance Fiction in the English Renaissance.* Cambridge: Cambridge University Press, 2000.

Hall, Kim F. *Things of Darkness: Economies of Race and Gender in Early Modern England.* Ithaca, NY: Cornell University Press, 1995.

Hampton, Timothy. *Literature and the Nation in the Sixteenth Century: Inventing Renaissance France.* Ithaca, NY: Cornell University Press, 2001.

Hannay, Margaret, ed. *Silent but for the Word.* Kent, OH: Kent State University Press, 1985.

Hardwick, Julie. *The Practice of Patriarchy: Gender and the Politics of Household Authority in Early Modern France.* University Park, PA: Pennsylvania State University Press, 1998.

Harris, Barbara J. *English Aristocratic Women, 1450–1550: Marriage and Family, Property and Careers.* New York: Oxford University Press, 2002.

Harth, Erica. *Ideology and Culture in Seventeenth-Century France.* Ithaca, NY: Cornell University Press, 1983.

————. *Cartesian Women. Versions and Subversions of Rational Discourse in the Old Regime.* Ithaca, NY: Cornell University Press, 1992.

Harvey, Elizabeth D. *Ventriloquized Voices: Feminist Theory and English Renaissance Texts.* London and New York: Routledge, 1992.

Haselkorn, Anne M., and Betty Travitsky, eds. *The Renaissance Englishwoman in Print: Counterbalancing the Canon.* Amherst: University of Massachusetts Press, 1990.

Herlihy, David. "Did Women Have a Renaissance? A Reconsideration." *Medievalia et Humanistica* n.s. 13 (1985): 1–22.

Hill, Bridget. *The Republican Virago: The Life and Times of Catharine Macaulay, Historian.* New York: Oxford University Press, 1992.

A History of Central European Women's Writing. Ed. Celia Hawkesworth. New York: Palgrave Press, 2001.

A History of Women in the West.
Volume 1: *From Ancient Goddesses to Christian Saints.* Ed. Pauline Schmitt Pantel. Cambridge, MA: Harvard University Press, 1992.
Volume 2: *Silences of the Middle Ages.* Ed. Christiane Klapisch-Zuber. Cambridge, MA: Harvard University Press, 1992.
Volume 3: *Renaissance and Enlightenment Paradoxes.* Ed. Natalie Zemon Davis and Arlette Farge. Cambridge, MA: Harvard University Press, 1993.

A History of Women Philosophers. Ed. Mary Ellen Waithe. 3 vols. Dordrecht: Martinus Nijhoff, 1987.

A History of Women's Writing in France. Ed. Sonya Stephens. Cambridge: Cambridge University Press, 2000.

A History of Women's Writing in Germany, Austria and Switzerland. Ed. Jo Catling. Cambridge: Cambridge University Press, 2000.

A History of Women's Writing in Italy. Ed. Letizia Panizza and Sharon Wood. Cambridge: Cambridge University Press, 2000.

A History of Women's Writing in Russia. Ed. Alele Marie Barker and Jehanne M. Gheith. Cambridge: Cambridge University Press, 2002.

Hobby, Elaine. *Virtue of Necessity: English Women's Writing, 1646–1688.* London: Virago Press, 1988.

Horowitz, Maryanne Cline. "Aristotle and Women." *Journal of the History of Biology* 9 (1976): 183–213.

Howell, Martha. *The Marriage Exchange: Property, Social Place, and Gender in Cities of the Low Countries, 1300–1550.* Chicago: University of Chicago Press, 1998.

Hufton, Olwen H. *The Prospect before Her: A History of Women in Western Europe, 1: 1500–1800.* New York: HarperCollins, 1996.

Hull, Suzanne W. *Chaste, Silent, and Obedient: English Books for Women, 1475–1640.* San Marino, CA: Huntington Library, 1982.

Hunt, Lynn, ed. *The Invention of Pornography: Obscenity and the Origins of Modernity, 1500–1800.* New York: Zone Books, 1996.

Hutner, Heidi, ed. *Rereading Aphra Behn: History, Theory, and Criticism.* Charlottesville, VA: University Press of Virginia, 1993.

Hutson, Lorna, ed. *Feminism and Renaissance Studies.* New York: Oxford University Press, 1999.

Italian Women Writers: A Bio-Bibliographical Sourcebook. Ed. Rinaldina Russell. Westport, CT: Greenwood Press, 1994.

Jaffe, Irma B., with Gernando Colombardo. *Shining Eyes, Cruel Fortune: The Lives and Loves of Italian Renaissance Women Poets.* New York: Fordham University Press, 2002.

James, Susan E. *Kateryn Parr: The Making of a Queen*. Aldershot and Brookfield, UK: Ashgate Publishing Co., 1999.

Jankowski, Theodora A. *Women in Power in the Early Modern Drama*. Urbana, IL: University of Illinois Press, 1992.

Jansen, Katherine Ludwig. *The Making of the Magdalen: Preaching and Popular Devotion in the Later Middle Ages*. Princeton: Princeton University Press, 2000.

Jed, Stephanie H. *Chaste Thinking: The Rape of Lucretia and the Birth of Humanism*. Bloomington, IN: Indiana University Press, 1989.

Jordan, Constance. *Renaissance Feminism: Literary Texts and Political Models*. Ithaca, NY: Cornell University Press, 1990.

Kagan, Richard L. *Lucrecia's Dreams: Politics and Prophecy in Sixteenth-Century Spain*. Berkeley: University of California Press, 1990.

Kehler, Dorothea and Laurel Amtower, eds. *The Single Woman in Medieval and Early Modern England: Her Life and Representation*. Tempe, AZ: Medieval and Renaissance Texts and Studies, 2002.

Kelly, Joan. "Did Women Have a Renaissance?" In *Women, History, and Theory*. Chicago: University of Chicago Press, 1984. Also in *Becoming Visible: Women in European History*, Renate Bridenthal, Claudia Koonz, and Susan M. Stuard, eds. Third edition. Boston: Houghton Mifflin, 1998.

———. "Early Feminist Theory and the *Querelle des Femmes*." In *Women, History, and Theory*.

Kelso, Ruth. *Doctrine for the Lady of the Renaissance*. Foreword by Katharine M. Rogers. Urbana, IL: University of Illinois Press, 1956, 1978.

King, Carole. *Renaissance Women Patrons: Wives and Widows in Italy, c. 1300–1550*. New York and Manchester: Manchester University Press (distributed in the U.S. by St. Martin's Press), 1998.

King, Margaret L. *Women of the Renaissance*. Foreword by Catharine R. Stimpson. Chicago: University of Chicago Press, 1991.

Krontiris, Tina. *Oppositional Voices: Women as Writers and Translators of Literature in the English Renaissance*. London and New York: Routledge, 1992.

Kuehn, Thomas. *Law, Family, and Women: Toward a Legal Anthropology of Renaissance Italy*. Chicago: University of Chicago Press, 1991.

Kunze, Bonnelyn Young. *Margaret Fell and the Rise of Quakerism*. Stanford: Stanford University Press, 1994.

Labalme, Patricia A., ed. *Beyond Their Sex: Learned Women of the European Past*. New York: New York University Press, 1980.

Laqueur, Thomas. *Making Sex: Body and Gender from the Greeks to Freud*. Cambridge, MA: Harvard University Press, 1990.

Larsen, Anne R., and Colette H. Winn, eds. *Renaissance Women Writers: French Texts/American Contexts*. Detroit, MI: Wayne State University Press, 1994.

Lerner, Gerda. *The Creation of Patriarchy* and *Creation of Feminist Consciousness, 1000–1870*. 2 vols. New York: Oxford University Press, 1986, 1994.

Levin, Carole, and Jeanie Watson, eds. *Ambiguous Realities: Women in the Middle Ages and Renaissance*. Detroit: Wayne State University Press, 1987.

Levin, Carole, et al. *Extraordinary Women of the Medieval and Renaissance World: A Biographical Dictionary*. Westport, CT: Greenwood Press, 2000.

Lewalsky, Barbara Kiefer. *Writing Women in Jacobean England*. Cambridge, MA: Harvard University Press, 1993.

Lewis, Jayne Elizabeth. *Mary Queen of Scots: Romance and Nation.* London: Routledge, 1998.

Lindsey, Karen. *Divorced Beheaded Survived: A Feminist Reinterpretation of the Wives of Henry VIII.* Reading, MA: Addison-Wesley Publishing Co., 1995.

Lochrie, Karma. *Margery Kempe and Translations of the Flesh.* Philadelphia: University of Pennsylvania Press, 1992.

Lougee, Carolyn C. *Le Paradis des Femmes: Women, Salons, and Social Stratification in Seventeenth-Century France.* Princeton: Princeton University Press, 1976.

Love, Harold. *The Culture and Commerce of Texts: Scribal Publication in Seventeenth-Century England.* Amherst, MA: University of Massachusetts Press, 1993.

MacCarthy, Bridget G. *The Female Pen: Women Writers and Novelists, 1621–1818.* Preface by Janet Todd. New York: New York University Press, 1994. Originally published by Cork University Press, 1946–47.

Maclean, Ian. *Woman Triumphant: Feminism in French Literature, 1610–1652.* Oxford: Clarendon Press, 1977.

———. *The Renaissance Notion of Woman: A Study of the Fortunes of Scholasticism and Medical Science in European Intellectual Life.* Cambridge: Cambridge University Press, 1980.

MacNeil, Anne. *Music and Women of the Commedia dell'Arte in the Late Sixteenth Century.* New York: Oxford University Press, 2003.

Maggi, Armando. *Uttering the Word: The Mystical Performances of Maria Maddalena de' Pazzi, a Renaissance Visionary.* Albany: State University of New York Press, 1998.

Marshall, Sherrin. *Women in Reformation and Counter-Reformation Europe: Public and Private Worlds.* Bloomington, IN: Indiana University Press, 1989.

Masten, Jeffrey. *Textual Intercourse: Collaboration, Authorship, and Sexualities in Renaissance Drama.* Cambridge: Cambridge University Press, 1997.

Matter, E. Ann, and John Coakley, eds. *Creative Women in Medieval and Early Modern Italy.* Philadelphia: University of Pennsylvania Press, 1994. Sequel to the Monson collection, below.

McLeod, Glenda. *Virtue and Venom: Catalogs of Women from Antiquity to the Renaissance.* Ann Arbor: University of Michigan Press, 1991.

Medwick, Cathleen. *Teresa of Avila: The Progress of a Soul.* New York: Alfred A. Knopf, 2000.

Meek, Christine, ed. *Women in Renaissance and Early Modern Europe.* Dublin-Portland: Four Courts Press, 2000.

Mendelson, Sara, and Patricia Crawford. *Women in Early Modern England, 1550–1720.* Oxford: Clarendon Press, 1998.

Merchant, Carolyn. *The Death of Nature: Women, Ecology and the Scientific Revolution.* New York: HarperCollins, 1980.

Merrim, Stephanie. *Early Modern Women's Writing and Sor Juana Inés de la Cruz.* Nashville, TN: Vanderbilt University Press, 1999.

Messbarger, Rebecca. *The Century of Women: The Representations of Women in Eighteenth-Century Italian Public Discourse.* Toronto: University of Toronto Press, 2002.

Miller, Nancy K. *The Heroine's Text: Readings in the French and English Novel, 1722–1782.* New York: Columbia University Press, 1980.

Miller, Naomi J. *Changing the Subject: Mary Wroth and Figurations of Gender in Early Modern England.* Lexington, KY: University Press of Kentucky, 1996.

Miller, Naomi J., and Gary Waller, eds. *Reading Mary Wroth: Representing Alternatives in Early Modern England.* Knoxville, TN: University of Tennessee Press, 1991.

Monson, Craig A., ed. *The Crannied Wall: Women, Religion, and the Arts in Early Modern Europe.* Ann Arbor: University of Michigan Press, 1992.

Musacchio, Jacqueline Marie. *The Art and Ritual of Childbirth in Renaissance Italy.* New Haven, CT: Yale University Press, 1999.

Newman, Barbara. *God and the Goddesses: Vision, Poetry, and Belief in the Middle Ages.* Philadelphia: University of Pennsylvania Press, 2003.

Newman, Karen. *Fashioning Femininity and English Renaissance Drama.* Chicago and London: University of Chicago Press, 1991.

Okin, Susan Moller. *Women in Western Political Thought.* Princeton: Princeton University Press, 1979.

Ozment, Steven. *The Bürgermeister's Daughter: Scandal in a Sixteenth-Century German Town.* New York: St. Martin's Press, 1995.

Pacheco, Anita, ed. *Early [English] Women Writers, 1600–1720.* New York and London: Longman, 1998.

Pagels, Elaine. *Adam, Eve, and the Serpent.* New York: HarperCollins, 1988.

Panizza, Letizia, ed. *Women in Italian Renaissance Culture and Society.* Oxford: European Humanities Research Centre, 2000.

Parker, Patricia. *Literary Fat Ladies: Rhetoric, Gender and Property.* London and New York: Methuen, 1987.

Pernoud, Regine, and Marie-Veronique Clin. *Joan of Arc: Her Story.* Rev. and trans. Jeremy DuQuesnay Adams. New York: St. Martin's Press, 1998. French original, 1986.

Perry, Mary Elizabeth. *Crime and Society in Early Modern Seville.* Hanover, NH: University Press of New England, 1980.

———. *Gender and Disorder in Early Modern Seville.* Princeton: Princeton University Press, 1990.

Petroff, Elizabeth Alvilda, ed. *Medieval Women's Visionary Literature.* New York: Oxford University Press, 1986.

Perry, Ruth. *The Celebrated Mary Astell: An Early English Feminist.* Chicago: University of Chicago Press, 1986.

Rabil, Albert. *Laura Cereta: Quattrocento Humanist.* Binghamton, NY: Medieval and Renaissance Texts and Studies, 1981.

Ranft, Patricia. *Women in Western Intellectual Culture, 600–1500.* New York: Palgrave, 2002.

Rapley, Elizabeth. *A Social History of the Cloister: Daily Life in the Teaching Monasteries of the Old Regime.* Montreal: McGill-Queen's University Press, 2001.

Raven, James, Helen Small, and Naomi Tadmor, eds. *The Practice and Representation of Reading in England.* Cambridge: Cambridge University Press, 1996.

Reardon, Colleen. *Holy Concord within Sacred Walls: Nuns and Music in Siena, 1575–1700.* Oxford: Oxford University Press, 2001.

Reiss, Sheryl E., and David G. Wilkins, ed. *Beyond Isabella: Secular Women Patrons of Art in Renaissance Italy.* Kirksville, MO: Turman State University Press, 2001.

Rheubottom, David. *Age, Marriage, and Politics in Fifteenth-Century Ragusa.* Oxford: Oxford University Press, 2000.

Richardson, Brian. *Printing, Writers and Readers in Renaissance Italy.* Cambridge: Cambridge University Press, 1999.

Riddle, John M. *Contraception and Abortion from the Ancient World to the Renaissance.* Cambridge, MA: Harvard University Press, 1992.

———. *Eve's Herbs: A History of Contraception and Abortion in the West.* Cambridge, MA: Harvard University Press, 1997.

Rose, Mary Beth. *The Expense of Spirit: Love and Sexuality in English Renaissance Drama.* Ithaca, NY: Cornell University Press, 1988.

———. *Gender and Heroism in Early Modern English Literature.* Chicago: University of Chicago Press, 2002.

———, ed. *Women in the Middle Ages and the Renaissance: Literary and Historical Perspectives.* Syracuse: Syracuse University Press, 1986.

Rosenthal, Margaret F. *The Honest Courtesan: Veronica Franco, Citizen and Writer in Sixteenth-Century Venice.* Foreword by Catharine R. Stimpson. Chicago: University of Chicago Press, 1992.

Sackville-West, Vita. *Daughter of France: The Life of La Grande Mademoiselle.* Garden City, NY: Doubleday, 1959.

Sánchez, Magdalena S. *The Empress, the Queen, and the Nun: Women and Power at the Court of Philip III of Spain.* Baltimore: Johns Hopkins University Press, 1998.

Schiebinger, Londa. *The Mind Has No Sex?: Women in the Origins of Modern Science.* Cambridge, MA: Harvard University Press, 1991.

———. *Nature's Body: Gender in the Making of Modern Science.* Boston: Beacon Press, 1993.

Schutte, Anne Jacobson, Thomas Kuehn, and Silvana Seidel Menchi, eds. *Time, Space, and Women's Lives in Early Modern Europe.* Kirksville, MO: Truman State University Press, 2001.

Schofield, Mary Anne, and Cecilia Macheski, eds. *Fetter'd or Free? British Women Novelists, 1670–1815.* Athens, OH: Ohio University Press, 1986.

Shannon, Laurie. *Sovereign Amity: Figures of Friendship in Shakespearean Contexts.* Chicago: University of Chicago Press, 2002.

Shemek, Deanna. *Ladies Errant: Wayward Women and Social Order in Early Modern Italy.* Durham, NC: Duke University Press, 1998.

Smith, Hilda L. *Reason's Disciples: Seventeenth-Century English Feminists.* Urbana, IL: University of Illinois Press, 1982.

———. *Women Writers and the Early Modern British Political Tradition.* Cambridge: Cambridge University Press, 1998.

Sobel, Dava. *Galileo's Daughter: A Historical Memoir of Science, Faith, and Love.* New York: Penguin Books, 2000.

Sommerville, Margaret R. *Sex and Subjection: Attitudes to Women in Early-Modern Society.* London: Arnold, 1995.

Soufas, Teresa Scott. *Dramas of Distinction: A Study of Plays by Golden Age Women.* Lexington, KY: The University Press of Kentucky, 1997.

Spencer, Jane. *The Rise of the Woman Novelist: From Aphra Behn to Jane Austen.* Oxford: Basil Blackwell, 1986.

Spender, Dale. *Mothers of the Novel: 100 Good Women Writers before Jane Austen.* London and New York: Routledge, 1986.

Sperling, Jutta Gisela. *Convents and the Body Politic in Late Renaissance Venice.* Foreword by Catharine R. Stimpson. Chicago: University of Chicago Press, 1999.

Steinbrügge, Lieselotte. *The Moral Sex: Woman's Nature in the French Enlightenment.* Trans. Pamela E. Selwyn. New York: Oxford University Press, 1995.

Stocker, Margarita. *Judith, Sexual Warrior: Women and Power in Western Culture.* New Haven, CT: Yale University Press, 1998.

Stretton, Timothy. *Women Waging Law in Elizabethan England.* Cambridge: Cambridge University Press, 1998.

Stuard, Susan M. "The Dominion of Gender: Women's Fortunes in the High Middle Ages." In *Becoming Visible: Women in European History,* ed. Renate Bridenthal, Claudia Koonz, and Susan M. Stuard. Third edition. Boston: Houghton Mifflin, 1998.

Summit, Jennifer. *Lost Property: The Woman Writer and English Literary History, 1380–1589.* Chicago: University of Chicago Press, 2000.

Surtz, Ronald E. *The Guitar of God: Gender, Power, and Authority in the Visionary World of Mother Juana de la Cruz (1481–1534).* Philadelphia: University of Pennsylvania Press, 1991.

———. *Writing Women in Late Medieval and Early Modern Spain: The Mothers of Saint Teresa of Avila.* Philadelphia: University of Pennsylvania Press, 1995.

Teague, Frances. *Bathsua Makin, Woman of Learning.* Lewisburg, PA: Bucknell University Press, 1999.

Todd, Janet. *The Secret Life of Aphra Behn.* London, New York, and Sydney: Pandora, 2000.

———. *The Sign of Angelica: Women, Writing and Fiction, 1660–1800.* New York: Columbia University Press, 1989.

Valenze, Deborah. *The First Industrial Woman.* New York: Oxford University Press, 1995.

Van Dijk, Susan, Lia van Gemert, and Sheila Ottway, eds. *Writing the History of Women's Writing: Toward an International Approach.* Proceedings of the Colloquium, Amsterdam, 9–11 September. Amsterdam: Royal Netherlands Academy of Arts and Sciences, 2001.

Vickery, Amanda. *The Gentleman's Daughter: Women's Lives in Georgian England.* New Haven, CT: Yale University Press, 1998.

Vollendorf, Lisa, ed. *Recovering Spain's Feminist Tradition.* New York: Modern Language Association, 2001.

Walker, Claire. *Gender and Politics in Early Modern Europe: English Convents in France and the Low Countries.* New York: Palgrave, 2003.

Wall, Wendy. *The Imprint of Gender: Authorship and Publication in the English Renaissance.* Ithaca, NY: Cornell University Press, 1993.

Walsh, William T. *St. Teresa of Avila: A Biography.* Rockford, IL: TAN Books and Publications, 1987.

Warner, Marina. *Alone of All Her Sex: The Myth and Cult of the Virgin Mary.* New York: Knopf, 1976.

Warnicke, Retha M. *The Marrying of Anne of Cleves: Royal Protocol in Tudor England.* Cambridge: Cambridge University Press, 2000.

Watt, Diane. *Secretaries of God: Women Prophets in Late Medieval and Early Modern England.* Cambridge, England: D.S. Brewer, 1997.

Weber, Alison. *Teresa of Avila and the Rhetoric of Femininity.* Princeton: Princeton University Press, 1990.

Welles, Marcia L. *Persephone's Girdle: Narratives of Rape in Seventeenth-Century Spanish Literature.* Nashville: Vanderbilt University Press, 2000.

Whitehead, Barbara J., ed. *Women's Education in Early Modern Europe: A History, 1500–1800.* New York and London: Garland Publishing Co., 1999.

Wiesner, Merry E. *Women and Gender in Early Modern Europe.* Cambridge: Cambridge University Press, 1993.

————. *Working Women in Renaissance Germany.* New Brunswick, NJ: Rutgers University Press, 1986.

Willard, Charity Cannon. *Christine de Pizan: Her Life and Works.* New York: Persea Books, 1984.

Winn, Colette, and Donna Kuizenga, eds. *Women Writers in Pre-Revolutionary France.* New York: Garland Publishing, 1997.

Woodbridge, Linda. *Women and the English Renaissance: Literature and the Nature of Womankind, 1540–1620.* Urbana, IL: University of Illinois Press, 1984.

Woods, Susanne. *Lanyer: A Renaissance Woman Poet.* New York: Oxford University Press, 1999.

Woods, Susanne, and Margaret P. Hannay, eds. *Teaching Tudor and Stuart Women Writers.* New York: Modern Language Association, 2000.

INDEX